I. S. Prokhanoff

# Autobiography

*of*

# IVAN S. PROKHANOFF

**with a record of the main facts of the Evangelical
Christian Movement in Russia.**

"The romance of the restoration movement in Russia is one of the most thrilling bits of church history ever recorded."
—James DeForest Murch
Author, *Christians Only*

"One of the most exciting and heroic stories  of the Christian unity movement found anywhere in the world."
—Victor Knowles
Editor, *One Body*

"This book could be the catalyst that would give rebirth to the restoration movement in Russia."
—Reggie Thomas
Evangelist, White Fields

# In the Cauldron

## of

# Russia

## 1869-1933

Autobiography of

## I. S. PROKHANOFF

Founder and Honorary President of the
All-Russian Evangelical Christian Union

The Life of an Optimist in the Land of Pessimism

*Together with an Interesting History of the*
*Russian Evangelical Christian Union*

ALL-RUSSIAN EVANGELICAL CHRISTIAN UNION
New York, 1933

Printed and Bound in the
United States of America


Cover by Paula Nash Giltner


International Standard Book Number: 0-89900-596-9

Mrs. Anna Ivanovna Prokhanoff

To Him Who gave me life
AND HAS MAINTAINED IT UNTIL NOW
and
In Memory
of my dearly beloved wife
ANNA IVANOVNA
devoted friend and fellow-worker in the field
of God, called home on July 31st, 1919,
this book is dedicated with humble
spirit, flaming soul, and
thankful heart.

By the Author.

# CONTENTS

# LIST OF ILLUSTRATIONS

# Introduction

THE book you now hold in your hands is an answer to prayer. It has been out of print for 60 long years. Now, by the providence of God, you are about to embark upon one of the most unforgettable reading adventures of your life.

Many people today are unaware that long, long before the collapse of Communism in the former Soviet Union, an amazingly successful movement to be "Christians only" was genuinely affected by brave believers like Ivan S. Prokhanoff. Born in 1869, the same year the movement began, this man was able to unite over 2 million believers into "one body."

James DeForest Murch has written, "The romance of the restoration movement in Russia is one of the most thrilling bits of church history ever recorded" (*Christians Only,* 1962, Standard Publishing, Cincinnati, OH). Prepare to be thrilled to bits!

What happened once can happen again. Few people, including Harvard scholars, ever thought that the Communist Party would one day self-destruct. Even fewer, including Christians in the West, believed that the church of Christ could ever survive the years of brutal repression and persecution.

Over 30 years ago, however, Murch noted: "Evangelical Christians in the border states report hundreds of thousands of their brethren who still meet in homes, barns, and cellars for the observance of the Lord's Supper and the study of God's Word. These men of faith look forward to the day when the Evangelical Christians can resume their role in Russia's destiny as progenitors of the restoration of primitive Christianity" (*ibid*). That day has at last come.

I am indebted to John Fisk, Director, Touchstone Russian Ministries, Akron, Ohio, who loaned me his set of photocopies of this book. I also appreciate Rod Huron, Director, North American Christian Convention, Cincinnati, Ohio, who loaned me his 1933 hardbound copy of *In the Cauldron of Russia* for the purpose of reprinting the original pages. Rod's copy was originally part of the late Russian preacher John Huk's library.

Victor Knowles
Executive Director
One Body Ministries
May 1993

# Foreword

*"Oh that my words were now written! Oh that they were printed in a book! That they were graven with an iron pen and lead in the rock forever! For I know that my Redeemer liveth."*

Job. 19 : 23-25.

FRIENDS who are familiar with the main features of my work have very often asked me to write my autobiography. In their opinion such a book would be useful as a contribution to the Evangelical Movement in Russia.

Though disinclined to write such a book, after deliberation I concluded that it would undoubtedly be helpful to the Reformation movement in Russia for which I have labored so long and so arduously. Perhaps the story of my life might also encourage others in times of unrest, persecution and tribulation such as we have suffered. The unfulfilled prophecies in the Word of God indicate that such times are still to come to the people of the world.

Thus I am inspired to write my recollection of facts in my life, especially those connected with the national Reformation movement in my country.

I am convinced that the right way in this case is the concentration of the writer's mind on all the facts that manifest the invisible power of God in the visible weakness of our human nature. Not our glory, but His glory, should shine through all our writings. Under this condition, the readers of this book will draw spiritual good for themselves; a weak worker will be strengthened, a sad one will be made to rejoice, he who is afflicted with doubts will have his faith strengthened, a young worker will draw some useful lessons for his work, and all will experience a sentiment of sincere gratitude to the Captain of all good things for the fact that He ever, and in all countries of the world, is the same.

In the later chapters of this autobiography I have written of my imprisonments and hardships experienced under the

7

old and new regimes for the faith's sake. Of course, I cannot now write about many things, because the partners in my sufferings are still there, inside of Russia, and my unwise statements here could do harm to them.

Therefore, in some places I have written tersely where I ought to have written at length. Perhaps at some future time I may feel free to do full justice to some things which are of necessity omitted here.

That the reader may fully understand the religious atmosphere and spiritual state of the Russian people during the time of which I write, it was necessary to describe at length the condition of the Greek Orthodox or State Church, and also to tell of the dissenters from the thousand-year-old Russian religion. This I have done in the opening chapter of the book.

I desire to write a wise autobiography, helpful to other Christians as they strive to "overcome evil with good," and knowing that without the Lord we can do nothing, my first thought is prayerfully directed to Him, Who alone can give a right inspiration and proper words to describe a not uneventful life.

"Not unto us, O Lord, not unto us, but unto Thy Name give glory." — Psalm 115 : 1.

# My Message to the People of Our Day

A SPECIAL message to the people of our day and to coming generations is contained herein.

In the days when this book is written, the world represents a scene of great tragedy, of unparalleled war and struggle between nations and classes of people; great revolutions, rivers of blood shed in all corners of the world, economic depression, unemployment, famine and starvation of great masses of men and women.

Under the influence of these calamities some thinkers of our day have arrived at theories of pessimism, saying that all our culture and the world itself are going to perish, and otherwise prophesying evil. One of them, the celebrated German scientist Spengler, wrote a book on "the coming ruin of the civilizations of the West."

The intellectual and spiritual condition of the greater part of mankind is a pure pessimism, which is growing and growing every day and everywhere.

If there were time, I could show that this pessimism is the result of the pessimism of the past and it may become the father of the pessimism of the future.

My autobiography is the description of the life of an optimist, who was saved from the depths of pessimism by the mighty and merciful hand of Him who said: "Be of good cheer; I have overcome the world." — John 16 : 33. All his life the writer has lived under the guidance of the golden teaching of Christian optimism. "All things work together for good to them that love God." — Rom. 8 : 28.

Almost all my life I have lived in Russia, the country of the greatest sorrows. The Russian people suffered severely under the old regime, but the change of the revolution has brought to my people still greater sufferings, and now our nation is in the pangs of unspeakable privations and hardships. From the human standpoint pessimism would be fully justified in those who have lived in Russia.

9

# MESSAGE TO THE READER

But owing to the accepted light from Christ, I have lived more than half a century in Russia, under both former and present conditions, with the radiant heart of an optimist.

On my life pathway I have shown to many pessimists the way to that glorious Christian optimism of faith, the way from darkness to light.

If I were able, I would like to broadcast on the radio to all the world, saying: "Be not pessimists; become optimists. Pessimism makes you weak; optimisim will make you strong and powerful to overcome the evils existing in the world." I would further declare through the world loud speaker: "The way to this is Christ."

This is my message to the world. But unfortunately there are pessimists even among Christian believers, — the most unnatural phenomenon in the world.

The teaching of Jesus Christ is a pure crystal-like optimism. How can His disciple be a pessimist? It is incredible, but unfortunately true. On my life's journey I meet many Christians who look through the dark glasses of pessimism upon the future of the world and Christianity, upon mankind, the culture and scientific achievements of men, and even upon Christians outside of their own circles. They are full of sorrow and walk everywhere as it were in a circle.

To these I say: "You misunderstand your Christ, Who said: "Can the children of the bride chamber mourn?" (Matt. 9 : 15); Who wished the joy of His believers might be full (John 15 : 11), and Who assured His followers: "Your joy no man can take from you." (John 16 : 22).

I summon the pessimists to reconsider their spiritual condition and they will find that their pessimism is a kind of disease, which it is necessary to cure. To them I say that as they come nearer to Christ He will heal them; they will forget their pessimism and will shine with the rays of the undying optimism of faith in Jesus Christ.

Yours ever triumphant in Him,

January, 1933.  New York City.          I. S. PROKHANOFF.

# CHAPTER I

## The Religious Condition of Russia in the Sixties of the Nineteenth Century

*"He discovereth deep things out of darkness and bringeth out to light the shadows of death."*
Job 12 : 22.

### General Features of Russian Life

SOME one has said: "Russia is a very big interrogation mark."

Throughout all its centuries of history Russia has been surrounded with mysteries. Russia is a mystery herself.

Unnumbered efforts have been made to draw a real picture of the country, to paint her actual role in the history of humanity, but all the results have been partial, weak and imperfect. Deep students have endeavored to recite her good qualities and her negative features, but they soon felt lost among her many contradictions. Beneath a very prosaic outward appearance every one has felt some deep, powerful and magnetic thing.

This was the impression of foreigners who visited Russia in the middle ages; it is the opinion of many contemporary writers.

Most of them end by saying: "Russia is the country of unlimited possibilities" or even "of impossible possibilities."

Russia has an enormous territory, equal to one-sixth of the land surface of the globe. Even after the war and revolutions she had a population of about 150,000,000, large enough to give her an enormous force for self defence, but at the same time not nearly sufficient to cover her immense territory, thus leaving ample opportunity for increasing her population for many centuries in the future.

11

## IN THE CAULDRON OF RUSSIA

Russia has made important contributions to science, through such great scientists as Mendeleeff, Mechnikoff, Lobachevsky, Pirogoff and others. Russian painters, such as Bruloff, Ivanoff, Verechagin, Makovsky, Ivasovsky, and Repin have been recognized throughout the world.

The Russian people have contributed to the development of music through such world-known composers as Glinka, Rubinstein, Rimsky-Korsakoff, Dragomizhski, Chaikovsky, Borodin, Igor Stavinsky, Rachmaninoff and others.

Russia has produced such great thinkers as Tolstoy and Solovieff, and an endless chain of mighty statesmen, such as Peter the Great.

The natural resources of Russia surpass those of all other countries of the world, and she has been the leading country in various branches of economic activity, producing heavily of rye, furs, leather, caviar, manganese, platinum and other articles of commerce.

Nobody can deny that the Russian people have created a literature that is among the richest in the world. The names of such poets as Pushkin, Lermontoff, and the writers Turgenjeff, Nekrassoff, Gogol, Dostojevsky, Tolstoy, Gorky and others are world famous.

The chief purposes of this literature have been disclosure of the mystery about the Russian people, description of the nation's character, its vices and gifts, and its destination in the world's history. The Russian people have been described by giants of the literary art, but all of them have felt their inability to solve finally the mystery, to probe the problem to its bottom. Something mysterious always remained.

The Poet Nekrassoff wrote of Russia:

"Thou art very abundant
And at the same time thou art poor;
Thou art all powerful
And thou art at the same time weak, —

Little Mother Russia!"

**I. S. Prokhanoff as a Student
in St. Petersburg**

1. I. S. Prokhanoff with Group of Young Engineers from the Westinghouse Company, St. Petersburg.
2. I. S. Prokhanoff with his Two Sons, Yaroslav and Vsevolod

Another poet, Tutcheff, wrote:

"It is impossible to understand Russia with our intellect,
It is impossible to measure it with the common arshin,*
She has a special destiny —
One can only believe in Russia."

Religious thinkers in Western Europe and in America have devoted a great deal of attention to Russia. Special investigations have been made in Bible prophecy, passages from Ezekiel, Daniel and Revelation being applied to explain Russia, but even for these religious teachers there still remains a great mystery.

From their predictions only one thing can be gathered for certain: Russia will play such a world-wide role in the destiny of humanity that it may surpass any other country on the globe.

But in what sense?

Here the opinions are divided.

1. One group of prophets speak pessimistically about the anti-Christian role of Russia, reminding us of Gog and Magog in Rev. 20 : 7.

2. Another group is quite uncertain and indefinite, among them Vladimir Solovieff, the celebrated philosopher and theologian, who in one of his poems asks:

"What will become of Russia!
An army of Artaxerxes
Or the country of Christ?"

3. The third group, optimistic in their writings, idealize the role of Russia and prophecy a great and glorious future for her. The first of these, the famous Russian writer-prophet Dostojevsky, speaking in 1887 at Pushkin's jubilee in Moscow, described the universality of the Russian character and its ability to understand the soul of every nation in the world, saying that the poverty of the Russian people is the cause of their nearness to God. As Christ was born the first time in a manger, so He will be born again in the

---

* The Russian Unit of linear measure.

souls of the Russian people, i.e., He will be revealed finally to the whole world through the Russian people.

The most interesting question is: What is the opinion of the Russian people themselves about Russia?

The very rich Russian folklore consists of *builiny,* i.e., songs of reality composed during centuries by unknown singers from among the common people and handed down orally from generation to generation. These songs are learned by heart and sung in the Russian villages.

In most of these builines a national hero, Ilya Muromez (Elijah of Murom, a town in the central part of Russia), has been glorified. His story is as follows:

"The first thirty-three and a half years of his life he was always seated, never standing up. He was extremely weak and quiet as a child, so that any one could abuse him and he could not even show any signs of resistance or take offence. But when he reached the above age he drank three pells of 'green wine' and began to perform great feats of strength, by which he astonished the whole world."

The general sense of this story is that for a considerable period of its history the Russian nation will be inactive and humble, but the time must come when it will rise with super-human power and amaze the whole world with its great deeds.

Thus the general opinion of statesmen and prominent men and women of the world, and especially of the Russian people themselves, is that an exceptionally great future role awaits Russia, surpassing all precedents in the world's history.

In the opinion of the author, this future role lies in the religious realm of life. The only condition is that she will accept Christ and His Gospel as the basis of life and will realize the restoration of primitive apostolic Christianity.

Toward the sixties of the nineteenth century, under the reign of Emperor Alexander II, great reforms in the political and economic life of Russia were introduced, resulting in the liberation of several millions of slaves, a new system of justice, etc. This was followed by a great uplift in the national life.

## The Greek Catholic or Greek Orthodox Church Division

But the religious life of the people, which might only be expressed under the all-embracing influence and control of the Greek Orthodox Church, was not affected at all by the changes in the State, and remained in exactly the same condition as in the previous centuries.

In 1888 the Nine Hundredth Jubilee of the acceptance of the Christian religion by the Russian people was celebrated. In 988 A.D., Prince Vladimir himself joined the Greek Orthodox Church by accepting baptism, and ordered all his people to be baptized in the River Dnieper at Kieff. Since that time the Greek Orthodox Church has been the State Church, established in Russia as a section of the Byzantine Church.

Reading the history of the Russian people for this almost 1000-year period, one is impressed with the outstanding fact that, while many changes have occurred in the political, economic, industrial and educational life of the Russian people, their religious state remained static.

Out of a small Slavonic tribe the Russian people were transformed into a big European Empire, exerting a very powerful influence on the rest of Europe. But practically no change took place in the religious realm of the national life. The same hierarchy, with its religious services and its rituals, was maintained.

The only changes concerned the system of governing the Church. In the beginning their hierarchy did not go higher than the metropolitan. Afterwards the patriarchate was established. Then Peter the Great abolished the patriarchate and established the Holy Synod. The church dignitaries maintained that their system was unchanged because unchangeable. Yet it became increasingly evident that "stagnation" more accurately described the condition of the Greek Orthodox Church.

15

Gradually, however, various grammatical mistakes crept into the sacred and church service books. The Patriarch Nikon, in the second half of the seventeenth century, ordered the books corrected. A group of priests considered this to be sacriligious and a great split followed, dividing the Russian Orthodox Church into two parts, the majority of which belonged to the State Church. The minority formed the Rascol (Dissent) and they were named Old Believers. The differences were very slight, the majority performing the sign of the cross in prayer with three fingers and the minority with two fingers. All the dogmas and rituals were the same.

The Slavonic language of the people was gradually changing into the specifically Russian, and the people began to experience difficulty in understanding the old Slavonic services in the churches; nevertheless it was forbidden to change or to translate the text.

In Western Europe great reformation movements took place, connected with the work of Wycliff, John Huss, Luther and others. Various theological schools were created, and a very rich religious literature originated, but religious Russia was untouched by any similar progress in all this time.

## No Revival, No Spiritual Growth

During centuries there was no revival, no spiritual movement and no religious literature was created. The history of the Orthodox Church was as a blank sheet of paper.

During these more than nine centuries of Russian history, the religious life of the Russian Orthodox Church may be thus characterized: There was no religious progress; there was stagnation, transformed into a principle. It was even taught, as I have said, that the Church could not change, that its traditions and practices were as unchangeable as its Founder. The moral and spiritual condition of the people could not develop, and they became gradually demoralized.

The question naturally rises in the mind of the reader:

Why was there no progress in the Greek Orthodox Church during that long period? The answer is simple.

By its geographical position, partly in Europe, partly in Asia, Russia was a bulwark for Europe against the waves of barbarism which flowed from Asia and pressed against civilization. As a result, Russia had to struggle continually for national existence and political independence.

At the same time Russia blocked the invasion of Eastern barbarianism and proved to be the guardian and defender of European culture. With all the energy of the Russian people involved in the political struggle, religious questions were left in abeyance.

When my life began, in the sixties of the nineteenth century, religious conditions were the same as in past centuries. The Church was nominally governed by the Holy Synod, consisting of bishops and archbishops appointed by the state government — by the Czar. The bishops and archbishops for the provinces were appointed nominally by the Synod, but actually by the Czar, through his representative, the procurator of the Holy Synod. The priests were appointed by the bishops, regardless of the wishes or the will of the parishes. There was no right of local selection in the Orthodox Church.

This explains the fact that the standard of morality of the Russian Orthodox clergy was not at all high. A priest-drunkard has been an ordinary sight in Russia until recent times, and such a priest could never be dismissed from his position, in spite of all the protests of the people of his parish.

The most important person in the Holy Synod was the procurator, a civil official appointed by the Czar, and he, through the Czar, could annul any resolution of the Holy Synod. This condition of affairs led to the subjection of the Orthodox Church to the State to such an extent that no measures of the Synod which did not please the Government could be made effective. On the other hand, no order of the Government which might be harmful to the Church could be prevented. The Holy Synod was an ecclesiastical

17

institution only in appearance, but in reality it was "an office of the government for the oversight of church matters." This condition, of course, had a very harmful effect upon the whole church life.

Bishops and priests felt and acted not like shepherds of souls, but like state officials, even serving as secret agents of the government. By their position they had to report on all actions or intentions unfriendly to the Government about which they could learn from the secret confessions of citizens in their churches.

Outwardly the Church was prosperous. There were huge rich temples and golden roofed churches. The services were conducted amidst the glamorous splendor of gold, silver, precious stones and ornaments and costly clerical garments. The outward appearance was brilliant, but what was the condition of the inner life? The services consisted chiefly of ritual and there was no religious instruction or preaching. *The people did not know the Word of God.*

Even to this day the majority of members of Greek Orthodox parishes do not know what the Bible or the Gospel mean. This is quite natural, for even now the Bible and New Testament are read only during the services and then not in Russian but in the old Slavonic language, which is little understood by the people. The reading was never interpreted to them.

The religious ignorance of the people is so extreme that if you should ask one of them:

"Who is greater, St. Nicholas or Christ?"

you would in most cases receive the answer:

"St. Nicholas, of course."

One of the Greek Orthodox Archbishops officially recognized the fact that the people did not know Christ and knew very little about the saints, *but explained that they prayed to and worshipped eagerly the icons,* viz.: images of saints, thereby admitting that their worship was idolatrous. Under these conditions is it any wonder that the moral and spiritual condition of the people degenerated and that corruption, drunkenness and immorality were found to be flourishing on a nation-wide scale? Like a sea, vodka was flowing on the plains of Russia, poisoning millions of people and ruining the family, economic, industrial and social life, and at the same time carrying away to the abyss the Orthodox Church with its priests, bishops, archbishops and metropolitans.

While maintaining an attitude of stolid indifference to social conditions all around it, the Orthodox Church system was so intolerant in its bigotry that no manifestations of free religious thought were allowed. They were thwarted in the very beginning. In this way the Orthodox clergy not only themselves did not shed the light into the life of the people, but forbade others to do so. The smallest effort toward religious progress was smothered by both Church and State.

## The Dissent or Nonconformity

The Russian people themselves could not be satisfied with such a condition of affairs. The immortal souls of men and women were hungry and thirsty for the truth and they tried to find it. But, having no shepherd, they went the wrong way. What they thought was truth really had nothing in common with truth, and so their last state was worse than their first.

We shall have to unveil here a very sad picture. The largest group of the Nonconformity was the so-called "staroobriadchestwo," i.e., people of the old ritual. It was made up of that section of the Orthodox Church which separated from it as I mentioned above in the seventeenth century, due to the Church's attitude in clinging to the mistakes in its books and rituals, when corrections of obvious errors were submitted by the Patriarck Nikhon.

Their morality was higher than that of the Orthodox people, but their religious fanaticism and ignorance offset that advantage, leading them to turn away from the light of knowledge and European culture introduced by Peter the Great, and from other educational movements. Most of them went to the remote forests and marshes of Northern European Russia and Siberia, and so finally lagged behind

19

other Russian people with regard to education and standards of living.

The next group to be considered was known as "Chlisti." It was a secret sect of a gnostic nature. Outwardly these people showed themselves to be most zealously orthodox. They fulfilled all the Church rituals with great eagerness, fasted a great deal, and traveled to the monasteries.

## Thousands of "Christs" in Russia

But within their own circle they propagated a gnostic doctrine, teaching that no historical Christ had ever existed, that Christ is spirit and that He always migrates from one person to another. In the old days He was in Jesus; after that He indwelt many other men, and now He may dwell in a John, a James, or any man. They recognized as Christs various men, mostly peasants having ordinary names, such as Nicholas and Matthew; these they hailed as sons of God, equal to Him, and worshipped them as Gods. There were hundreds and even thousands of such "Christs" in Russia, and their friends and disciples were called apostles and prophets.

Among the women were Marys, mothers of God! Under the cover of night they held secret meetings, in which they worshipped their "Christs," the apostles, prophets and prophetesses leading the other members of these congregations in their devotional exercises. There was much singing and the melodies were generally of the dancing hall variety. "Prophecy" and speaking in unknown tongues characterized their meetings, and then a practice known as "radenie" crept in — religious dancing to exhaustion on the part of the prophets and prophetesses. While dancing they sang:

> "I flog myself, I flog myself,
> I seek God."

From the verb "Chlishu" — flog myself — is derived the name "chlisti."

Members of this sect were vegetarians. They propagated a doctrine which claimed to exalt a purely spiritual relationship between men and women, and declared child bearing to be a sin. But as was to be expected, this unnatural relationship between the two sexes under the circumstances of their ecstatic meetings resulted only in mass adultery.

## Russians Accepted the Jewish Religion

There was also a sect called "jidowstvuuchie" — Jew followers — composed of Russian people who, being unable to find any consolation in the Christian faith as practiced by the Orthodox Church, simply accepted the Jewish religion, circumcising themselves, observing Saturday instead of Sunday, and keeping the Jewish Easter.

The fourth sect was still more peculiar, and in some respects even more terrible. This was the sect of "scopzi" — *eunuchs.* As the basis of their faith they took Matt. 19 : 12:

"For there are eunuchs which were so born from their mothers' wombs; and there are eunuchs which were made eunuchs by men, and there are eunuchs which made themselves eunuchs for the kingdom of heaven's sake."

They made themselves eunuchs for the kingdom of God. They believed that only eunuchs would be saved and therefore they did not hesitate to perform the necessary operation on themselves (Matt. 18 : 8-9). In other respects their doctrine was similar to that of the Chlisti. One of the first Russian eunuchs — Selivanov — was worshipped by them as God. They called themselves "white doves," and also had secret meetings at which the "radenie" (religious dancing) was featured. They had various fantastic legends, among them one about the Emperor Peter III, who, according to their tradition, was also a eunuch. As a result of their self-inflicted operation, these people had special distinguishing features in their appearance. In the case of the men, for instance, no beard could be grown on their faces, and in this respect they somewhat resembled women.

These groups of the Russian Dissent represent something more awful than the Orthodox Church itself. Deciding to leave a dark house, man, left to himself, is liable to fall into an abyss of error which is still worse.

## Tragic Condition of the Russian People

These sects could originate only under conditions fostered by a spiritually dead State Orthodox Church and in the absence of enlightenment which should have come through education and religious instruction. Their existence well illustrates the tragic religious condition of the Russia people.

Still one other Russian sect should be mentioned. This is *the sect of the Doukhobori,* or literally *spiritual wrestlers.* The Doukhobors originated in the province of Tamboff, as a result of teaching by a peasant named Pobirochin, at the end of the eighteenth century. Their doctrine is fairly well known, owing to the comments of Tolstoi and through their immigration from Russia to Canada.

The Doukhobors are somewhat similar to the Quakers; they deny the written Word of God and claim to be led by the unwritten Word of God; they also stress prophecy in their meetings. They deny any responsibility for military service and are consistent vegetarians.

Unfortunately they have gone to extremes in many ways. Indeed, many of them refuse to use such animals as horses and oxen in domestic service and have tried to draw their plows themselves, men and women yoked together! Some others of the sect even gave up wearing clothing made of wool, and some of them, preferring to be naked, gave up clothing of any kind. Practically all parents in this sect have been persistent in their refusal to send their children to school.

## The Sect of Milk People

There was, however, another group of Dissenters which kept free from such extremes. We refer to *the sect of the Molokans* (milk people). They were called by this name because, during the fasting periods established by the Orthodox Church, they drank milk and ate milk food, which was strictly forbidden. This sect originated in the same province as the Doukhobors, Tamboff, and Peasant Uklein, a relative of Pobirochin, was the founder.

The main features of their doctrine are: The Bible is the guide in questions of soul salvation; no rituals, no ikons, no dead bodies of the saints to be worshipped; no fastings, no temples. The worship of God must be performed in spirit and in truth. The practice of good works and acquirement of virtues are the main duty of a Christian and the only way to salvation. The Old Testament has had some influence upon the Molokans. All of them refrain from eating the meat of swine, and some of them keep Saturday as a day of rest instead of Sunday.

They do not practice baptism or observe the Lord's Supper, interpreting these in a spiritual sense. Biblical teaching concerning the way of salvation has not been clearly understood by the Molokans. They have worked out a special order of service in their congregational meetings and have created a characteristically Russian type of melodies.

All of the above sects exist at the present time, almost in the same condition as in the sixties of the last century. It is true that in some respects these sects were superior to the Orthodox people, but as they were not in favor of education and intellectual enlightenment (this seems to be a weakness common to all), they could not develop and gradually began to decay. Such was the religious condition of the Russian people in the sixties of the last century.

## The Age of Pessimism

It was spiritual night — deep night.

Those years may well be called "the time of pessimism." The Russian educated class — the so-called intelligentia — imbibed pessimism from the theories of materialism and from the philosophy of pessimism of Schopenhauer and Hartman, who were very popular at that time.

A very deep pessimism reigned in the political life because everything was suppressed and oppressed by the autocracy and because hopes and plans for political liberties were frustrated.

But especially pessimism prevailed in the realm of religion. The Greek Orthodox Church, pretending to be the Church of Christ, really had pessimism as her cornerstone. This Church taught the people that the Czar was far and God was too high, that He was a severe judge, and that no one could directly approach God, that one must do that through the ranks of priests and saints.

The truth that God is love was never explained and the people were kept in the condition of trembling souls. The general doctrine of the Church was that in order to please God one must fast, make long pilgrimages and feats of asceticism in monasteries, deprive one's self of food and clothing, and give much to the Church. This was the source of the great wealth of gold, silver, jewels and embroideries which nearly every church possessed. The Church taught that man is justified and saved by his works, but at the same time the Church said that *no one can know on earth that he is saved.*

Justification by faith, salvation by Christ's death on the cross, purification from sin by the blood of Jesus Christ, spiritual regeneration (new birth), the forgiveness of sin directly by God, the work of the Holy Spirit in the hearts of men — all this was absolutely omitted and unknown.

## A Church Without the Gospel

In a word, the Greek Church omitted and lost the whole Gospel, the source of joy and life, and left its people in the darkness of hopeless life or spiritual pessimism, everlasting fear; no salvation, no eternity.

The people who belonged to the various separating sects — the "staroobriatzi," "chlisti," "scopzi" and others, not excluding the "molokans," unfortunately overlooked the joyful truths of the Gospel and lived in the condition of the same darkness of pessimism.

Not even one of them has believed in his salvation through Christ. They lived without hope. They were in the condition described by St. Paul in I Cor. 15 : 19: "If in this life only we have hope in Christ, we are of all men most miserable."

I repeat: It was night; deep, dark night.

Then out of that darkness of night came faint glimmerings of the dawn. It may not be out of place to remember now a verse from the book of Isaiah, 21 : 11-12: "Watchman, what of the night?"

The watchman said: "The morning cometh and also the night." In some other translations this verse reads: "The morning cometh, although it is night."

Although it was very dark in the religious world of the Russian people, the morning had really begun to dawn, for during the sixties the last books of the Bible were translated from the old Slavonic language into the Russian.

## The Word of God Brings Light

The Word of God had a great influence upon the religious condition of the people. It was like the first rays of the rising sun in the early morning. Simple workmen and peasants began to read the Bible and the New Testament, and as the blessed truths gripped their hearts and transformed their lives, they began to preach the Gospel to their neighbors. Thus it was that the Gospel was let loose and the Evangelical Movement began in the late sixties of the nineteenth century. It has taken but few words to tell of its coming, but more will be written in later chapters, for my own life, year after year, seems to have been bound up in the new religious life that followed, its growth, its joy, and even its persecutions and suffering and hardships, its imprisonments and its victories also.

———•———

# CHAPTER II

## My Life up to the Time of My Conversion

*"I will lead them in paths that they have not known."*
*Isa. 42 : 16.*

I WAS born on the seventeenth day of April, 1869, in the city of Vladikavkas, in the Caucasus.

The province of Caucasus is in some respects one of the most remarkable parts of Russia. Geographically it occupies the isthmus between the Black Sea and the Caspian Sea. From the peninsula of Taman on the Black Sea along the Caucasus Mountain Range to the peninsula of Apsheron on the Caspian Sea this province is about 700 miles long.

This mountain range is sometimes regarded as part of the boundary line between Europe and Asia, but the region is really Asiatic in character. The highest peaks in the central ridge greatly exceed the highest Alps, at least six of them being well over 16,000 feet high. Mount Elbrus attains an elevation of 18,000 feet above the sea, while Kasbek reaches a height of more than 16,500 feet. Here the line of perpetual snow is generally found between 10,000 and 11,000 feet above sea level.

Historically the Caucasus was a gateway for the tribes and nations of Asia on their way to Europe. History recites that during the period of the emigration of nations, they traveled through the Caucasus passes. At present the Caucasus mountains are populated by nearly sixty nationalities, speaking as many different languages, so that they cannot understand one another. Ethnography says that they are the remnants of those tribes which passed through the Caucasus many centuries ago.

If you visit Tiflis, which is the capital of the Caucasus, you will observe in the street life of that cosmopolitan city an ethnographical museum, for Georgians, Emeritins, Abhasces, Ossetins, Tavlins, Armenians, Tartars and many others walk to and fro in the streets, clad in their picturesque costumes, their conversation suggestive of the Tower of Babel. In ancient times the legendary Argonauts traveled from Greece to the present Georgia (Colchis), in search of the golden fleece. The Caucasus is a favored country with regard to its natural resources, oil, manganese, etc.

## Charm of the Mountainous Landscape

But the most salient feature of this province is its great natural beauty and charm. If on a day of bright spring sunshine you were privileged to look toward the mountains from the city of Vladikavkas, you would see first a range of green verdure-clad mountains; above and beyond that a second range of towering rock seen through a violet haze; then a third range of white snow-capped mountains and above them the bright blue sky, from which the burning sun shed its golden rays upon the whole grand panorama.

Riding along the Georgian military road connecting Vladikavkas and Tiflis, you would see fertile valleys, very high perpendicular rocks, native villages perched eerily among the mountain peaks, tumbling cascades of white foam, and the wild raging torrent of Terek. Amid such picturesque surroundings you would feel charmed and awed by the greatness and beauty of God's handiwork.

It is not, however, the peaceful pastoral beauty of gently undulating slopes, but rather the austere grandeur of silent giants, who for centuries have witnessed the desperate struggle of many hundreds of nationalities and tribes, making roads for themselves through the narrow passes of these forbidding mountains. When one looks upon these snowy giants, one cannot help but imagine how many thrilling stories they could tell to the present generation. Every corner, every stone, every tower, every ruined wall — everything there is replete with legends and traditions.

## The Shepherd Sings an Ancient Song

Looking upward, you may often see, standing high on a rocky projecting shelf, a young shepherd, singing an ancient

27

popular song which exalts the great deeds of his forefathers, the music of his song uniting with the wild roaring of mighty Terek, flowing in its deep bed far below.

It will thus be readily understood why the celebrated Russian poet, Pushkin, devoted several of his finest poems to the Caucasus, while another great Russian poet, Lermontoff, also wrote very powerful poems on Caucasian life, such as "The Demon," which afterward became the text for a very well-known opera by Rubinstein.

Both of these writers described in an intensely dramatic manner the life of the natives — Chircassians, Georgians, etc., and pictured in living words some of the most beautiful scenes in the Caucasus, such as Dariel Pass, the Castle of Tamara, etc.

The Caucasus province was added gradually to the Russian territory, as a result of the voluntary subjection to Russia of Georgia in the beginning of the nineteenth century, under the reign of Emperor Alexander I. Being a Christian (Orthodox) country, surrounded on all sides by Mohammedans, Turks and Persians, Georgia joined Russia in order to get rid of the yoke of these barbarous hordes.

## Dissenters Peopled the Caucasus Region

The Caucasus was gradually colonized, partly by the emigrant peasants from the interior of Russia, partly by the Cossacks, and also by dissenters who were banished by the Government for religious reasons. The Doukhobors, at first banished to Crimea, were afterward sent to Transcaucasus, while Molokans, Chlisti, Staroobriatzi, etc., found their way to all parts of the Caucasus. Thus it came about that toward the sixties of the last Century the Caucasus was populated not only by the natives, but also by a considerable number of Russians, among them dissenters of various sects.

The dissenters formed large villages in the Caucasus, such as Voronzovka, a town near Tiflis, populated by the Molokans and *renowned for its cheese factories.* The Molokans occupied special quarters in such cities as Vladikavkas, Baku and Tiflis. Vladikavkas, where I was born, is a small city situated at the very foot of the main Caucasus range, and consisting of wide streets with boulevards of acacia trees and many parks and orchards. My parents belonged to the Molokans. They lived as peasants in the province of Saratoff, in the villages of Kopeni and Slastucha, of the Atkarsky District. Severe persecutions on the part of the Orthodox priesthood and the police were the main cause of their emigrating to the Caucasus. They hoped to find there the religious freedom denied them elsewhere in Russia.

My father and mother arrived at Vladikavkas in the year 1862, together with his mother and her sister, so that I had two grandmothers in my childhood.

### The Physician Pronounces Me Dead

My mother has told me many times that when I was ten days old I fainted and lay apparently lifeless, so that she went for a doctor. The doctor looked and said:

"Why have you come? He is dead."

Bitterly weeping, my mother brought me home, ordered a coffin, laid me therein, and prepared me for burial. The people came and wept, as usual.

In such cases the Molokans call their old men and elders, who read the Bible, sing the psalms and perform the funeral rites. But before the elders came I began to move quite unexpectedly, opened my eyes and started to cry! Of course, the change in the picture was sudden.

When I heard about this for the first time, I thought: Surely the power of the Omnipotent appointed me to live and to solve a special problem set by Him for my life; another power, the power of death, wanted to cut my life short in its very beginning, but the power of the Omnipotent overcame (of course, it could not be otherwise), and I was left to live on earth. Let His will be done! Job once said: "I should have been as though I had not been." — Job 10:18.

Sometimes moments of depression came before my conversion when I began to think: "Why did I not die during those first days of my life?" But the thought of His supreme will, which is always good, stopped my thinking further in that direction, and I learned to repeat joyfully: "Not my will, but Thine, be done," and the sense of subjection to His supreme will filled my heart with joy.

When I was about eight years old my brother Alexander and I were put under a private teacher, an old Bohemian, who taught us to read and write. He was very severe and sometimes punished his pupils by putting them on their bare knees on grains of rock salt strewn on the floor. After leaving his tutorship we entered the primary school, and being twelve years old, I was accepted for the high school (third class), from which I graduated in 1887.

## Thoughts of a Serious-Minded Youth

Even as a boy I was serious-minded and inclined to reflection, and from the early days of my youth, as I recall them, I tried to imagine "the being" or "the absence of being;" infinite space, eternity, the heavens, angels, and above everything God, Creator of all things. Another characteristic was an acute pity for poor and suffering people. In this connection I remember an incident which produced upon me an impression which has influenced my whole life and made it impossible for me to deny the poor.

It was mid-winter, in the city of Vladikavkas. My brother and I were playing in the street. A neighbor was coming from a ride on horseback. A very poorly dressed man, in rags, evidently a drunkard, belonging to the class called in Russia "bosiaki" (vagabonds), approached him and asked for a few copecks in order that he might go to a shelter for the night. The horseman turned and sneeringly said: "You will use the money for drinking. I am not going to give you anything," and went to his house.

The beggar remained with outstretched hand, and then began slowly to descend a sloping street into the broad market square. I so greatly pitied him, but neither my brother nor myself had any copecks at the time and so could not help him. The next morning when we came up the street some boys said to us:

"Yonder, at the market square, a frozen man is lying."

We ran and saw there the cold body of the man to whom our neighbor had on the previous day refused to give a few copecks! He had really asked for money to enable him to spend the night in some shelter. Having no money to pay, he tried to spend the night under a scale shed at the market place, and was frozen.

## "Give to Him That Asketh of Thee"

Since that time I have understood the words of Christ: "Give to him that asketh thee" (Matt. 5:42), in an unconditional sense.

In many cases we decline requests where a real need exists, for various reasons connected with the faults and defects of those who ask. If we were omniscient and could read the thoughts of men, we might be justified in so doing, but as our knowledge of man is extremely limited and we may make a mistake by refusing a really needy person who can through that refusal perish, we must not refuse anybody. We must "give to them that ask of us."

If some of those whom we help abuse our help, the responsibility for that rests entirely with them, while we do not incur the risk of doing an injustice to somebody by a refusal to help. But if we judge those who ask for help, and give to some while we refuse others, we may make a mistake in both ways — by giving to those who will abuse and by refusing those who are really in need. Therefore the wisest thing, according to Christ, is "to give to him that asketh."

Of course, we have a right to determine the measure of our help in proportion to the need and in accordance with our means, but we must "give to him who asketh" and not refuse.

## A Help to Backward Pupils

I also pitied the poor backward pupils, who through some disability could not prepare their lessons and in consequence had various unpleasant experiences with the teachers. Especially do I remember one Armenian pupil who was diligent but somewhat weak-minded, could not

31

understand, could not remember, and very often received an unsatisfactory note or mark for his answers. He often remained after the lesson period and wept. I was so touched by his sorrow that I offered him my help gratuitously. We remained together at the class and I spent hours with him to help him in his efforts to understand and to remember.

This characteristic brought me a popularity at school which was entirely unsought, particularly among those pupils who found it difficult to understand or to learn. They came to me and I tried to do my best to help them.

In the same way I felt a great compassion for dumb animals. One incident will illustrate: There was an old rifle in our house, and one afternoon I took it and went out on a hunting expedition. Soon I saw a little bird sitting on a very high stalk of grass. Unthinkingly I lifted my rifle and shot. Looking in that direction, I did not see the bird, but when I reached the spot I saw it lying on the ground, still alive but with blood on its wings. Its eyes were closing and it was dying.

### I "Murder" My First and Last Living Thing

I cannot describe what I felt at that moment. The word "murderer" flashed into my mind, and I blushed from the sense of a crime committed. The inner voice said to me: "Why hast thou stopped this life, which glorified its Creator?" I blushed, even trembled, and prayed in despair.

When the bird died, I buried it in the sand. I did it without analyzing my motives, but now I quite understand my action. It was an instinct to hide, to conceal the traces of the crime from the shining sun, the blue sky, from the heavens. But of course, nothing was concealed.

I determined then and there never to go hunting again, never to take into my hands any rifle. Since that time I have abhorred everything that is connected with the deprivation of life.

Very often I experienced, quite suddenly and spontaneously, a great exaltation of spirit, and would begin to pray to God or to talk earnestly with my brother on the improve-

**Typical Molokan Elders**   (See page 22)

Engineering Staff and Central Power House of St. Petersburg Electric Railways   (See page 120)

ment of human relations and of social and spiritual conditions generally. Although I enjoyed being with my little friends and comrades, I preferred to find myself among adults and to listen to their conversation. When guests came to my father's house, as they often did, I asked for permission to be present in the room, and enjoyed their earnest talks, especially when they were discussing religious topics.

### Attending a Session of the Municipal Board

At one time my father was elected a member of the municipal board. I asked, indeed, insisted that he should take me to one of the meetings of the Board. He did so, and after the meeting some of the members expressed their surprise to see among them a boy attentively listening to the municipal debates.

Various influences combined to form my character and general view of life, but foremost among them must be placed the influence of my father and the Molokan people.

We lived in the city of Vladikavkas, but father had a large orchard and kitchen garden in a suburb which was in the foothills of the forest mountains. The orchard was situated on the shore of a stream. In such a setting the orchard presented a very beautiful picture, particularly in the autumn, when the apple trees, pear trees and plum trees were laden with fruit. There was an apiary, too, and always plenty of honey. In the great virgin forest there were many beasts, such as hares, foxes, wolves and bears. On many well remembered occasions, when my brother and I were walking from the city to that orchard, we saw young bears going into the forest.

### Happy Days Spent in the Country

My brother and I enjoyed very much to visit the orchard and found much pleasure there. It was a great joy to me when my father used to say: "We are going to the orchard." I liked to talk with my father while sitting in his wagon.

He told me stories from the Bible — about Joseph and his brethren, and others. Listening to that story I wept. I liked also to hear his singing of the Molokan hymns.

When we came to the orchard we were met by one of the grandmothers, who made their home at the orchard during the summer. Beside them there lived in the orchard an old man called "Gavrilich," whose life story was remarkable. In his young days he was a soldier and was taken a prisoner by the "chechenzi," a wild tribe in the Caucasus.

He was given to a prominent "chechenez" as a slave, and did for him all kinds of work, brought water and wood, and cooked his food. Once his master was so angry with him that he wanted to murder him, but his wife pleaded for him and he was saved. For twenty-five years he was a prisoner, forgot Russian, talked only the "chechensky" language and even began to resemble a "chechenez" in appearance!

At last a report reached his master that the Russian troops were approaching, whereupon his master and most of the inhabitants of the village ran away, leaving him alone. "Gavrilich" liked to tell the story of his sufferings as a prisoner and to speak about his liberation; how he wandered in the woods and mountains, before he found a company of Russian soldiers.

He finally came to Vladikavkas and visited a religious gathering of Molokans. It was customary to make announcement to the congregation whenever occasion warranted that there was such and such a homeless stranger, and the elder would ask that members of the congregation who were able to do so should receive such a man and give him refuge.

So at this meeting the elders told about an "old man" who was a "chechenez" prisoner and homeless. My father took him and placed him as a watchman and gardener in the orchard. My brother and I had a great esteem and even awe for "Gavrilich." Reading the poem by Pushkin, "The Caucasian Captive," we looked upon him as a hero, and it gave us great pleasure to hear his stories.

# THE DAYS OF MY YOUTH

## The Story Period of My Life

I will never forget those happy summer days and the evenings when we sat out of doors around the table with a samovar (tea set). Father, grandmothers and "Gavrilich," told their stories in turn and we listened to them with glowing eyes and trembling hearts. All the stories about the sufferings, especially of innocent men, strongly appealed to my heart. I liked so much to hear the story of Job's sufferings, told by one of my grandmothers.

My father told me the story of his boyhood orphanage. Both grandmothers told touching stories of the sufferings of the Molokans in the province of Saratoff, where they were arrested and imprisoned. This thought, that here were people who were righteous and innocent as angels, and still suffered bitter persecutions at the hands of wicked people, fascinated my mind and melted my heart.

My old grandmothers, who in their youth suffered imprisonments, seemed to me to be "saintly women," utterly incapable of wrong doing. The stories of religious persecution produced an especially strong impression because they coincided with the thoughts of my own boyish mind.

At the primary school all the pupils knew that my brother and I were sectarians — Molokans — and often an unfriendly spirit was displayed; various sneering remarks and all kinds of insults were leveled at us. There were even occasions when boys attacked us on the streets, shouting: "sectarians" and "Molokans," and tried to beat us.

But this persecution for the faith's sake did not discourage me, nor did it make me ashamed of the faith of my father. On the contrary, I felt instinctively that those persecutions, however small, made me a member of that holy multitude who suffered for Christ and for the truth. To comfort my brother Alexander I used to say: "Nothing is to be feared, Sacha; we are higher than they are."

Another strong influence of those early days was that of the school, which broadened my horizon and developed my mind by imparting various kinds of knowledge. Of all the sciences I liked best to study history, literature and particularly poetry. I read very much, especially our national poets, Pushkin, Lermontoff, Nekrassoff and others. The first two poets delighted me with their beautiful thoughts and the exquisite artistic style of their poems. Nekrassoff appealed to my mind through his description of the people's suffering. Especially I liked his poem:

"Go to the Volga!  Whose groan\* is heard there?
Upon the great Russian river?"

## Appeal of the Literature of Suffering

But more than any other writer Dostojevsky captivated my mind, because he was the greatest of the poets describing the suffering of the people.  His novels, "Notes from the Dead House," "The Crime and the Punishment," "Evil Spirits," "Brothers Karamazoffs" and others vividly portrayed these sufferings in all their forms.

This literature of suffering awoke in my heart a deep pity, love and admiration for every sufferer and martyr. The whole Russian people seemed to me to be the martyr nation.  I idealized the simple Russian peasants as sufferers and began as it were to worship in my heart the Russian mogik (peasant).

At that time, all over Russia, a secret literature, emanating from various political writers, was spreading.  As it was impossible to discuss freely in Russia political and social questions, the leaders of the liberation movement, such as A. Gerzen, Lavroff, Prince Kropotkin and others, emigrated to other countries and began to print various periodicals and books on political and social questions.  These books were secretly spread all over the country.

Like other people, I read some of these books, such as "What is to be done?" by Chernishevsky.  This liberation movement, however, became extreme.  A left wing of it was called "nihilism."  This word comes from a Latin word

---

\* Here he refers to an old Russian method of transport on the Volga. A boat was moved on the river by a rope hauled by a group of workmen, called "burlaki."

"nihil," meaning nothing, and being applied to this movement meant that the people belonging to it recognized nothing and denied everything.

Types of such men were pictured by all the celebrated Russian writers, notably I. S. Turgeneff in his novel, "Fathers and Sons." They denied the State, social, family and re-religious forms of life, and propagated anarchism, terrorism and universal destruction as the way to ideal life.

Of course, these extreme doctrines did not appeal to fair-minded men, but the general principles enunciated by the leaders of the liberation movement were generally approved. That the state order should be changed; that the country should be governed by the people (democracy); that all social injustice should be removed (socialism); that the right of education for all should be recognized and realized; that all the freedom and liberty of cultured nations should be introduced — in all these aspirations the leaders of the liberation movement who lived at that time abroad had the moral support of the intelligent classes of the Russian people.

## Disagreed With Socialistic Attitude Toward Christ

Of course, I fully sympathized with all these ideals and wished that they might be attained in the shortest possible time. But instinctively, from my very boyhood, I could not become entangled with political movements. I could not agree with one aspect of their doctrines. They denied Christ and every kind of religion. I thought this was il-logical, because their ideals of liberty, equality and fraternity and socialistic principles were borrowed from the teachings of Christ and His religion (Acts 4 : 32). It is surely il-logical to accept the teaching and to reject the Teacher.

It was also impractical, because for attaining every pur-pose there exists one correct and effective method. If you do not want to use that special method and employ another, it must bring failure or result in only a partial attainment of your purpose. The method of attaining the ideal social life of humanity is surely by love and good will. I reasoned that all who adopted the method of hatred and revenge took an impractical course, one impossible of realization. Thus, I was convinced, it was powerless. It would be in vain to change the outward conditions of the life of men and not to reform them spiritually.

Political and social workers can work out ideal reforms for the outward life of men, but they cannot change a wicked man into a good one. This can only be done by religion. *In rejecting religion, leaders of the liberation movements in Russia have rejected the only power by which their purpose could be attained.*

While hailing with all my heart the liberation movement, I instinctively felt, and afterward expressed in clear written form, my conviction that the cardinal and final solution of the question lies not in revolution only, although that might take place as an act of necessity, but in a great spiritual reformation.

## Another Influence on My Life

The third influence on my early life came through the powerful but silent appeal of the beauty of nature.

We lived on the shore of the famous Caucasian river torrent, Terek. I liked to sit on a big stone amidst the waves of the roaring waters and to look on the gorgeous beauty of the green, violet and white ranges of mountains and that romantic peak Kazbek, and so to muse for hours. In those moments most poetic thoughts peopled my mind and I felt inspired to write. Thus some of my poems originated.

Here I recall the theory according to which every man is a product of various earthly circumstances and influences. I do not believe in that theory at all. These influences were strong, but they were only instruments of the still stronger influence of the Invisible Spirit, because beside me at the same time and in the same city of Vladikavkas were other young men under the same influences, who did not feel them and did not answer to them.

This invisible influence of Him, Who saved me in the moment of the attack of death during the first days of my earthly life, has directed all my impressions, feelings and experiences to fulfill His own purposes.

While in the sixth grade of the high school in 1886, my character and the inner part of my nature began to take definite form. A characteristic which must be set down as a simple statement of fact was my noted intellectual development and erudition. Teachers and pupils were often astonished to hear from me quotations which it was considered impossible to expect from one of us. At that time I was reading almost all the classics of Russian literature and the works of such foreign authors as were accessible to me.

### Inspired to Write at an Early Age

It soon became evident to the teachers and others that God had given me a certain amount of literary ability. As in other schools, the pupils of our high school were obliged sometimes to write compositions on set themes. My compositions were usually pronounced to be the best and some of them were sent as models to the Caucasian Board of Education. I remember we wrote compositions on Russia. In the Bulletin of the School Board was quoted one passage from my composition, running something like this:

"The area of the Russian territory is at present one-sixth of all the continental surface of the globe and equal to the surface of the moon. But there is one difference between the surface of the moon and that of Russia: Whereas the surface of the moon is always the same and does not increase, the surface of Russia has always been growing and will grow. . . But our faith goes farther. We believe that not only the surface of Russia, but its soul, will grow and flourish."

Until a few years ago I preserved a manuscript written in my brother's hand which contained some of my first writings. Without any suggestion from others I began to write poems and prose compositions. Among them there was, for instance, a story of "Gavrilich," his experience as a slave. Some of the pupils learned about that fact and reported it to the teachers. The result was that one of my poems was read at the high school reception day exercises and was so well received that I became popular and my poems began to be published in the local papers.

The writers on the sufferings of the Russian people awakened in my heart a great love of people and put a democratic imprint upon my spirit, creating in me an inextinguishable desire and aspiration to devote all my life to a self-denying service in the interest of the millions of suffering Russian people. My observations of that time represented Russia as a big stuffy prison, in which millions of people were fettered, and of course the first thing that was needed for this unfortunate country was liberty, freedom.

I desired to devote all my life to the cause of freedom for my people, and I felt that some how I would participate in this great task, though without the necessity of aligning myself with any political group. My soul was permeated with religious sentiment. I often read the Bible, reflecting on its passages, prayed and even had some religious dreams. One of these dreams seemed to have a practical application. It was as follows:

## A Dream of Labor Under Christ

I was in a public park in Vladikavkas, and many people were gathered there. A report was spread: "Christ has come." I ran to the gates and saw Christ with His face shining with meekness, peace and love, standing on a staircase leading from the street to the park. He was throwing gold coins in great quantity to the people. I had a sack and the greatest number of coins seemed to flow to me. But when I looked below they were flowing through my sack to the people. A friend standing by my side said: "Look, all the coins have gone!" I said: "All right; they were for the people."

This dream strengthened my feeling that God's purpose for my life was that I should be a transmitter of His gifts to needy humanity. This dream, or more correctly vision, has never been obliterated from my mind. I often remember it — the face of the Saviour beaming with heavenly joy and good will — and although not yet converted, I felt that some how I should come under the yoke of the Divine Teacher of humanity. After my own conversion this vision took on special significance for me. Really it was the call of God for the ministry of distributing His riches to a suffering world of poor sinners.

## Ministering to Those in Prison

All that I had heard about the sufferings for the faith from my father and grandmothers created in me a desire to devote my life to the service of persecuted Christians and to the struggle for freedom of conscience. My personal experience only served to strengthen this desire.

Father had a water-driven flour mill on the shore of the Terek River, which was not far from the government prison. Sometimes we received messages from the prison to call there. These were calls from the prisoners, dissenters who for the sake of their religion were sentenced to be exiled to the Transcaucasus. They were in the prison of Vladikavkas on their way to the place of exile, and used to send word to my father to come and see them.

Their power of suffering but unconquerable faith impressed me strongly. Of course, in our visits to the prison we brought to the prisoners food, money and other help. I liked to go among the prisoners and called very often at the prison to ascertain whether there were any prisoners for the faith, and if I found any, I invited my father or somebody else and we visited and aided them.

Thus it came about that these early influences finally confirmed me in my resolve to make the chief purpose of my life the struggle for freedom of conscience for all.

Toward the end of the sixth class of the high school, in the spring of 1886, my character and qualities became more or less determined. But my spiritual condition was still unsettled and any strong influence, political, religious or even atheistic, could carry me away. Indeed, that is what nearly occurred in this period of my life, as the next chapter tells.

41

# CHAPTER III

## My Conversion

*"In the day when I cried Thou answeredst me."*
Ps. 138 : 3.

MY conversion took place in the autumn of 1886 in the city of Vladikavkas. The following circumstances preceded this most important event of my life.

In picturing the religious condition of Russia in the sixties of the last century, I only briefly mentioned the religious condition of the intelligent classes generally and of the students of the colleges and universities. They were usually in opposition to the great Orthodox Church.

It is true that in the high schools religion was taught, and in the colleges and universities there were studies in theology. But all this teaching was so obviously official and so far removed from revealed truth as contained in the Scriptures that it aroused only antipathy or actual resistence in the minds of the students. There was no subject in the curriculum more unpopular than religion and theology in nearly all the schools and colleges.

Intelligent people were therefore opposed to the Orthodox Church, first of all because it had grown so corrupt that they ascribed to it all the crimes of the Government with which it was so vitally connected; secondly, on account of its heathenish practices, and thirdly, on account of its inability to approach them in scientific thought or language. The result was that in high schools and colleges infidelity was widespread. Among students were to be found organized groups, who read together the works of such writers and philosophers as Voltaire (skeptic), Feierbach (atheist), Buchner (materialist) and others.

### Reading the Pessimistic Philosophers

At our school there was such a group, the members of which studied especially the works of the pessimistic philosophers, Schopenhauer, Hartman and others. At the head of that group was a very talented young man, by the name of Korsh. I began to read writings by Schopenhauer and liked some of his thoughts. I can now understand why they appealed to me. It was because my mind was inclined to ponder over the sufferings of others and I liked to discuss the problem with others who were interested in it, particularly when they seemed to offer a solution.

There was at our school a teacher by the name of Shulgin, who was deeply engrossed in the teachings of Sakia-Muni (Buddha), that great teacher on the sufferings of humanity, and incidentally one of the strongest pillars of pessimism in the world. I remember how Shulgin picturesquely argued, according to Sakia-Muni, that the whole of life is nothing more than an endless chain of sufferings, and that the only method of getting rid of it is the Nirvanna —which nobody could really understand and which ordinary men, when pressed for a definition, described as a place of absence from any existence.

All this prepared the soil of my soul for the pessimistic teaching of Schopenhauer and Hartman, and I became a member of that group. We had our meetings in the evenings, read some of the books, tracts or manuscripts of these pessimistic philosophers, and discussed various questions. I found it at that time a very fascinating atmosphere.

### Our Leader Attempts to Overcome Life

At one of these meetings our leader, Korsh, stood up and exclaimed:

"I am going to overcome life by death!"

We saw a bottle of syanic kabi in his hands, which he was about to drink! I succeeded in knocking the bottle out of his hand by a blow, but apparently without weakening his determination to "overcome life," for he tried it again soon afterwards.

During all these experiences my mind was constantly occupied with one question:

"What was the real purpose of life?"

## IN THE CAULDRON OF RUSSIA

I could not shelve the question by indifference, as many of my companions seemed to do, and the daily recurrence of the problem caused me to suffer very much. The people who lived without finding an adequate answer to this great question seemed to me to be like passengers in a train with no knowledge of where they were going. I felt it was unworthy for a man as a reasoning human being to live on day by day and year by year with no knowledge of the purpose of his existence. I heard all possible philosophical answers to this question, but not one of them satisfied me.

The great Russian poet Pushkin wrote:

"Gift occasional, gift superfluous, —
Life! Why was it given me?"

and, replied to his own question:

"Life was given to me for life."

But this reply was not really a reply at all and, of course, could not satisfy my mind.

One of my fellow-students said to me: "There is no question about it: I live in order to support my mother and sisters."

I replied: "Men do not live to eat, but eat in order to live," and reminded him that even to acknowledge the validity of his purpose would be to deprive his mother and sisters of purpose for their lives.

There are, happily, answers of a nobler nature: We live for society, for our nation, for the good of humanity. But none of these answers could satisfy my mind, for I was still confronted by the question:

"What is the purpose of society, of the nation, of humanity itself?"

Some people claim to have something higher in their minds. They say that they live for art or for science. But this is not a cardinal answer, because the same question concerning the purpose of the arts and science is raised and remains without answer.

In my investigations I insisted upon one idea: That all

men must have one guiding purpose of life independent of individual environment. Not finding an absolutely satisfactory solution to my problem, I suffered bitterly and came to the verge of despair.

When I recall now my mental struggles of that period of my life I ask myself: How could I have so spent myself in searching for an answer to this question when I was so near God and my heart felt Him near? It must have been because of a darkened mind, dark to spiritual light because seeking truth by natural means. I have absolutely no doubt of the depravity of man. "The natural man comprehendeth not the things of God; they are spiritually discerned." — 1 Cor. 2 : 14.

## A Sudden Change From Pessimism to Optimism

Every one knows that the age of sixteen to nineteen years is a transition period for every young man. At this age they are restless, experience inner storms and often go to extremes. These features of the age had their effect upon me, but of course, beyond all this, there was also a reason of a purely spiritual nature. My heart was unconsciously crying out for the living God. Fighting against this hunger for God was a temptation from the same invisible power that made the effort to deprive me of my life in its very beginning, shortly after my birth, and which now again sought to bring death upon me in this transition period of my life. I became gloomy and obsessed with the idea that my life had no reasonable purpose or object, and I began to think seriously of some method by which I could get rid of the burden of life! How close I was to the right solution, and how near to the loss of eternal life!

In my room a rifle was hanging, and I thought that it might answer my purpose. One evening I came home from a meeting of pessimistic friends in a very distressed condition, and almost decided to make use of that rifle to "overcome life." On my way home I tried to imagine the impression which would be produced by my act. I entered my room and lighted the lamp, but what was my surprise on looking at the place where the rifle usually hung, to find that it had disappeared!

Afterward I learned that my father, acting on some inner prompting, had taken the rifle to another room. On the table I was surprised to see a small slip of paper, on which was written in large characters the question:

*"Do you love Jesus Christ?"*

These words pierced my soul. At once I remembered all my previous spiritual experiences. I was so struck that I could not move for some minutes. I took the New Testament then, and began to read such well remembered verses as John 14 : 6:

*"I am the Way, the Truth and the Life."*

and Phil. 1 : 21:

"For me to live is Christ, and to die is gain."

Of course, I was familiar with these verses before, but now they were revealed to me in a new light. A sweet voice said to me:

"Here is the answer to your life question."

## All the Darkness Cleared Away

In a flash the Gospel truth lighted my consciousness. All was as plain as day: Yes, I must live for Him, Who gave me life in my creation (birth), Who gave up His life for me on the cross, Who now, with His Son, gave me everlasting life, Who would assuredly give me all things necessary for my present life. I now saw clearly that the purpose of a life is to return to Him from Whom it came. — Gen. 2 : 7.

Such a simple truth made me happy beyond words to express, and I felt as though I had found my life anew. That night I prayed for the first time with all my heart and soul, asking the Lord for forgiveness of my unbelief, and sincerely thanking Him for saving me from the abyss which was before me and for opening for me such undreamed horizons of life, real life, new life. Not even one trace of the dark pessimism remained in my mind or heart.

## EFFORT TO OVERCOME LIFE

It is needless to say that after my conversion I left the group of pessimists and tried to persuade them to forsake the path which had been so dangerous for me and to accept the everlasting optimism of the Gospel.

*Since that day the salient feature of my life has always been and it is at the present time a pure optimism of faith.*

### Choosing the More Difficult Way

My conversion had a most favorable effect upon my relations with my fellow pupils. Although some of them spoke jokingly about my change, most of them began to feel an especial esteem for me, because it soon became evident that my highest aim was to combine in my life the ideals of the Gospel and Christian philosophy with the most practical helpfulness.

According to this new purpose I began to shape my life. On submitting my certificate from the high school I was accepted by two State institutions, Riga Polytechnic Institute and Moscow Academy of Agriculture. But I was not satisfied with either school. I heard an inward voice, which called me to go to St. Petersburg and to enter the Institute of Technology. The terms of admission there were very difficult. There were never more than 200 vacancies; generally there were more than a thousand candidates. I had, therefore, to pass competitive examinations. I remained at Vladikavkas one year, from 1887-1888, and spent the entire time in preparation for the competition. In August, 1888, I arrived at St. Petersburg. There were about twelve hundred candidates for the two hundred vacancies!

I passed the examinations with honors, being among the first five who received the highest marks. I was accepted as a student, and on the 25th of August I put on the student's uniform. This fact had an influence upon my whole life. It was the first step in realizing the practical ambition of my life. As to the spiritual side, from the day of my admission to the brotherhood, and until my departure from St. Petersburg, it was as active as it was joyful.

———•———

# CHAPTER IV

## Preparation for Future Service

*"That the man of God may be thoroughly furnished unto all good works."*

2 Tim. 3:17.

MY conversion took place in November 1886. On the 17th of January, 1887, I joined the local group of Christian believers, having been baptized in the river Terek at Vladikavkas.

The optimism of faith not only filled me with the joyful decision to devote all my life to Christ, but also gave a vision of the glorious goal toward which to aim and the assurance that He would give the necessary power to overcome all the hindrances and difficulties and to gain the final victory. I felt so assured of these truths that I was led in the same year, 1887, to make a program of my future life, and to take for my motto:

"Life for Christ!"

An incident of my school life caused me to put this life program into written form. The St. Petersburg Committee of Education published in the newspapers an announcement inviting literary men to write an essay on the Russian proverb:

"Education is light; the lack of it is darkness."

### An Essay on the Value of an Education

I wrote a story, the broad outlines of which, briefly stated, were as follows:

"Through a village rode a very rich man, a 'pomeshik,' the proprietor of one of the neighboring estates. A bag fell down from his wagon containing a very large sum of money. There was a moujik in the same village, Antonoff by name, who had three sons. The eldest, Wania, ten years old, saw the lost bag on the street, picked it up, and as he saw

I. S. Prokhanoff and his Closest Group of Fellow Workers
in Leningrad    (See page 157)

I. S. Prokhanoff with his Mother and Son at Leningrad    (See page 161)

1. **Guerusi Exile Prison Camp.**—(See page 115)
2. **Center Square of Vladikavkas.**—(See page 29)

the estate proprietor riding along the street, he thought that the bag must have been lost by him. Without any delay he ran to the estate and gave the lost bag to the 'barin,' who asked him who his father was and told him to come with his father on a certain day.

"When the father came, the rich man said that he would like to take his son to a school to give him a good education if the father would consent. When he hesitated, he was told to think the matter over and to come later with a definite answer.

"Moujik Antonoff went home and called some of his friends to ask for their advice. 'Diachek,' the junior deacon, said:

" 'Do not give your son to the school; he will be an atheist.'

Old man Potap said:

" 'Do not give him to the school; those who learn sciences do not esteem their parents.'

Another said:

" 'You will have no assistant in your farm work.'

"Only one, Moujik Grigory, who had been for some time in the military service, said:

" 'Do not listen to anybody. Send your son to school. He will become quite another man, for education is light, the lack of it is darkness. While in the military service I knew a man who was a dissenter and read the Gospel and explained it in a wonderful way. We are illiterate, and if that Book were here we would not be able to read it.'

"Antonoff decided to accept the propostion of the estate proprietor, and gave his son to him. The boy was sent to the town school. He finished there the grammar and high school courses of study, and then entered an Institute of Technology and became a mechanical engineer. He built the factories on the estate, founded hospitals, schools, libraries, bureaux of agricultural improvements, etc. Beside that, he arranged for a hall for scientific and religious lectures. A special feature for the people was his religious lectures. He and his assistants explained to the people the

49

Gospel in a simple and clear manner and called the people to follow the precepts of Christ. The report was spread that under the influence of his preaching drunkards became sober and lives were transformed. The name of the Engineer Antonoff became very well known throughout the whole province.

"One day 'Diachok' visited old Antonoff, who now lived in the town, in a good house given him by his son. 'Diachok' said: 'Grigory was right when he told us that education is light, the lack of it darkness.' "

## The Program of My Future Life

In this story I had pictured the program of my future life as I desired it to be.

Out of many striking features of St. Paul's life one always appealed to me with special power, of which mention is made in Acts 20 : 34:

"These hands have ministered unto my necessities, and to them that were with me." Also Acts 18 : 3:

"Because he was one of the same craft, he abode with them and wrought: for by their occupation they were tent makers."

## Following After the Apostle Paul

The Apostle Paul was a great worker in the field of God, yet at the same time he earned his living with his own hands, at least for a considerable period of his life. I took this for my ideal — to be as devoted a worker for the Gospel as the Apostle Paul, but at the same time to earn my living with my own hands.

This does not mean that I denied a paid ministry or paid missionary work. Not at all. "The workman is worthy of his meat." — Matt. 10 : 10, and "They which preach the Gospel should live of the Gospel." — 1 Cor. 9 : 14. I always was and am at present a sincere supporter and promoter of paid missionary work. But for myself I chose the way pictured in the words of the Apostle Paul.

I decided that I would gain a practical education in technical engineering and make my living by it, but at the same time I would serve the Lord with all my power and ability by spreading His Gospel.

It was as well that such was my purpose, for in Russia at that time Gospel preachers were not encouraged. Indeed, no Russian religious meetings nor congregations outside of the Orthodox Church were allowed by law, and preachers or ministers of such congregations simply could not be supported as such. The only way was to have ordinary occupations for income and to minister to churches in secret.

I chose mechanical engineering especially because I admired the great achievements of practical science in bringing forth inventions so helpful for the facilitation of human labor and because I hoped it would give me access to the masses of working people in factories and elsewhere.

As previously stated, I acted accordingly, and was admitted to the St. Petersburg Institute of Technology in 1888. During the time after my conversion, while I still remained at Vladikavkas, I began to take part in the spiritual work of the local church of believers and even gave Bible lessons to the children. About this time I also began to preach.

### Preaching My First Sermon

My first sermon, very appropriately, was on the text: "Blessed are the meek." — Matt. 5 : 5.

"I rely upon the Lord and I know that He will help me," were my words. And He did help. As I remember, my sermon produced a favorable impression.

On my arrival at St. Petersburg my life began in accordance with my program. On the one hand, I diligently studied in the Institute of Technology; on the other, I had always in mind the fact that I was dedicated to a certain definite program for my life. It enabled me always to judge clearly and to choose wisely when I brought every question to my Father and asked for His guidance in view of my life plan.

# CHAPTER V

## The Light Begins to Dawn

*"The people which sat in darkness saw a great light."*
*Matt. 4 : 16.*

IN a previous chapter I stated that the Evangelical movement in Russia had its beginning in the late sixties of the
nineteenth century, — about the time of my birth. The chief
manifestations of the movement appeared almost simul-
taneously in three different parts of Russia.

1. In St. Petersburg, the national capital, the Evangelical
movement had a very interesting beginning. There resided there at that time an aristocratic family by the name
of Chertkoff. The father was a general in the Russian
armies, while his wife was a society lady, devoted to the
pleasures of life. Among their children there was a son by
the name of Misha, whose tutor was a Christian believer.
Misha was taught by him to believe in Jesus Christ and to
love Him.

When Misha's mother called at his room, which was not
often, he would tell her about Jesus Christ. As can be
readily imagined, his mother was surprised to hear such
words from him, especially as he could not be prevented
from giving his witness. He also liked to read the Gospel
and to pray. The boy became seriously ill, and during his
illness he read the Gospel and prayed more often. When
his mother came he talked enthusiastically about the love of
Jesus Christ.

"O, how He loves me, mother. Do you know, mother,
He saved me. He can save you. Do you believe that,
mother? O, how sweet to be with Jesus! I would like to
see Him. By and by I will see Him. Mother! How I
would like to see you there with Jesus. Will you be there?"

Such ardent love and pleading from the sick boy produced a deep impression upon the mother, but it was still

stronger and overwhelming when the boy's condition became really serious and he lay dying. But his end was peace and his last word a benediction. As he prayed, asking Jesus to take him, his face was shining with joyful expectancy of the eternal blessedness, and he continued inviting his mother to believe in Jesus Christ until his lips were silent.

## A Search for Christian Happiness

His death had so deep an effect upon his mother that she left her pleasure-seeking worldly life and began to read the Gospel and to seek for herself that joy and happiness which her boy had found. She was joined by other anxious souls, to whom she spoke about Christ. Thus, the burning candle of one boy's faith lighted candles of faith in several souls, and opened the way for the Gospel in Russia.

Madam Chertkova began her search for that living power revealed in the Bible, which makes human souls happy, and as a first step she talked with eminent clergymen of the Orthodox Church. Of course, they could not satisfy her. Then she left Russia and began to visit various famous preachers in different countries. She was very deeply impressed by the preaching of Lord Radstock in Switzerland, whose sermons were simple and spiritual. She invited him to Russia, where he arrived in the early seventies. He began to preach in the home of Madam Chertkova among her friends and relatives.

Through his preaching, Col. Pashkoff (her brother-in-law), Count M. M. Korff and other members of the Russian aristocracy were converted. These new converts opened their houses for meetings, in which the Gospel was preached to aristocrats. Soon W. A. Pashkoff, M. M. Korff and other converts themselves began to preach. The conversion of these aristocrats was sincere and lasting. Col. Pashkoff left his service in the army, changed his mode of life altogether, became a preacher of the Gospel, and began to give great sums of money for the spreading of the Gospel and for various forms of social work.

Through his instrumentality cheap boarding houses, workshops of various kinds and homes for orphans were opened. At the same time he gave large sums for the printing of evangelistic tracts and for the distribution of Bibles and New Testaments.

Thus in the religious life of Russia almost the same thing happened as in its political history. The political liberation movement was started in Russia by men and women of the high aristocracy, such as Princess Volkonsky, Trubezkoi and others, who were called "Decabrists*." Though both Col. Pashkoff and Count Korff were soon banished from Russia for their religious activities, the Evangelical movement continued to expand and grow.

## Gospel Among the Russian Peasants

2. Now let us turn to the southwestern part of Russia, where, in the province of Odessa, the new religious movement began among Russia peasants who commenced to read the Scripture which had been translated into modern Russian from the Old Slavonic language. In that district of Russia there were many German colonies, and among these colonies were Lutherans, Mennonites and other believers. The Russian peasants naturally came into contact with these colonists and asked them for the interpretation of the Bible.

Bible and prayer meetings were arranged, which were called in German, *"Die Stunden,"* meaning *hours.* This term as applied to these mixed religious meetings of Russians and Germans was the origin of the name given later to the whole movement: "Stundism," i.e., *the movement of meeting hours, or the movement of meetings.* This name well characterized the movement.

## The Word of God Teaches New Converts

In the Orthodox churches there were only pompous ritualistic services in which the clergymen took part "like actors." The people did not and could not participate, be-

---

*Literally "December men," because their attempted revolution took place in December, 1826.

cause they did not understand anything of what was going on in the service. It was the Bible alone, accepted at its face value by the people, which taught the Christians in Odessa to arrange these meetings, with their simple faith in the words of Christ:

"Where two or three are gathered together in My Name, there am I in the midst of them." In these gatherings all felt that they were the children of one Father, brothers with One Great Teacher, and all who attended participated in comforting one another with the Word of God, in prayer and spiritual fellowship.

These meetings were a startling revelation to the clergy of the Orthodox Church itself, because they indicated a new conception of the Church, — a New Testament Church as a society of those who were redeemed by the blood of Jesus Christ, saved by His Grace and living according to His teachings.

Every meeting of this kind carried in itself the living seeds of a future reformation. They meant the founding of Evangelical churches with the right of election, control and discipline of the spiritual life. They meant the beginning of the new Christian social order. No wonder, therefore, that Stundism so terrified the Greek Orthodox Church clergy.

### Spiritual Movement in the Caucasus

3. In the Caucasus also a spiritual movement started in 1869. At Tiflis, the chief city of the Caucasus, there were two or three congregations of "Molokans" (see page 22). Nikita Veronin was one of their elders. Searching the Word of God, he found various points of difference between his own beliefs and the teachings of the New Testament, and as a consequence he began to inquire more diligently into the Scripture.

About this time he became acquainted with a German colonist named Kalveit, who lived at Tiflis and who explained to him the fundamental truths of the Gospel. The result was that Veronin was baptized by Kalveit in 1869, and the new movement resulting was called "Baptist." Almost at the same time another young man, Vassily Pavloff, was baptized. These two were the first preachers of baptism in the Caucasus.

These three streams of spiritual awakening began almost at the same time, although quite independently, humanly speaking. For some years there was no communication between these three groups. They knew of the existence of one another through the papers, but they had no relations between themselves. There was no transmission of this new spiritual movement from St. Petersburg to Odessa or the Caucasus. Each group was entirely independent of the others and unaware in the beginning that a similar work was going on elsewhere in Russia.

It proves that the time was fulfilled and "the hour had come" for the spiritual revival in Russia. The same Spirit breathed at the same time on people in different places and produced really spiritual movements, which were later to blend in widespread blessing. Gradually these believers came to know each other, and the necessity of fellowship sprang up. The initiative in this movement was taken by the representatives of the Gospel movement in St. Petersburg, W. A. Pashkoff, M. M. Korff and others.

## Aristocrats and Peasants Unite

In 1884 a conference was called in St. Petersburg to which the representatives of the Odessa movement (Stundism) and those of the Caucasian movement were invited. Those who took part in that Conference still speak about it with great enthusiasm. Aristocrats of Russia and simple peasants and workmen embraced each other as "brethren and sisters" in Christ. The love of God removed all social barriers. But the Conference could not last more than a day or two, as the police ordered it to be closed! Some of the members of the Conference were arrested, and finally W. A. Pashkoff and M. M. Korff were banished from Russia.

In spite of the fact that the three branches of the movement started in different parts of Russia, under different conditions, they were akin to each other with regard to their doctrines.

The Orthodox Clergy were alarmed at this beginning of the religious movement among the Russian people. Here history repeated itself. Being powerless to struggle against it with spiritual weapons, they had recourse to political expediency.

They wrote various reports to the Government, painting lurid pictures of imaginary political dangers connected with the religious movement. The Government of Alexander II evidently did not attach much importance to the reports of the clergy, and therefore the persecutions were not very severe. But the reactionary Government of Alexander III, at the head of which was such a retrograde as Pobedonostzeff, who filled the office of Procurator of the Holy Synod, was very friendly with the Orthodox clergy and developed a system of extremely bitter persecutions about the year of my arrival at St. Petersburg (1888).

# CHAPTER VI

## Persecutions

*"If they have persecuted Me, they will persecute you."*
John 15 : 20.

THE Government of Alexander II prepared a law which would have granted religious liberty to dissenters. This law was to have been proclaimed on Easter, 1881, as part of a cautiously worded Constitution of Rights. But the Emperor's assassination on the first of March of that year made the publication of this most important act impossible.

Alexander III declared in his manifesto his intention to proclaim the liberties intended by his father, but the influence of such reactionary men as Pobedonostzeff and others prevented him from doing so, and the Constitution was never promulgated. Count Loris-Melikoff, who was the Prime Minister and author of this Constitution, was dismissed; retrograde men were appointed to all the ministerial offices and the reaction soon began to set in.

In order to better understand the conditions under which the spiritual and evangelistic work was carried on in those days it will be necessary to picture the persecution which took place.

### Difficulty of Organizing for Worship

Out of all the new laws which were to have been issued together with the Constitution, only the law pertaining to dissenters and sectarians was proclaimed. It gave permission for dissenters and sectarians *who were born such* to hold their meetings if they constituted a considerable part of a certain village. But this permission was hedged about with many formalities and restrictions, so that only a very few could be benefitted by the law.

As a matter of fact the permission depended on the will-

58

ingness of the local authorities, but as those authorities were everywhere subservient to the local priests, bishops and archbishops, it will be readily understood that official permission was almost unheard of. In the places where the sectarians were exiled, if there was a considerable number of them, they assembled for the prayer meetings without permission, on the strength of their natural right. In all other places the dissenters either did not gather for public worship at all or they gathered secretly. If the police discovered such meetings, the partakers were fined or imprisoned and exiled.

As to other expressions of the religious life of the people anywhere, there was only one word: "Forbidden!"

According to the fundamental laws of the Empire it was forbidden for any man to have religious convictions differing from Greek Orthodox Church dogmas, or to separate from the church. Those who were guilty were liable to be exiled and their children were taken from them to be educated in monasteries.

## Protest of Count Tolstoy to the Government

One case of this kind came to public knowledge in 1892, when the children of the sectarians (Molokans) were taken to the monasteries, and the celebrated writer, Count Leo Tolstoi, wrote an open letter about it to the highest authority. The children of those who became dissenters were not always taken from them, but a great many were banished from their homes to Siberia, Caucasus and elsewhere. The idea was to isolate such men from the Orthodox population.

There was a law forbidding a sectarian or anybody else to talk on religious topics not in accord with the doctrines of the Orthodox Church or to persuade anybody to accept any doctrine differing from that of the Greek Orthodox Church. All who were guilty of this, and especially when somebody changed his religious beliefs under the influence of such a talk, were to be banished to Siberia. This crime was called "proselytizing." The same punishment, or one even more severe up to "hard labor" exile, was extended to those who spoke disrespectfully about the holy ikons (images), the dead bodies of saints, and the rituals of the Orthodox Church.

These laws were very unjust in themselves, but one condition was even worse than might have been reasonably expected from their general interpretation. The clergy of the Orthodox Church, being powerless to struggle against the religious movements with spiritual weapons, transformed these laws into weapons of offense against any display of free religious thought. If the clergy knew that in a certain place there was a man who thought or spoke like a dissenter, their first move was to send some one to the dissenter or sectarian, that he might talk with him on religious matters in the presence of a witness. Then an application to the law court was filed, charging him with proselytizing, and the man would be tried, convicted and exiled. Of course, in all these cases, "false witnesses" played a prominent role.

If, however, no offence could be found in such a sectarian for which he could be prosecuted by the law, another means remained in the hands of the clergy to get rid of him. It was the so-called "administrative process." In such cases the clergy applied to the highest local administrative official with a complaint against such and such a dissenter for being a dangerous propagandist of his heresy and with a request to exile him. And such a dissenter was always exiled.

## Sectarians Had No Legal Standing

As separation from the Orthodox Church was considered to be an unlawful act, the sectarians themselves were deprived of many rights. Their marriages were considered to be unlawful, their children were illegitimate. The children of sectarians were not registered, had no documents and therefore were not accepted into the schools. If a sectarian died, the clergy forbade burial in an Orthodox cemetery. On the other hand, no special cemeteries were allowed for dissenters. Therefore, in many cases, the dead bodies remained in the houses for a long time and the families of the dead had to suffer.

Sometimes such bodies were buried in the Jewish cemeteries or in a lonely place in a field. Sometimes the dissenters buried their own dead in their courtyards or kitchen gardens. One can imagine what sufferings such actions by the clergy caused to the dissenters. Very often the priests incited crowds to make attacks on the Stundists and others. From this it is clear that not even the slightest semblance of religious liberty existed in all that time, and the condition continued almost up to 1905.

## Propaganda Prohibition Was Complete

Any kind of religious propaganda was forbidden; any public service or religious meeting apart from the Orthodox Church was considered unlawful. No religious book, paper or tract (except only those of purely Orthodox contents) could be printed. No school for the education of children of the dissenters was allowed.

But the Orthodox clergy were not satisfied with that. They brought influence to bear upon the secular authorities, so that on the 3rd of September, 1894, a circular by the Minister of the Interior was published, according to which the adherents of the new religious movement (Stundism) were proclaimed to be dangerous to the State and by this act they were denied the protection of the law.

The result was that toward 1895 (two years after I had finished my course at the St. Petersburg Institute of Technology) all the prisons and places of exile were filled with dissenters and their families. The dissenters were exiled mostly to Siberia and Transcaucasus. The Armenian village of Guerusi, in the Transcaucasus, became the principal place of exile for dissenters. I will have to mention this place later.

Journeying to the places of exile was very trying. Our brethren were herded together with criminals, thieves and murderers. Many of them in chains, with half shaved heads, suffered under the rough treatment, the most unsanitary conditions and the lack of food. Some brethren died on their way to the places of exile, and others in their banishment.

# CHAPTER VII

## Student and Organizer

*"I must work the works of Him that sent me, while it is day."*

John 9 : 4.

I HAVE already mentioned that, being guided by an unseen will, and energized by a joyous optimism of faith, I made a program for my whole life. Since that time it has always been my aim to make programs for my future, as well as for short periods of my life, in connection with every new situation in which I found myself. I was accustomed to make a program for a year, for a summer vacation, etc.

It has always been my rule to make a program for the work of each day at the close of the previous day. Every evening I usually wrote on a slip of paper what I would have to do on the next day. This made all my days most productive. Arising in the morning, I would look at my program and proceed to attend to all the affairs noted thereon. This saved me the necessity of thinking what should be done next and gave me a speed and precision with my work which I would not otherwise have been able to master. I can highly recommend such a program to every reader, especially to all young men. By adopting this method your efficiency may be increased as much as fifty per cent.

When I grew more intimately acquainted with my daily routine as a student at the Institute of Technology, I made a program for spiritual work in St. Petersburg.

At that time in Russia public gatherings were impossible. All the meetings were secret. Every Friday brothers from the principal parts of the city gathered and arranged for secret meetings in private houses. Every Saturday believers in different quarters were personally informed by brethren of the places of meeting. Every week the program was changed. The meetings took place under very trying conditions, often in the poor rooms of workmen or craftsmen.

Especially do I remember one meeting that was arranged in a basement room occupied by a waiter in a military school. The room was approached by means of long, dark corridors, which made me think of the catacombs. The waiter himself stood at the entrance of the corridor. The visitors came one by one, careful that nobody should see them. The waiter passed only those whom he knew or on the recommendation of a known brother. Keeping silence, he led visitors through a very gloomy corridor to his room, where from fifteen to twenty-five people were gathered. No singing was indulged in, for fear of drawing the attention of the police. After the meeting was over all the visitors retired one by one, with the same measure of precaution.

Another meeting that I recall was held at the house of the Countess Shuvaloff, at Moika and Zimnia Kanavka streets. The meeting was in the basement of the house, in a room occupied by the coachman. The believers came in and went out of the meeting one by one, striving to keep their movements hidden from police agents. The Countess herself came to the meeting with the same precaution. The coachman was one of the preachers. Usually he and some one else, two or three brethren, delivered short sermons. There was prayer, sometimes the breaking of bread and Bible reading, but there was no singing, or very little in a low tone.

### Risking Arrest and Exile

On my arrival in St. Petersburg I began to take part in these meetings, and I preached in them very often. As I remember, I broached the idea to the brothers that we should extend the meetings all over the city, using every opportunity to enlarge the preaching of the Gospel, even though we were restricted to secret gatherings and ran a continual risk of arrest, imprisonment and exile.

I proposed that in the summer the meetings should be arranged in the woods and forests surrounding St. Petersburg. But at the same time I laid special stress on the importance of private visits to those interested in the Word of God, and of holding personal conversation with them. Together with other brethren I visited many families and individuals in their houses, sometimes in the basements, sometimes in the attics, persuading them to believe in Jesus Christ. How many really suffering souls we found, and what joy we saw in their faces after our reading of the Word of God and prayer! Of course, these meetings and even the visits of individuals were not at all safe.

One such meeting, arranged in a forest, was raided by the police and one of the preachers, Mr. S. A. Alexeef, was arrested and exiled to Transcaucasus, where he spent eight years, being then moved to another place of exile, where he was compelled to spend five years more. But we did not hesitate to arrange new meetings, remembering the promise that "Not a hair of our head shall perish" without the Will of God.

The second branch of my religious work was connected with the alleviation of the sufferings of believers throughout Russia. It was perhaps only natural that, being in St. Petersburg, I received a great many letters and personal communications through individual Christians arriving in the city from all parts of Russia. These letters told harrowing details of all kinds of persecutions. As during the time of Christ, so also in Russia we had our Nicodemuses and our Josephs of Arimathea, secret disciples in all departments of the State Government.

## Secret Aid by Government Officials

There were members of the Senate and the State Council who sympathized with the movement; there were lawyers who were always ready to help gratuitously with their advice. Of course, at that time it was very difficult to do much by correspondence, because there was a constant censorship of letters. Many such communications did not reach their destination at all, and most of them undoubtedly found their way to the secret rooms of the post offices, there to be read for the discovery of evidence against the writers or recipients. Suspicious letters were always sent to the secret police or to the gendarmes, and in many cases trials and persecutions followed.

Nevertheless, God helped us to arrange a very satisfactory line of communication with the main places of suffering of believers, and especially with Ukraina, where the persecutions were the most bitter.

Among the Christian believers of that time there was a very remarkable man named Vassily Nicolaevitch Ivanoff. He had been one of the gendarmes of the Czar's Government, but on his conversion he left the service and became a worker among the Stundists. He lived at Kharkoff, the present capital of Ukraina, and chose a special bit of service for himself.

Dressing always as a simple peasant, he traveled in secret all through Ukraina, penetrating into the most remote and lonely villages and "khutors" (hamlets), most of which were well guarded by the police and gendarmes. Owing to his knowledge of police practice, he managed to visit places which nobody else could have reached.

## Our Secret Ambassador at Work

In each of these places Brother Ivanoff did four things: 1. He comforted the persecuted brothers and sisters with the Word of God, and encouraged them to stand fast for Christ. 2. He delivered to them inspiring messages and greetings from other churches. 3. He brought material help for the sufferers from Christian believers in other districts. 4. He gave to the sufferers advice as to the laws by which they could be benefitted; wrote petitions for them and gathered information or written material about the persecutions. This written evidence he sent to friendly officials at Kharkoff, and also to us at St. Petersburg, by trusted brothers.

Very often Brother Ivanoff came to St. Petersburg himself, with heaps of papers and documents. We studied all this material and carefully worked out the measures to be taken in each case. In many instances our influential friends wrote private letters to their friends among high officials in the provinces, suggesting the mitigation of severe measures which had been taken against the Stundists. Sometimes these letters helped in a remarkable way, but mostly in individual cases, and the general persecution continued to be very severe.

## Always Escaped the Secret Police

Brother Ivanoff visited the Caucasus, which was the chief place of exile, and other provinces outside of Ukraina, where the persecution was raging. During many years he kept on traveling in this way, and never was arrested. The secret police and gendarmes often knew of his visits to the places of persecution and tried to capture him, but they could not manage to do so. Often he was about to be taken, but always managed to escape. Evidently the hand of God protected him as he continued to carry on his important work among the brethren all over Russia.

Being at St. Petersburg, I was in constant communication with him and aided in the direction of all these matters pertaining to the persecution of our brethren. Beside Brother Ivanoff there were brethren who took care of the persecuted, and gradually at St. Petersburg we came to have a secret executive office on the religious persecution. In connection with this work we considered it our duty to make collections so as to secure material help and send it to the suffering brothers through Brother Ivanoff and others.

## The Work of Correspondence and Evangelism

The work described above was conducted mainly by correspondence. At that time there were not very many groups of Christian believers, but they were increasing and the correspondence grew heavier month by month. Letters concerned not only the persecutions, but also all kinds of economic, social and spiritual questions. Accordingly my answers touched all the phases of Christian life. A considerable portion of my time was devoted to such correspondence.

All this time I had a clear understanding that the Evangelical movement must exert a continuous influence upon all classes of the Russian population and upon an increasing area of the country. The first method for spreading the Gospel was, of course, by word of mouth. I remember that at the time I had a rule not to live one day without saying something to some one about the love of God. In all my letters and intercourse with the believers I used continually to urge them to fulfill their duty of preaching the Gospel.

But at the same time I began to think about the necessity of using the literary method of spreading the Gospel. At that time it was apparently impossible to plan for the printing of anything concerning our labor, it being against the law to produce or distribute anything that was not strictly in conformity with the doctrines of the Greek Catholic Church.

## The First Periodical

One day in the spring of 1889, in the midst of my examinations at the Technological Institute, I was thinking of the difficulties we were having in maintaining our correspondence with Christian believers scattered in places of exile and throughout the whole country. Suddenly the thought came to my mind:

"Why not found a periodical for that purpose?"

As I was very busy just then with my examinations I postponed the realization of this much needed project until I should return to Vladikavkas. At the end of May in that year I was again in that city and immediately I began to work out the details necessary to produce a periodical. But how could my plan be realized? It was impossible to receive permission from the Government for a printed paper or magazine. What was to be done? I decided to make use of the hectograph for the purpose, but even so, a permit was required, which, of course, I knew would not be granted when the authorities discovered what use I proposed to make of the outfit. Then I decided to start the periodical and to use a hectograph in spite of the Government regulations. We planned to send copies to the brethren all over

67

Russia by means of registered letters. So as the first step in our important undertaking my younger brother and I made the hectograph at home.

We had already decided that the periodical was to be published monthly, under the title of "Besseda," meaning a conversation or talk. We deliberately chose the most innocent title possible, so as to allay suspicion should any of the letters be opened by the police. Copies of the periodical were sent to the main Evangelical churches and preachers and even to places of exile. The joy with which the first copies were received and the deep impression produced as their reading progressed may be better imagined than described. Every Christian was thus strengthened and was encouraged by this periodical.

These copies of "Besseda" contained a considerable amount of spiritual help and encouragement, and we were told over and over again that to read the little pages, full of brotherly comfort, amidst all kinds of persecution, brought the greatest delight to the hearts of the believers.

Amid the dangerous condition of the times the writers of articles could not, of course, sign their proper names, and so we used Biblical cognomens, such as David, Timothy, Luke and others, or certain Christian words, such as believer, laborer, etc. The name of Zaccheus was given to me, quite in contrast to my stature.

## Connecting Link for All Believers

This little magazine, appearing regularly month after month, drew all the believers close together, and almost instantly the feeling that the Gospel movement had become a real power crystalized into a joyous conviction. While I remained at Vladikavkas, my younger brother, Alexander, co-operated with me in issuing this periodical, but on my return to the Institute at St. Petersburg in the fall I made another arrangement, since it was necessary to use greater caution as the quantity increased month after month and many numbers were still in circulation among the believers in all parts of Russia. Among my friends at St. Petersburg was H. I. Fast, a Mennonite* brother, tutor to the young Count Orloff-Denisoff. A Russian by the name of Gorinovich, who in his youth had belonged to the party of Terrorist Socialists, was converted and joined our Christian group. The sister of Brother Gorinovich was Mr. Fast's wife, and she was a very good and clever Christian lady. On my return from Vladikavkas to St. Petersburg I told these good friends about the periodical "Bessada," and they were much interested and expressed their willingness to aid in the publication work. For convenience in the work of issuing the publication, I moved to their house, where I occupied a small room. Thus we continued this most important part of our ministry, using the hectograph my brother and I had made, and sending out the consecutive issues of our periodical in registered letters.

## Work at the Institute

While deeply devoted to and active in the various branches of the spiritual work, I had, of course, to work very hard at the Institute of Technology. Study in the technical faculties or engineering school was always more difficult than in the other departments of our universities, for the reason that not only theoretical but practical branches of the work were required. The practical branch included tests with machines and mechanisms of many kinds, drawing designs and plans of all sorts of engineering projects, steam engines, bridges, factories, etc. All this required much time, great energy and persistence.

Every student had to serve an apprenticeship in some practical line of work, according to his specialty, and also to pass examinations in the same line. My course was in mechanical engineering, and in 1890 I chose to be an apprentice to an assistant engine driver. Accordingly I spent

---

*During the reign of Catherine II, Mennonites emigrated from Holland and Poland to the Southern part of Russia, in Taurian, Kherson and Ekaterinoslav provinces. Their colonies were flourishing there. During the sixties of the nineteenth century a new movement started among them, resulting in the formation of the "Mennonite Brothers' Church," kindred in belief and practices to the Gospel (Evangelical) Christians.

two months of my summer vacation on the Novorossyisk branch of the Vladikavkas Railroad.

In the summer vacation of 1892 I decided to secure practical experience on a steamship. The Board of the Russian Steamship and Trade company in Odessa accepted me as an apprentice on one of their steamers, and I made the voyage on the "Russia" to Constantinople, Smyrna, Alexandria, Joppa and Beirut, and so back again to Odessa. I will never forget the impressions on my mind and heart caused by this first voyage.

I cannot describe in these pages all my impressions, but that trip on the steamer "Russia" had a great influence on my intellectual development. Needless to say, my horizon was immensely extended.

I passed my final examinations at the Institute of Technology and finished the prescribed course in 1893.

# CHAPTER VIII

## Days of Broadening Views

*"Prove all things; hold fast that which is good."*
*1 Thes. 5 : 21.*

FROM my reading of the Acts of the Apostles and their Epistles I saw that in preaching the Gospel they not only did not avoid contact with the various social and religious groups, but sought fellowship with as many as possible. The Apostle Paul not only sought out the heathen temples at Athens, but encountered certain of the Epicureans and of the Stoics, who brought him to the Aeropagus, where he preached the Gospel with much power.

Deciding to follow this example, I did not avoid intercourse with other social and religious groups, but endeavored to come into contact with all of them, to the end that I might show to them the saving power of the pure Gospel, insisting also that it was the necessary basis for any religious work.

This brought me into contact with that old sect, "Chlisti," of which I have previously spoken. A Kazak from the Caucasus, a member of the Imperial Guard, came to one of our secret meetings. He showed me a letter from one of my friends in the Caucasus, and so we allowed him to remain and to associate himself with us.

It is a general characteristic of the "Chlisti" that they do not say openly what their religious connections are, but leave this to be discovered afterward. Very soon the father and mother of this man arrived in St. Petersburg and opened a little workshop for the sale of ornaments for the Kazak uniforms. They zealously attended our meetings and always prayed very earnestly.

As we become better acquainted with them we found that they were strict vegetarians. They prayed very often that God might give us the "fulness." We endeavored to guess

71

what fulness it was, but could not find a satisfactory explanation. The "fulness" was finally discovered in this manner:

At one of the Sunday morning meetings, when all the believers were engaged in prayer, the mother of the Kazak suddenly raised her voice and began to shout and cry, uttering
unknown words, interspersed with some plain words. This
produced a sensation. Every one stood up and one of the
brothers took her by the arm and asked her to quiet herself.

When asked, she and her husband explained that it was
a prophecy in an unknown tongue. After the brethren had
explained to them the Scriptural teaching on prophecy and
tongues they left the service.

Afterward many conversions of the "Chlisti" were reported in various parts of Russia. Even prophets of that
sect were converted through faith in the Gospel.

## We Gain Converts from the Chlisti

Toward the close of my course at the Institute of Technology I was told that a "Chlisti" prophet named Riaboff
had arrived in St. Petersburg and that he and a group of his
followers were operating a lace factory. Their meetings were
closely guarded and it was almost impossible to receive permission to visit them. One of his followers, however, was
the brother of one of our members, and he finally secured for
us permission to visit one of their meetings. It was late at
night — about 11 o'clock — when we reached the house and
were shown into the room.

The Prophet Riaboff was a tall, black-haired man about
forty, with magnetic eyes. When we entered, they were
singing their hymns, the melodies of which resembled dance
hall music. After singing, the prophet began to speak. What
he said was vague, but most of his utterances were quotations
from Old Testament prophets. His manner of speaking was
calculated to captivate the minds and to sway the emotions
of his followers.

One young man, who was sitting on the bed, suddenly
fell on it and became apparently unconscious. After a little
while he began to utter strange incomprehensible words. The

prophet stood over him and addressed his audience in words like these:

"He sees the third heavens and angels."

When the young man awakened, Riaboff asked him:

"What did you see, my dear?"

The young man answered him in the exact words of the prophet: That he had beheld the third heaven and angels. It was clear to me that here we had an example of purely hynotic influence or even a case of religious cheating.

Afterward I talked with this prophet several times, endeavoring to convince him of the necessity of believing the pure Gospel in the way in which the Apostles believed it. We discovered, however, that among these people he was looked upon as more than a prophet. They honored him as Christ.

We decided finally to make a spiritual attack on his group. As a result, some of them were really converted, Riaboff left St. Petersburg and his congregation ceased to exist. We found special difficulty in dealing with the "Chlisti," since, although they might come to a knowledge of the Gospel truth, it was very difficult for them to leave their group and their false teachers, owing to the fact that their hypnotic influence over them was often very strong. But the power of the Gospel always proved stronger for those who really desired to be free from this error.

## Attitude of Students Toward Religion

The students of the Institute of Technology, as well as those attending all other colleges and universities in Russia, were either indifferent or even hostile to religion. As I have said, their attitude was largely due to their indifference or opposition to the Orthodox Church, with its almost heathenish practices, or on account of its inability to approach them in scientific language and on their own mental ground.

Materialistic theories were very prevalent among the students, but political and social questions stood preeminent and quite naturally claimed the most attention among our educated young men. In those days the despotism and oppression of the autocratic government in Russia reached its highest limits. No social activity was allowed. The literature, the press and science were put under severe restrictions and inhibitions. Prisons and places of exile were filled with the exponents of free political thought and their followers. Nevertheless various political parties were formed among the intelligent classes for the purpose of overthrowing the czarist regime. These parties were: "Zemlia i vola," (Land and Liberty); "National Socialist," "Social Revolutionary" and others. Most of these organizations were of a socialistic nature.

The leaders generally emigrated abroad and published in other countries the organs of their parties. Secretly these publications were imported and spread among the Russian workmen and students. Many pamphlets and tracts were printed in secret in Russia itself, and spread in the same manner. Various groups were formed among the students for propagating political ideas. The students of the Institute of Technology were especially known for their political activity.

Very often we would hear that one of our fellow students was under arrest and had disappeared. After a time the report would reach us that he had been sent to somewhere in Siberia.

## Unsuccessful Political Reformers

There was a motto among the students: *"to go to the people!"* It meant that the student left his institute or university, became like a peasant and went to a certain chosen village to propagate liberation ideas among the peasants in a secret manner. More often these young men went to the factories and endeavored to influence the workmen. Usually these attempts did not last long. The police were so watchful and severe that such propagandists were soon arrested and exiled. Some of them were sentenced for life in prisons and fortresses like Petropavlovsky and Schliesselburgsky.

In this way many noble young men voluntarily sacrificed their lives with only one objective in mind, the great cause of political freedom for their country. They went to prison, to exile and very often to death with this idealistic sentiment and self-denying enthusiasm as the great incentive and driving power. They were great lovers of freedom for their people and they idealized the simple gray "moujik" (peasant), the great sufferer of the centuries.

Of course, I admired these young men and had a great sympathy for them, but I could not join them on account of their anti-religious views. Most of them, if not all, were opposed to religion of any kind.

Since my conversion the religion of Jesus Christ was all in all to me. Only when viewed in the light of the Gospel did the real meaning of life burst upon my mind. For me the teaching of Jesus Christ was the only real way to the spiritual regeneration of an individual, of society, of nations and the whole of humanity.

In debates with my fellow students of the political group I always argued that, although extreme political and social reforms were necessary for the Russian people and must be obtained, the regeneration of the spiritual life was still more necessary. I maintained that no political reform could be put into practical effect if the people remained in the darkness of the Orthodox Church with its fetishism. No social or political reforms could prove successful unless a moral and spiritual reform in the people themselves was first realized.

I continuously made an effort to preach the Gospel among those students, two of whom joined me and afterward became members of our Evangelical churches and my fellow workers, Theodor S. and X. E. Z.

I felt that my continual message to our educated class was to "repent and believe in the Gospel," a call to take that Gospel and to build a new life on its foundation. Really that was my message even to Tolstoy and his followers (about whom I write in the next chapter), because what he preached was not the Gospel — good tidings about salvation — but a kind of Moses law perfected by Christ.

# CHAPTER IX

## Tolstoy and His Followers

*"Fulfill the Law and Thou Wilt Have Life."*

EVEN before my entry into the Institute of Technology I was, of course, acquainted with the main theses of Tolstoy's doctrine. But my practical acquaintance with Tolstoism took place while I was a student there. My first meeting with a Tolstoist took place under the following circumstances.

While under appointment as an apprentice according to the rules of the Institute of Technology, and serving as an assistant locomotive engineer on the railroad, at Novorossiisk, I contracted malaria, which is very prevalent in that part of Russia. I was lying ill in the house of a brother carpenter. This house was in process of construction, being almost finished, so that the carpenter and his family were able to live there.

One day the wife came and said to me: "A Tolstoist has come to see you." Although I felt very ill, I said: "I want to see him; let him come in."

A tall man about thirty-eight years old entered the room and we greeted each other. He was large and with a massive head, almost bald, with broad shoulders and wearing spectacles over his large eyes. He wore a simple peasant shirt and his shoes were covered with dust. But while his clothing was that of a peasant, it was apparent after a brief scrutiny that he was not a peasant. His name was Alekhin.

One could understand at once that he was learned and had a philosophical mind. His people were descendants of a very old noble family. Clothed in a vagabond's costume, he spoke as a distinguished philosopher. It was very interesting to listen to him.

Afterward Alekhin visited me and other brethren in St. Petersburg, and very often we had long talks with him. We soon began to notice that he was somewhat disappointed in Tolstoism. We spoke to him a great deal of the simple Gospel teaching, about the necessity of regeneration as a sound basis for spiritual life and other spiritual topics. I will never forget how at one of our secret meetings Mr. Alekhin prayed earnestly in commanding tones, giving vent to a desire to be converted.

This was not at all a Tolstoist action, as the Tolstoists do not recognize verbal prayers. It was the result of the influence of the Holy Spirit, working through the Gospel preaching. Mr. Alekhin was very powerful in debates with infidels. But I felt that nothing could be solid or permanent in the life of this man, since he would not acknowledge definitely his allegiance to Christ. He belonged to the type of men who are numerous in Russia, but rarely met with in the rest of Europe. They like to seek the truth, not because they want to apply it to their own lives, but because they enjoy the process of "seeking" it. I had a presentiment that his convictions would change often in the future, with changing circumstances, and my presentiment was amply fulfilled.

## Always Changing; Never Changed

Some years later, about 1902, I met Mr. Alekhin on Nevsky Avenue, the finest street in St. Petersburg, exquisitely dressed and wearing a silk top hat and fine gloves. He told me that he was at that time the Lord Mayor of the city of Kursk, and that he had changed his religious and political views, and was now an ardent follower of another Russian Philosopher, Vladimir Solovieuff, a great mystic and an Orthodox Church writer, and that he longed for theocracy in the church and for autocracy in the state!

I met him again on the streets of St. Petersburg in 1905, after the State Duma was organized. On this occasion he was also finely dressed, but now he expressed quite new ideas. He declared himself to be a member of the party of "Trudoviky," a moderate socialist party. Before he had eloquently taught, "Do not resist evil;" now he said: "Resist evil."

Generally speaking, I gathered one definite impression from all the Tolstoists whom I met — that the religious conviction of most of them was not strong, and that they were subject to a change of mind and heart on the slightest provocation.

## My Meeting with Tolstoy

After we had received from the Institute of Technology our diplomas as mechanical engineers, my friend S. and I decided to visit our homes in the Caucasus before beginning our future work. Our railroad route to the Caucasus took us through the city of Tula, in the neighborhood of which, in Yasnaia Poliana, Leo Tolstoy lived, and we decided to visit him.

It will undoubtedly be of interest here to recall some features of that memorable visit. We had hired a cab from Tula, which brought us to the estate Yasnaia Poliana. Among the big trees of the park, as we arrived we saw a white house and a group of ladies, who were playing lawn tennis. An old man with large features, gray hair and beard, was walking in the direction of the veranda. On his head he wore a large white cap. He was dressed in a white blouse, gray trousers and rough boots, and looked like a gardener. We recognized in him Leo Tolstoy. He carried a walking stick, and he was engaged, as he walked, in eating a piece of dry bread!

When Tolstoy saw us, he came toward us, and we introduced ourselves to him. He asked us of which institute we were students, and then said:

"Would you like to walk a little with me on the avenues of the park?" Of course, we eagerly assented. We said to him:

"We are aiming at being disciples of Christ, and we would like to have a talk with you about Christ."

After our conversation Tolstoy asked us whether we preferred to go with him for a walk to the forest to gather mushrooms, or to read the manuscript of his new book, "The Kingdom of God Is Within You."

We preferred to see the manuscript, of course, so Tolstoy climbed through a window into his room, got his copy, gave it to us, and went to the woods with a basket, to gather mushrooms.

## We Read Tolstoy's New Manuscript

With an eagerness which you will readily understand, we read that manuscript. After a few hours, Tolstoy entered our room and invited us to take dinner with him in his room. He treated us to his mushrooms, picked by himself, which we ate with relish. The dinner was laid in his own special room in a house situated at some distance from the main buildings, where his family lived.

Of course, we could not persuade Tolstoy to change his mind. Still less could he influence our convictions and beliefs.

After the conversation with Tolstoy, I became more firmly convinced that the salvation of the world is in the simple Gospel, not in a part of the Gospel, but in the whole Gospel; not even in the highest and most clever interpretation of the Gospel, but in the Gospel itself; that the wonderful substance of the Gospel can be understood, not by philosophers, but as it is revealed to the humblest childlike heart (Matt. 11:25-26 on) by the Holy Spirit; that for every unprejudiced mind it is clear that the teaching of Christ cannot be separated from His person; that the highest moral precepts and ideals of Christ cannot be separated from His teachings or from the dogmatic contents of the Scriptures; that the doctrine of Tolstoy, if separated from some peculiarities, is simply a moral teaching, which transforms Christ's grace into the Mosaic law or the Stoic principle, because it brings men to an inaccessible mountain and without imparting to them any power says: "Climb up." Of course, they cannot climb up.

When Moses sent men to a mountain, it was Sinai; but Tolstoy sends his disciples to a still higher mountain, the mountain of Christ's perfection, and says the same thing. Of course, there can be no other result than the consciousness of utter helplessness and despair. Unfortunately Tolstoy did not study or he did not understand the seventh and eighth chapters of Paul's Epistle to the Romans.

In saying "good bye" to us, Tolstoy said that he believed us to be sincere young men and wished us all good things. He accompanied us to our coach and we departed. Our coachman, Alexei, said that in our absence Tolstoy himself had come and invited him to the house, where he had his dinner with the servants.

## The Mystery of Tolstoy's End

The sharp contrasts and changes of front by Alekhin, Prince Khilkoff and others among the Tolstoists can be very easily explained. Even their leader, Leo Tolstoy, was not exempt. A few days before his death on the 7th of November, 1911, under very peculiar circumstances, Tolstoy left his house without saying a word to anybody. In fact, he disappeared quite unexpectedly, and it is hinted that he "ran away."

His wife and sons were in great distress. Police officers were sent everywhere to seek him. They could not find him for several days, but he was finally located in the home of the master of a railway station, lying ill in bed. After a few days he died there, in the presence of his closest friends and most intimate disciples, but neither his wife nor other members of his family were allowed to approach him at the time. It was later revealed that before reaching the station master's house Tolstoy had visited a monastery where lived a very old monk, widely known for his saintliness and wisdom. Tolstoy spent considerable time in conversation with this hermit. What was the nature of that conversation? What was the state of mind of Tolstoy after he left the monastery? No one knows except his nearest friends, but it is generally conceded that this visit and conversation could not have been possible if no change had been wrought previously in the mind of this great thinker. One can easily guess the nature of that change!

Some people were carried away with his teachings, but generally speaking, they were soon disappointed. As for myself, I recognized in Tolstoy a great writer and thinker. I admired him for his great literary ability and his writings on the moral phase of Christianity, but I could not follow him as a religious teacher, because he really misunderstood Christ, throwing away nearly all of the Bible, entirely overlooking the problem of sin and rejecting the necessities of conversion, faith and prayer — the cardinal elements of the spiritual life.

## CHAPTER X

# The Mission with Regard to the Orthodox Church

*"My shepherds did not search for my flock."*
*Ezek. 34:8.*

IN the eighties of the nineteenth century the condition of the Orthodox Church was no better than it had been in the sixties, as described in Chapter I. It was still characterized by the same predominance of ritualism and even fetishism among the people; the same absence of spiritually alive individuals among its highest clergy; the same subjection of clerical authority to the secular power, and, in short, spiritual stagnation and death everywhere.

These clerical leaders needed the preaching of the Gospel even more than the lay members of the Orthodox Church did, and the Gospel *was* preached to them. In St. Petersburg there lived a very old lady named Chernilevsky. She was in good health and quite strong, in spite of her seventy-five years, and she felt a special call from God to preach the Gospel to the highest members of the Orthodox Clergy. She succeeded in visiting the Archbishops and the Metropolitans and speaking to them about the simple Gospel faith. Some of them listened attentively and put down all the texts which were quoted by her, together with her own comments. Especially was this true of the Metropolitan Antonius. But as far as could be seen there were no practical results among the clergy.

No activity of the Orthodox Church showed to such an extent its spiritual poverty as the work of so-called "Orthodox missionaries." The most reactionary of the Holy Synod's Procurators, K. R. Pobedonostzeff, founded a movement called "The Orthodox Inland Mission," the purpose of which was officially stated to be the struggle against all kinds of sectarian teachings.

## ORTHODOX "MISSIONARY" PERSECUTION

These "missionaries" really made of themselves "police agents," and as a result of their reports, many preachers of the Gospel were shut up in prison or exiled. Among the most zealous of these missionaries was one, *Skvortzoff*. This name means in Russia a "starling." Later, among the persecuted Stundists all the orthodox missionaries were called "starlings." If in their letters there occurred such an expression as "starlings arrived," everybody understood that the Orthodox missionaries had arrived and there would be persecutions and arrests.

The condition of the Orthodox Church just described inspired me with great enthusiasm, for I felt assured that in its failure to bring "the Bread of Life" to the people were the seeds for a final glorious victory for Christ, and so my faith was confirmed.

### I Make a Startling Prophecy

I attended meetings in the city of St. Petersburg very often and took an active part in them. One Sunday morning in the meeting there were about twenty people present. I felt inspired to preach my sermon from the very well known text, Luke 12 : 32, in the words spoken by Jesus Christ:

"Fear not, little flock, for it is your Father's good pleasure to give you the kingdom."

I described how small and weak and insignificant was our flock as compared with the pompous organization of our persecutors. During the course of my sermon I made a prophecy which has since been fulfilled, though at the time it seemed to be most unlikely, even impossible of fulfillment. I said:

*"The days will come when we will preach in the churches and cathedrals of the Greek Catholic Church!"*

After the meeting some of the brethren and sisters came to me and said: "What did you say, Ivan Stepanovich? Is it possible? Can such things ever happen?" In the midst of the persecutions we were suffering at the hands of a strong and powerful enemy it seemed altogether incredible, one of the things the least likely to happen to us.

And yet thirty-two years later I actually preached in a well known ancient Greek Orthodox Church at Moscow and in a temple which was presided over by the Metropolitan. You will find that interesting story later in this book. Surely this prophecy was dictated by the Holy Spirit and by the optimism of faith, which as we know is the substance of things hoped for. Through the present atmosphere of persecutions, dangers and fears, God helped me to see the glorious victory of the Gospel that was to come.

# CHAPTER XI

## I Gird on My Armor

*"Put on the whole armor of God that ye may be able to stand."*

Eph. 6 : 11.

GRADUATION days are full of joy — always and everywhere. What bright hopes are entertained! The future seems to be a path strewn with roses. My friend S. and I were no exception. I have already spoken of his conversion. Now I may add that on his conversion he joined our brotherhood and was a very zealous Christian. He even began to preach in our meetings.

We were so closely united in spirit and in our ideas that we decided to endeavor to find employment in the same institution. Through the Society of Technologists we secured employment at the estate of Neplueff, a very big land owner in Chernigoff Province.

My position was assistant director of the sugar factory on Neplueff's estate. My friend S. was given a situation as manager of a small mechanical factory. Both factories were in the same place, Svessa, so that our desire to remain together was realized.

We passed our final examinations at the Institute in the spring. Then we had to serve in a workshop until the end of July. In August we received our diplomas as Mechanical Engineers.

### Working for a Rich Russian Land Owner

Before going to Neplueff's estate we decided to visit our homes in the Caucasus. My friend S. proved to be a native of Ekaterinodar, the capitol of the Kuban district in the Caucasus, while my native city, Vladikavkas, was the administrative center of the Terek district. It was on this journey that we stopped off at the city of Tula for our memorable visit with Count Leo Tolstoy.

After meeting him we continued our journey and, having visited our homes and spent a little time with our parents and friends, we returned to our labors on the estate of Neplueff, who, we discovered, was one of the richest land owners of Russia and also one of the most interesting personalities among the social workers, because of his attitude toward the laboring class of Russia.

He published a number of pamphlets describing his scheme of labor brotherhoods and endeavored to persuade other land owners to do the same thing with their land and peasantry. Of course, since the whole plan was acceptable to the Greek Orthodox Church, there was little opposition and his theories became widely known.

On our arrival at Neplueff's estate S. and I began our work in the factories, where we came in close contact with their Brotherhood. We visited their meetings and, of course, tried to teach them how to read the Bible and to interpret it, and also how to pray according to the Gospel, i.e., not according to certain formulae, but spontaneously, as dictated by the heart's desire and led by the Holy Spirit.

We had conversations also with Neplueff himself, explaining to him the New Testament Christianity and pointing out the necessity of removing all traces of compromise with the clerical authorities.

### Priests Alarmed by Two "Stundists"

As young Christians we could not reconcile his compromises with many of his beliefs and practices. On the other hand, the local priest was alarmed by the presence of two "Stundists" in the Brotherhood. Among the members of the Brotherhood we became more and more popular, but as for Neplueff himself, the priest and other zealous Orthodox employes, we soon became dangerous men in their sight, so that our further stay with Neplueff became impossible.

In our final talk with Mr. Neplueff we explained to him our opinion with regard to all his work. He said to us quite frankly that he could go no further in his practice than he had. The result was that we resigned and left his estate.

Our parting with the members of the Brotherhood was most touching. Some of them wept, saying to us: "Good bye. A spiritual tie was created during the time of our fellowship."

From Neplueff's estate we went, in February, 1894, to the Ijorsky Admiralty Works, at Colpino, near St. Petersburg. We were employed there as assistant manager engineers of some workshops in a large mill, where steel plates for ironclad ships were manufactured. We looked upon this employment as temporary, not being at all satisfied with it.

The nearness of the works to St. Petersburg made it possible for us to renew our Christian work at the capital. We attended meetings and I continued my wide correspondence and also issued the periodical "Besseda."

## We Found Our Own Landed Estate

Under the general oppression of the regime we all felt that we ought to seek other conditions for our spiritual work, and our thoughts were directed toward the advisability of founding a special settlement on Gospel principles. We were inspired in this by the example of the Jerusalem Church, as described in the second and fourth chapters of the Acts of the Apostles. Brothers F. and S. and I discussed the question between ourselves, and finally decided that we would endeavor to found a Christian agricultural community somewhere in the south of Russia, in the Crimea, if possible.

Brother F. was to go first, making all preparations, and we were to follow him later. While our plans were being perfected, a lady, Mrs. Z. N. Nekrassova, joined us. She was the widow of the celebrated Russian poet, Nekrassoff, who was very popular on account of his descriptive poems dealing with the sufferings of the Russian peasants and workmen. Two nieces of the widow visited one of our meetings, and being deeply impressed, invited their aunt also. She was converted and later became a member of our church. She was about forty-five years old at the time. Becoming interested in the scheme of founding an agricultural community, she heartily joined our enterprise, bringing to it a certain investment of financial means.

After some consideration of various properties we bought an estate in the neighborhood of the city of Simferopol, in Crimea. The name of the estate was "Kirk." It had been occupied by a group of German colonists called "Jerusalem Brethren," who emigrated to Palestine on the basis of a certain prophecy.

Brother F. with his family, Mrs. Nekrassova and her two nieces, went to "Kirk" first. They completed all the arrangements for the purchase of the estate, and I followed later, with S. and his wife. I should have said that Brother S. had married one of the members of our church. Our fellowship together was both pleasant and profitable.

## Happy Days of Labor and Study

Soon a peasant brother, Egor Syromiatnikoff, joined our group. He was a good bee keeper. Our community was given the name of "Vertograd" (the Vineyard). As previously stated, we were guided by the records of primitive Christianity and endeavored to realize the example of the Apostles, Acts 4 : 32: "None of them said that aught of the things which he possessed was his own, but they had all things in common."

Everything belonged to all. There was a peculiar spiritual exaltation in the realization that here everything, as well as oneself, belonged to others, that no one could use anything without the consent of others. One felt as though he had lost his "self," his freedom, his personality. But as it was done in accordance with the example of the Apostles and with the words of Jesus Christ concerning *self denial* (Matt. 16:24) joy filled our hearts and all the time we were in the brightest state imaginable spiritually.

There was a certain distribution of labor. I had to take care of the cattle, horses and oxen. I used to water them, bring them food, straw, etc., and so I was called Solomonos. i.e., a straw bearer. I had also to make pits for planting vines and have dug as many as 180 such pits during one day, which was a record for that class of work.

In addition to this, I worked at bringing clay from a distance on my wagon, which was drawn by oxen. It was a very difficult labor, but I worked with great pleasure and joy. I was always singing and was told that the sound of my voice was often heard for a considerable distance over the hills. To spend our evenings usefully, I proposed to arrange Bible courses on interpretation of the Word of God, on Church History, etc.

After a hard day's work and our evening meal, we all gathered together. I would read or tell something of Church History; the sisters would be quietly sewing or knitting, while they listened with the brethren. Those were memorable evenings, and I remember them now with the liveliest satisfaction. This was, in reality, the beginning of the Bible School. We were very happy in our Vertograd, but happiness on earth is never lasting.

## Circumstances Disrupt Our Community

The local authorities, who opposed at that time all kinds of social movements, became interested in our organization, and we knew that we were being watched. Then difficulties arose. I received a telegram from Vladikavkas, informing me that my father had been sentenced to exile. My mother asked me to come and help her in her difficulties. Of necessity I had to leave our community. All felt very sad about my departure, and Brother F. said: "We lose our best workman." We hoped to meet again soon, at Vertograd, but in the will of God that was not to be.

On my arrival at Vladikavkas, I learned that my father and two of the brethren had been exiled to the Transcaucasus, having been accused of disseminating harmful religious propaganda. This was done by order of the Governor General of the Terek Region, General Kochanoff. Beside exiling the brethren, he strictly forbade any religious meetings and put all kinds of restrictions on the remaining brethren.

I aided my mother in arranging her household, and in the meantime, with great secrecy, arranged some meetings with the brethren and sisters. We comforted one another from the Word of God and also conferred on our unhappy situation. The brethren finally asked me to go to St. Petersburg and plead through our friends for the liberation of the exiled ones and for the removal of the severe restrictions inflicted upon us by General Kochanoff. In the meantime, a report was spread that the police were planning my own arrest.

## Persecuted Sectarians Left Friendless

In a secret way I was transported to a small station further to the north of Vladikavkas, where I took a train for St. Petersburg. But here all my efforts to see our friends in the Government and to present a petition were useless. No one dared to raise a voice for the persecuted "sectarians."

Just at that time — September 3, 1894 — a circular was issued by the Minister of the Interior, to the effect that the "Stundists" were "the most dangerous sect, and therefore the greatest vigilance and watchfulness were to be exercised and all possible measures taken, in order that the sect should be prevented from spreading!"

This circular was understood in the provinces to mean that all kinds of persecutions would be allowed with regard to these "sectarians," and was only one more indication of the powerful influence of Pobedonostzeff, the favorite of Emperor Alexander III and Nicolas II. He was the Procurator of the Holy Synod, and the outstanding supporter of all reactionary political measures, the most cruel of all who stood for the prevention of free religious thought and the persecution of "dissenters."

## "Vertograd" Estate Disintegrated

The oppression became so severe that it was impossible to do anything in the way of relief for the exiles or those who remained behind. I discussed the whole situation with the brethren in St. Petersburg, and we decided the only thing left to do was to transfer the center of our work to some foreign country and endeavor to organize help from abroad.

Our sister Kirchner, of Saratoff, was asked to emigrate to Stockholm, which she did. There she undertook to continue the publication of our periodical, "Besseda," printing and sending its issues into Russia in registered letters. She carried on this work faithfully, but unfortunately a considerable number of the letters — and consequently complete issues of the periodicals — were lost. Some of them, however, reached their destination, often in the most remote parts of Russia, and brought messages of deep spiritual comfort to the prisoners in the great "jail" of Russia.

Under the conditions described, further existence of the community "Vertograd" proved to be impossible. Brother F. sold what could be disposed of and emigrated, first to Roumania and afterward to Canada. Brother Syromiatnikoff, the bee keeper, returned to his home in Ekaterinoslav Province; Sister Nekrassova went to Saratoff, where she lived to the end of her life. Brother S. secured employment as a mechanical engineer on a railroad. Under other conditions, with freedom for the simple practice of Gospel faith and Gospel living, who knows what the outcome might have been.

# CHAPTER XII

## Experiences Abroad

*"That your love may abound more in knowledge: that ye may approve all things that are excellent."*
*Phil. 1 : 9-10.*

A S for myself, the brethren strongly urged me to go abroad, advising me to publish there information about the persecutions in Russia, to obtain spiritual and financial help for our cause and our brethren, and to send from the outside literature for the moral support of the believers.

Even while I remained in St. Petersburg, making arrangements to carry out the advice of the brethren, I was sought by the secret police. Once I paid a visit to Brother Bernikoff. A few minutes after I had left his lodging a secret police agent, together with the janitor, came and asked for me! Surely it would not be wise for me to tarry any longer in this place, and so immediate plans were laid for me to go abroad.

I made the acquaintance of an American who was the Russian representative of the Worthington Pump Company and the Westinghouse Air Brake Company. He planned to open an office in St. Petersburg. This acquaintance occurred in a characteristic Russian way. His American wife was greatly interested in the Evangelical mission work, and they hired a servant girl who was a member of our St. Petersburg Church. She told them about her Gospel faith and of our secret meetings. Thus the American lady visited one of our meetings, bringing her husband to a second meeting a little later, and so we became acquainted.

This man invited me to visit his office, together with the Finnish Pastor S. We discussed the matter, and the latter consented to make arrangements for me to go abroad through Finland.

## SEEKING FREEDOM ABROAD

On the prearranged evening in January, 1895, Pastor S. awaited us at the station. I came hurrying to the train, while some steps after me Brother Meshaninoff followed, carrying my bag. Silently I entered the train. With a very few words we parted with Brother Meshaninoff. Thus Pastor S. and I safely commenced our journey. Finland was at that time a province of Russia, and the gendarmes carefully scrutinized all passengers on the Finland Railroad just in the same manner as they did in all parts of Russia. Fortunately I was not regarded with suspicion by those who saw me and was able to begin my journey.

We went at first to a place called "Akenes," where we spent the night at the pastor's house. After that we visited Helsingfors, where I stayed for some time with a family named Amerikanianz.

### Concealed for Ten Weeks by Friends

At Helsingfors a further discussion of my affairs was held, and it was decided that I should leave Finland for abroad on the first steamer sailing from Abo, the largest seaport of Finland. But I was in Helsingfors by the middle of February, and navigation from that port would probably open only at the end of April, so I had to be provided for somewhere in the country during this ten weeks interval.

Within a few days Pastor S. returned to Helsingfors and announced that a decision as to my stopping place had been reached. He escorted me to a station called "Binas," and from there to the castle of Baron H., a sincere Christian brother, sympathizing with all sufferers for Christ's sake.

I had a small but clean room on the third floor, where I spent my time reading books, studying the English language and writing poems. Three times every day I was called downstairs for meals: breakfast, lunch and dinner. All the meals were served very sumptuously. It was impossible for me to leave the castle, even for a short walk, because my presence there was a secret. Once a Russian official paid a visit to Baron H., but I was hidden safely in the loft.

Although I was virtually a prisoner in the castle, the

time passed very rapidly. In the interval I wrote various poems and hymns, many of which are now being sung by my people. At the castle these hymns were finally put into shape and still others were composed.

As I remember, some of the hymns which are now very popular among the believers in Russia were written during the period of time from the day of my leaving Vladikavkas to the day of my crossing the frontier in Finland. For instance:

### HYMN NO. 74—CHRISTIAN'S SONGS *

1. No pow'r on earth, no pow'r in heaven,
   Shall rob us of our freedom now!
   The flesh may tremble, ever feeling
   A prison shadow on its brow.
   But those held captive long in darkness
   The love of God sets free again;
   No one may bring us into bondage,
   For He has broken every chain.

2. No pow'r on earth, no pow'r in heaven,
   Shall take away our wealth untold.
   What tho', in this most holy conflict,
   We lose our silver or our gold?
   We know of treasures hid in secret,
   The riches of a heart at rest!
   One day, thro' us, if we are faithful,
   The World with Him shall still be blest.

3. No pow'r on earth, no pow'r in heaven,
   Shall turn our glory into shame.
   The world may still despise, reject us,
   Blaspheming our most worthy name.
   The truth is our eternal standard,
   And perfect love shall cast out fear.
   The sacred hope, unchanged, unchanging,
   Abides with us from year to year.

This hymn was composed by me while riding in the train between Vladikavkas and St. Petersburg, after my father had been sent to exile. It has been sung during all the time of the persecutions as the march song of the Evangelical Christians.

---

* All the poems in this autobiography were translated from the Russian by Miss Catherine Ruth Smith.

## SEEKING FREEDOM ABROAD

The following hymn was composed during the journey from St. Petersburg to Finland, while under the possibility of being arrested by the gendarmes. Hymns No. 239 and 336 of the "Gusli" song book and others also belong to the same period.

### HYMN NO. 325 — GUSLI

The way is clear before me,
To some unearthly land;
A guiding power still leads me
By the hand.

No gaily colored flowers
My rugged path adorn;
The thicket lies before me
And the thorn.

I hear no more the singing
Of the clear-voiced nightingale;
The jackal's howl is dismal
In the vale.

I cannot pause to slumber
In any cool retreat,
Though long the way, and weary
To my feet.

The pathway is not peaceful
Through which I must be led;
The hurricane is raging
Overhead.

I make no pleasant journey
Beside the murmuring rill,
But through the lonely mountains,
Dark and still.

And yet I see before me
The footprints, stained with red,
Of those who trod this pathway,
And who bled.

Enfolded by the darkness,
I tremble now with fear;
One beacon in the distance
Brings me cheer.

Though terrors may beset me,
My way has all been planned —
A Guiding power still leads me
By the hand.

# IN THE CAULDRON OF RUSSIA

The surroundings were dark and gloomy, but I saw one beacon in the distance which brought me cheer. This was a song of optimism of the faith among all kinds of trial and with the future all hidden from view.

Toward the end of April, Pastor S. again came and took me from the castle. Observing every possible precaution, we went to the railroad station at Binas, and from there to the seaport Abo, from whence I was to sail for Stockholm. Usually all the passports of the passengers were inspected by a gendarme, but it was so arranged that I was taken to the steamer without my passport having been demanded.

Pastor S. and I had a short prayer together on the steamer; then I said "good bye" to him and began to feel very lonely.

## Meeting Foreign Christian Friends

At Stockholm I found Mr. Stadling, a very well known reporter of a big Swedish daily paper, who had visited Russia in 1892, during the time of the famine on the Volga. He was a fine Christian man and had shown himself to be very deeply interested in the Russian Evangelical movement. He aided me in various ways. At Stockholm I was very much impressed on seeing, for the first time, a group of Eskimo huts in the public garden.

From Stockholm I went on to Hamburg, where I saw Jacob Kroeker, Heinrich Braun and other young Mennonite preachers, who had previously come from Russia and were studying for the ministry. These men afterward became prominent leaders among the Mennonites.

From Hamburg I went to Paris, where my younger brother, Alexander, was studying at the Faculty of Medicine, and also attending lectures on Theology at the Faculty of Protestant Theology. I was surprised to find that the French Government supported a Faculty in connection with the University of Paris devoted to studying Protestant theology. As a matter of fact, this was the highest theological school for the French Protestant churches, descendants of the Huguenots.

Among the professors at the Faculty there was one, M. Bonnet-Maury, a very sympathetic man. He was deeply interested in the Gospel movement in Russia. My brother and I gave him much information concerning Russian Stundism, and he published a good article on religion in one of the French periodicals.

From Paris I went to London. I will not describe here my first impressions of this great city, which may be briefly expressed in the words, "big city!" I had letters of introduction to Dr. Baedeker and to Mr. Adams, secretary of the Evangelical Alliance.

Both Mr. Adams and Dr. Baedeker conferred with me as to future plans. I had hoped to enter an English University and to attend some lectures on theology, but now I discovered that this was a most impractical desire. With my lack of knowledge of the English language, those lectures would not have given me a sufficient grounding in the subject to pay for the time and expense. It was, however, proposed that I should enter the Baptist College at Bristol, and I accepted this proposition. Mr. Brooks, a prominent member of the Society of Friends (Quakers), promised to pay the cost of my scholarship.

## "At Home" at Hackney Downs

After remaining for one year in the Baptist College, I went to London and entered the New Congregational College. The reason for such a change was my desire to come in contact with other denominations. I desired to gain as comprehensive a view of all the Protestant Christian denominations of Western Europe as might be possible.

I lived at a small Friends' boarding house (Missionary Home), at Hackney Downs, and attended the lectures at Hamstead New College. My brother Alexander came from Paris to engage in practical work at the London Hospital, and I was able to arrange for him to stay with me at the "Friends' Home."

It was really a happy time. We studied diligently and cheerfully, and I continued to maintain a very wide correspondence with the Russian brethren. The publication of our periodical, "Besseda," was transferred to London and again came to my own hands, since Miss Kirchner had emigrated from Stockholm to Roumania. It was with the greatest difficulty that I carried on this publication work in London and sent the literature throughout Russia by means of registered letters.

## A Taste of Real Liberty

As a Russian refugee, I enjoyed immensely the liberty of the European countries, something entirely lacking in my own country. It was so amazing to find that in England any one could arrange, anywhere, religious meetings without asking permission from the authorities. Especially was I impressed by the religious meetings which were held on the streets by the Salvation Army.

As to the political liberty, I had also some discoveries to make. The most popular public park in London was Hyde Park, in which unrestricted open air meetings were permitted. I saw there various groups of people. In one of these groups a man spoke on the subject of "Education." In another group an address was being delivered on some financial topic. In a third group the discussion was on a religious subject, while to a fourth group a speaker was delivering an address against the whole policy of the Government. He bitterly assailed the Government, and only a few yards away stood a policeman, calmly directing the traffic on the street! I wished I were an artist, that I might depict the scene as it impressed me. Coming from the country where all sorts of religious meetings were forbidden as a great crime, I saw all this with a sense of incredibility.

I was overwhelmed with conflicting emotions. I thought of my own country, in which at that time it was impossible to arrange even a small religious meeting, not to mention any sort of political meeting whatsoever, and I was overcome with a great feeling of shame for the Government of Russia and compassion for my own people. I repeated just one single word: "Liberty!" "Liberty!"

I endeavored to get acquainted with the English religious literature. Of course, I was overwhelmed with its bulk, variety and riches.

The material richness of Great Britain also deeply impressed me. The London Museum, the Crystal Palace, Westminster Abbey and many other buildings produced upon me a feeling of wonder. But especially do I remember the impression made by my visit to the stores of ivory at London, in a warehouse on the Thames. I saw an enormous shed, almost a mile long, filled with big elephant tusks (ivory). "Oh," I said, "here is wealth indeed!"

## I Toast Great Britain — and Russia

I remember once, at the Bristol Baptist College, there was an annual dinner being held. Every student was to give a short address. In my speech I said: "England is a land of contrasts. On the one hand, it is one of the leading commercial and industrial countries; on the other hand it has created the greatest poets in the world, such as Shakespeare and Byron. Again, it is undoubtedly one of the most religious countries, while at the same time it has produced the greatest rationalists and materialistic scientists, such as Darwin and Spencer. And examples of such contrasts could be multiplied. "After all," I said, "England is the best country in the world. . . ."

All the audience began to applaud very loudly. I was quietly standing and smiling. When the applause ceased, I quietly added: "after Russia!" The audience again burst into applause, still more vigorously.

The longer I staid abroad the stronger grew my desire to return to my dear suffering Russia, in order to devote all my powers and energies to evangelization work. I dreamed about the extension of that work in all the Slavonic countries.

About this time a proposal was made that I should go to Galicia, a province of Austria-Hungary adjacent to Russia, and make there the headquarters for my evangelization work. But a resolution was growing in my heart to return to Russia at all costs, and to make St. Petersburg the center of the work.  I remember once, while a student at the Stokes Croft Baptist College of Bristol, thinking during my study about Russia and the spiritual ignorance of my people, and of being overcome with such a desire to return home that I knelt and prayed, asking God to help me to return to St. Petersburg and to make that city the center of my evangelization work. Afterward this prayer was fulfilled in a remarkable way.

But before going back I wished to make proper preparation.  I had a plan to get better acquainted with both German and French schools of theology.  Accordingly, I decided to study for half a year at Berlin University and half a year at Paris University.

# CHAPTER XIII

## Experiences Abroad

### (MY STAY IN GERMANY AND FRANCE)

*"The desire accomplished is sweet to the soul."*
Prov. 13 : 19.

WITH the aid of Mr. E. W. Brooks I was able to go to Germany. Through letters of introduction from Dr. Baedeker and Mr. Adams, Secretary of the Evangelical Alliance, I found a room in the same house in which were located the German Baptist Church and the office of the German Baptist Cameroon Mission. Rev. Mr. Scheve, his son Alfred, the musical composer, and their family showed me all possible kindness. The fact that my father was in exile touched their hearts.

I remember one Christmas night when they invited me to their family circle. There was a Christmas tree, much singing, prayer and real joy. It was a rare pleasure thus to be made at home by this German Christian family. Everybody received a Christmas present. The father addressed me in a few warm words and also gave me a present. This was quite unexpected and produced upon me a strong impression.

I was registered at the Berlin University as a student in the Faculty of Theology. Just at that time — in the autumn of 1896 — Professor Harnack delivered lectures on the "Substance of Christianity" (Wesen des Christentums), which were published later in book form. I also attended his lectures on the Introduction to the New Testament. I also heard Professor Pfleiderer on Christian Ethics and other subjects. There were at that time a great many Russian students in the Berlin University. Most of them studied social and economic subjects, such as political economy and sociology, the latter a new science then. Most important of the questions that interested me during this period was:

101

"What do the most rationalistic theologians say about the origin of the books of the Bible?" I wanted to sift it to the bottom. In England the so-called "higher criticism" had just begun to take root in the minds of some English theologians. This higher criticism was, of course, the child of German Rationalism, resulting from the writings of Strauss, Bauer and others.

After mature acquaintance with the theories of Karnack, I came to the conclusion that he and theologians generally of the new Tubingen School took a considerably milder position toward the question of the origin of the books of the New Testament than I had expected. In fact, they almost approached the traditional view.

## Weighing Some Theological Opinions

I endeavored to make a tabulation from the figures given by different professors concerning the time of the origin of every book, and found such a variety of opinions that I said to myself: "They contradict each other and therefore do not deserve any following." Although the criticism itself is helpful for certain prejudices, no disputes against the affirmations of the critics are necessary, for they contradict each other, and thus the safest way is to stick to the general data of the Universal Church. Since that time whatever I read could not make me change my mind.

I attended lectures in the Berlin University during one term. After that I went to Paris and spent one term there, the first half of 1897, attending lectures at the Faculté de Theologie Protestante.

At first I could not follow the lectures, but I studied the languages very diligently, as well as keeping up my studies in theology, and at the end I could speak fairly well and understand when others spoke in either the German or French language.

At the Faculté de Theologie Protestante there was a great friend of Russia in Mr. Bonet-Maury, previously mentioned, professor of Church History. He published a small booklet on the persecutions of the Stundists and attempted to arouse public interest in the Russian evangelical movement by delivering lectures. During all my studies I continued my Russian evangelistic labors, having a wide correspondence and often obtaining financial help for the persecuted Christians and sending it to Russia.

## The Homeland Tugs at My Heart Strings

But again I began to feel that it was not the best course for me to stay abroad and study; that the time had come for me to return to Russia and to resume there my work again in an extensive way. I knew, of course, that the extent of the theological knowledge which I might obtain abroad was very great and that much more useful knowledge could be attained than I had gained already, but I felt that for the work which was to be done in Russia the studies which I had pursued were sufficient and therefore there was no necessity to spend more time and the best way would be to return home as soon as possible. I did not, however, see how this was to be done. My father was in exile; I myself was under sentence of exile. How could the path be cleared of these difficulties, so that I could return to my country?

In this case, being again aided by the optimism of faith, I prayed, asking God to realize for me what seemed to be so impossible. Of course He found the way, as will be seen.

Looking back over my experience abroad, I consider it to be of the utmost importance for the interests of the Kingdom of God and for my future work of evangelization in Russia. Undoubtedly my experiences brought me face to face with many vital problems. As I mentioned before, one cardinal question concerned the spiritual value of Protestantism.

Some of the critically-minded Orthodox men used to say: "You strive to bring about a kind of reformation, to establish a Protestant form of religion in Russia, but look at the present condition of Protestantism in the lands you have visited. Is is worth while striving for that end for Russia?" It was a really difficult problem to decide, considering the fact that I was still quite a young man.

Unquestionably there were many weaknesses in the practical life of the Protestant churches abroad. With a certain pessimistic inclination of mind, the negative side of Protestantism might conceal from the sight of the observer, especially if he were a young man, the positive side. Thus he might easily arrive at the conclusion that it would be unwise to attempt to erect in Russia the same sort of spiritual building. Of course, he would be wrong, but it might have happened. In this case, as a Russian proverb says, "One could not see the forest for the tree."

## My Optimistic Mind Sees the Better Side

But I thank God that He led me in this case in the right path. In spite of considerable differences between the Protestant denominations the cardinal principles were common to all of them, such as faith in the Scriptures, the doctrine of God as the Father of men, of the mission of Christ, the atonement, salvation, etc. Nearly all denominations accepted the Apostolic Creed.

The differences consisted largely of varying interpretations of Bible truth. Even in this variety there was something good. The Apostle Paul wrote: "There must be also heresies among you, that they which are approved may be made manifest among you." (1 Cor. 11:19). With regard to the variety of methods of preaching the Gospel, the Apostle Paul's attitude was remarkable: "Notwithstanding, every way, whether in pretence or in truth, Christ is preached; and I therein rejoice, yea, and will rejoice" (Phil. 1:18). So looking from this standpoint I could see something good in every difference. It was clear to me that the general principle which was the basis or foundation of all the Protestant denominations was the effort to practice primitive Christianity.

## Protestantism Favorable to Science

The more I studied other denominations, the more I became faithful to my own Russian Evangelical conception of Christianity, which I regarded at that time and still believe to be the form nearest to the primitive Christianity of the Apostles.

I realized, however, that this variety of creeds in Protestantism is the result of freedom of conscience, freedom to read the Bible and to make our own interpretation of it, and freedom of personal initiative and religious activity for every man according to his own views.

I saw that this principle of religious liberty so influenced the life of the Protestant nations that it became the basis of political and scientific liberty. The Roman Catholic clergy used to burn great scientists for their discoveries. Such a thing was made impossible in the Protestant world. The freedom of scientific research was the source of wonderful achievements. From the political standpoint the Protestant countries are the most free in the world.

From practical comparison I concluded that morality in the purely Protestant countries is higher than in other non-Protestant countries, and that morality is low in those parts of the world where the influence of Protestantism does not penetrate to its full measure. Besides, Protestantism has various powerful methods for struggling against immorality and to educate the people morally and spiritually which are not practiced in the non-Protestant countries.

The first method is the moral and spiritual instruction of the people by preaching and exposition of the Bible in meetings and in family circles. In the Roman Catholic and Greek Catholic Churches there was very little instruction of this kind, because too much emphasis was placed on ritual and ceremonials. As a matter of fact, in the Greek Orthodox Church there was almost no preaching and little or no Bible exposition during centuries, and no effort was made to teach the Scripture to young or old.

### Social and Spiritual Education Important

It was deeply impressed in my conviction that this enormous work of social and spiritual education was the outstanding accomplishment of Protestant Christianity in Europe and America. The Greek Orthodox Church and the Roman Catholic Church paid no attention to these branches of Christian service, and in fact knew nothing about them!

## IN THE CAULDRON OF RUSSIA

My experiences abroad in connection with Protestantism brought me to the unshakeable conclusion that only the Bible and the Gospel freely distributed and freely accepted could create the highest welfare of my fatherland and make it a foremost country in all senses. Thus I became still more inspired with the desire to spread the Gospel in my own country.

Of course, the first impulse for my decision came from the lips of our Saviour: "Preach the Gospel to every creature." (Mark 16 : 15). Whatever may be the practical results of the preaching of the Gospel among the people largely depends on men themselves. But one truth is unshakeable: "One who has been saved will save others; one who has found everlasting life through the faith of the Gospel will share it with others."

With this sentiment of great joy and optimism, I thought more and more about my return from abroad to my dear suffering Russia.

# CHAPTER XIV

## With the Doukhobors and Return to Russia

*"Choosing rather to suffer affliction with the people."*
*Heb. 11 : 25.*

IN September of the year 1898, while in Paris, I received a letter from Mr. E. W. Brooks, proposing that I should go to Cyprus to aid the Doukhobors.

I have mentioned before that the Doukhobors living in the Transcaucasus, under the influence of the Tolstoists, withdrew their soldiers from the army, publicly burned their guns and rifles and declared to the Government that they would never take up arms again. Some of the Doukhobors' leaders were punished and they decided to emigrate from Russia.

After much negotiation Canada was chosen as the country to which they would migrate. The first party of Doukhobors, numbering 1150 people, took ship at Caucasus, but they were held up en route because of an epidemic which broke out among them. All the Doukhobor passengers were disembarked on the island of Cyprus. There the epidemic continued.

There was on the island only one man who could act as an interpreter for the Doukhobors, Mr. Birukoff, but he had to leave Cyprus for some reason and return to England. Somebody was required to take his place, and the committee, of which Mr. E. W. Brooks was the chairman, proposed that I should go there. Count Sergius L. Tolstoy, son of the celebrated Russian writer and philosopher, came to Paris to see me on this question. I gave my consent, and in a day or so a peasant Doukhobor came to Paris from London in order to travel with me to Cyprus.

We sailed from Marseilles on a steamer of the "Menageries Maritimes" line. For the first time I voyaged over the western portion of the Mediterranean Sea and I enjoyed the experience immensely, delighting in the beautiful scenery, particularly the shores of Italy and Sicily, the groves of oranges and lemons and other things of interest.

## Egypt, the Nile and the Pyramids

On our way to Cyprus the steamer called at Alexandria, where it lay for two days, and we also anchored at Port Said for two days. I took the advice of one of the ship's officers and, with my Doukhobor friend, made an excursion to Cairo and from there to the Pyramids. At Alexandria we saw the column of Pompeus and also some remarkable orchards belonging to a rich Greek. For the first time I saw bread as thin as linen. When a servant approached our table, I thought he was carrying napkins on his arm, but it proved to be bread! The small coffee house where we dined had a veranda covered with grapes, large and very sweet.

With a feeling of awe I looked for the first time upon the River Nile and its fertile estuaries where the land of Goshen is situated. My awe increased when I beheld the Sphynx and the pyramids. We went out from the city of Cairo on hired donkeys, attended by Arab boy drivers, who ran behind, shouting very loudly. The donkeys were so small that I had much difficulty in keeping my feet from dragging along the ground.

The highest of the pyramids, as is well known, is that of Pharao Kheops. Special Arab guides took both of us and a group of other tourists to see this pyramid. We had to climb up a narrow subterranean passage, all the time ascending in the darkness. Our Arab guide was climbing ahead of us with a torch in his hand, the smoke from which was very unpleasant. The greater part of the way we had to climb on "all fours." It was a very arduous journey.

When at last we attained our objective, the guide lighted a magnesium lamp and we saw a spacious room, much dust and flying bats. The atmosphere was stifling. It was the burying place of ancient kings. The coffins themselves, with the mummies, had been taken to a museum and we saw only the room. Of course, our impressions here were very strong! Were there not the odors of four thousand years in that cave!

The remarkable thing to me was the fact that the regular outlines of the pyramid had been preserved during forty centuries! For the first time I saw Arab Bedouins on their camels, and away in the distance the great Desert of Sahara. Sand! Sand! Sand without any end! This sight also inspired in me a feeling of awe. We returned from Cairo by railway to Port Said and again boarded our steamer.

On our arrival at Larnaka, the port of Cyprus, I found there Mr. Sturge, the commissary of the Society of Friends, who was supervising all the help that was being rendered by them to the Doukhobors. He introduced me to the British Governor of Cyprus. I also saw Mr. Birukoff and I entered upon the fulfillment of my new duties.

## An Oasis in the Sands of Cyprus

The population of Cyprus consisted of Turks, Greeks and Armenians. The tall and handsome figures of the fair-featured Doukhobors were conspicuous among these natives. The camp of the Doukhobors was in the interior of Cyprus. I traveled to the encampment on the back of another small donkey, like the one I had ridden in Egypt. When we left Larnaka I saw a wide, flat level of sand that became very hot from the rays of the burning sun, although it was in November. There was not even one tree and no grass. Sand! Sand!

After traveling several hours we saw at a distance a group of trees and vegetation. When we approached we found a grove of pretty palms, and also orange and lemon trees laden with their fruit. There was a small stream of water coming from the ground, and this was the reason for such luxuriant vegetation. I thought, "What a fine illustration of the living water of the Word of God, which regenerates men's hearts!"

Among these trees we found tents and small wooden barracks, in which the Doukhobor families lived. At a distance of a few miles there was another small colony, also housed in wooden barracks.

I found the Doukhobors in a very sad condition. Most of them were ill with a strange disease, something like dysentery. A man would have blood issues, some swelling on the legs and in a few days he would die. Entering one of the barracks, I saw a low wooden platform built along one wall for the full length of the room, on which they usually slept, but on which now there were sick people lying, with some dead bodies in between them! About one hundred men and women had already died. A Russian cemetery had been made a short distance from the Doukhobor colonies.

### Ministering to Sick Doukhobors

The doctor was an Armenian. He prescribed opium. The medicines were usually brought from Larnaka by an old man Mark, a Jew from Odessa, who spoke Russian, Greek, Turkish and even Armenian, all languages badly enough, but he was an indispensable person to the Doukhobors. He brought to them not only medicines but also small articles and all kinds of goods. Once more I was convinced that as long as our people remained uneducated they would need the services of Jews, who are always practical and energetic wherever they are.

My duties were to look after the general conditions of the Doukhobors, to secure improvements and to help them with their medicine. At once I insisted on putting into effect some measures which seemed practical and most important:

### Simple Rules to Combat the Plague

1. To remove all the dead bodies from the barracks immediately.

2. To isolate the sick ones from those who were in good health.

3. To keep the windows open as much as possible to secure ventilation. Usually they kept the windows closed and the air in the rooms was very stuffy and close.

4. To keep the rooms and clothing clean.

5. I tried to enforce upon everybody the necessity for

observing many simple rules of home sanitation which were being neglected.

6. I asked the doctor to increase the doses of opium for the sick ones, telling him that for a Russian treble quantity of medicines was required as compared with an Armenian. The doctor somewhat increased the portions and a beneficial effect was soon noticeable.

Whenever I had any free time I gathered around me the boys and girls and taught them the English language. Almost thirty years later, in 1926, when I visited the Doukhobors in Canada, one of them recognized me and said he would never forget my help in teaching him the English language.

By doing this work among the Doukhobors I attained some intimate relations with them. Mr. Sturge and Mr. Birukoff lived at the town of Larnaka, at some distance from the Doukhobors, and the latter left Cyprus soon after my arrival. Nobody really knew the conditions under which these people were living. I decided to live in their largest colony and so I was able to closely observe their mode of life and to decide on means to overcome the plague and also to improve their condition.

## I Fall Ill in a Strange Country

I endeavored to banish all kinds of uncleanness and disorderliness, and gradually the condition of the Doukhobors began to improve, but I became ill myself with the same disease which was ravaging their colonies. I fell sick while in the town of Larnaka and lay in the house which had recently been occupied by Mr. Birukoff.

During my illness no one came to visit me. To become ill with a mortally dangerous sickness in a strange land, far away from friends, is a very trying experience. But the optimism of faith helped me through this time also. I did not give way to despair, but during my illness I thought a great deal about my country and my life, and I prayed to God that He might dispose of me according to His will. It was God's will that I should recover. Gradually I began to mend, almost without any help, and at last I recovered. After this I resumed my work among the Doukhobors until a message reached us that a steamer was to come from England to take them to Canada.

I was asked by the English Committee whether I would be willing to go to Canada, but I felt that after the recovery of the Doukhobors they could very well get along without me, whereas the whole Russian people were in need of energetic workers and messengers of Christ. I felt I must return to Russia, where, although my father was still in exile and arrest might await me, and although many others were suffering oppression and persecution, there were great possibilities for Christ.

Perhaps the call to service among the Doukhobors was the means God used to prevent my premature return to Russia during the time I was liable to be sent to exile. But now the call to return to my country was irresistible, and so I declined to accompany the Doukhobors on their long journey to Canada.

### My Decision to Return is Confirmed

Knowing the circumstances, Mr. E. W. Brooks and the others were greatly surprised at my decision, but I felt that it was the will of God with regard to me. Shortly after the decision had been made, a telegram came to Larnaka from my brother Vasily from Vladikavkas, calling me back home. The telegram itself surprised me more than the message, for under the conditions in Russia at that time I never thought such a message could have been sent. I took it for the voice of God, confirming my decision.

After final conferences with the Doukhobors, Mr. Sturge and others, I boarded a steamer bound for Constantinople and to Odessa, and with a prayer I sailed for home. All my thoughts were directed to my poor country suffering for centuries and bound by the chains of spiritual darkness. I was ready to accept the worst things for myself if only I could be among my own people and have the privilege of preaching the Gospel to them.

## IN THE DOUKHOBOR COLONY

On arrival at Constantinople all the passengers were asked to produce their passports before the Turkish authorities. I had no passport and the Turkish official ordered two policemen to take me, which they did. They conducted me along the narrow streets until we came at last to a two-story brick building which was probably a police station. A large room was divided in two parts by a grating. On one side of it there were prisoners and in front of it the authorities were sitting on a wooden platform.

A big Turk, smoking his Valian, heard reports from the policemen about the criminals and at once decided the question of their punishment. The prisoners looked through the grating toward their judge. The severe-looking judge heard the report of my policemen, and told them something in Turkish, which, of course, I could not understand. I was again taken by the policemen through the strange streets. Suddenly I saw a signboard: "The Russian Consulate," and I rejoiced! Soon the Turkish policemen left me and I found myself in a room of an ordinary Russian official establishment.

An official asked me several questions, wrote down my answers and told me to go to a certain hotel and spend the night. "To-morrow," he said, "we will decide what to do with you."

Of course, I understood that this hotel was a Russian institution and that I was there under watchful supervision, but still I found it very good that I had not been put in a Turkish prison.

The next morning I was called to the Consulate and the same official told me that I must be ready to leave Constantinople for Odessa by a Russian boat that would sail on the following day, which was better than I had expected. After another night as a "guest" at the Russian hotel, I was handed over to a Turkish policeman, who took me to a small boat which brought me to the Russian steamer. The policeman handed his papers to one of the officers of the steamer. I was allowed to buy a second-class ticket and was my own master during the voyage. This also was better than I had expected.

113

Owing to my long stay abroad, all my impressions on the Russian boat gave me peculiar pleasure. The Russian language itself sounded in my ears like the sweetest music. When the sailors, according to their custom, began to sing their evening prayer, I was almost ready to weep, so deep and sweet were the emotions that overflowed me. What a wonderful emotion, unlike any other, is love for one's own country!

On my arrival at Odessa I was taken by a gendarme to the Gradonachalnik (the governor of the city), whose name was Count Shuvaloff. I was kept waiting a long time in a lonely room. I did not know what would be done with me. After some hours the Gradonacholnik arrived, looking at me very severely but asking no questions. Some time later an official came and said that I was to be forwarded to my home town of Vladikavkas under the supervision of their agents, with a special forwarding document. They ordered me to stop at a specified hotel and to sail on a certain steamer. My way was through Sebastopol, Yalta, Theodosia, Novorossiisk and then by railway through Ekaterinodar to Vladikavkas, which is the principal town of Terek Province.

On my arrival at Vladikavkas I went to the chief of the local police. He read the papers through and said: "You will stay in your father's house; all right, we know." And once again I said to myself: "This is better than I expected."

Soon I learned that General Kochanoff, who was the Governor of Terek Province and had sentenced my father to exile and who wanted to do the same thing with me, had been dismissed. Therefore all his orders and plans with regard to those whom he had intended to banish had remained without effect. Soon I received permission to move freely in the country.

# CHAPTER XV

## Renewed Labor and Marriage

*"It is not good that man should be alone."*
Gen. 2 : 18.

THE brethren at Vladikavkas and other places rejoiced greatly at my return. Meetings were arranged at which I spoke on the privileges which we have through our faith in Jesus Christ and our duty to preach His glorious Gospel to our people. I also preached at crowded meetings of the Molokans.

Soon I decided to visit my father in exile in a small Armenian village, Gueruzi, in the Transcaucasus. It was in January, 1899, that I left Vladikavkas and went by way of the Georgian military road to Tiflis, passing through ranges of the Caucasian Mountains.

At Tiflis I preached in the meetings of brethren and tried to do something toward securing the right to hold religious meetings, which were still prohibited. I went to one of the best lawyers to ask his advice, and he said to me: "Your question can be decided in a very simple way. I do not go to church from one year's end to another, and I do not feel any privation. You also could do without any meetings!"

What inability on the part of the representatives of the law to understand the needs and the spirit of participants in the Evangelical movement!

### Visiting My Father in Exile

From Tiflis I went through the station of Dzeham toward the ancient Armenian town Shusha, and on horseback through the ranges of mountains to the Armenian village of Guerusi, where I found my father and other brethren who had been banished from home for faith's sake. At many places along our route we had to negotiate narrow mountain paths, below which were deep abysses. Dipping down into the fertile valleys at other points, I plucked the sweet dry grapes from the vines of the vineyards. It was January and so this experience gave us especial pleasure. The grapes grown in this district are justly famed for their excellence.

My traveling companion on this journey was a brother from Vladikavkas, Kazakoff by name. Great was the joy of my father and the other exiles when we arrived in that remote Armenian village. Situated in a deep valley between very high mountains, it formed a natural prison.

No work could be obtained in that village, and the exiles had to live on what they received from their families or brethren from other places. But shipments of relief were necessarily infrequent, and therefore the condition of most of the exiles was very trying. Meetings among them were forbidden and the spiritual condition also suffered.

We comforted these brethren with the Word of God and helped them with some contributions which we had brought from other brothers and churches. The authorities gave us permission to stay only five days.

I remembered the words of the Apostle Paul, speaking of persecuted Christians: "Of whom the world was not worthy. They wandered in deserts." Here was a modern example, for there were in this place of exile noble and cultured men who would have exerted a great influence for good on their country if they had been permitted their liberty. I was so overwhelmed with the tragedy and pathos of it all that the tears glistened on my cheeks.

The parting with my father and other brethren was most touching. We prayed, and then, mounting our horses, reluctantly followed our guide along the winding mountain paths. As we passed down the village street I looked back and saw my father, standing on the staircase of his house, looking toward us and waving his hat. The other brethren with him did the same thing. We also waved to them with our handkerchiefs.

My message to them — that not only in Russia, but also abroad in European countries, there were Christians praying

116

for them and thinking about them in their exile — produced upon them a most cheering impression.

While toiling up the mountain paths I thought: "Guerusi is in reality a miniature picture of all Russia, for the whole country has been turned into a prison for those who love liberty and righteousness!"

## Resuming Activities at St. Petersburg

On returning to Vladikavkas I began to think and plan for the commencement of my work. At that time no Nonconformist minister was recognized by the Government, and all the preachers and pastors had to do their work secretly while engaged in some other occupation. Accordingly I began to look for a position and applied to the Society of Engineers and Technologists, of which I was a member, asking for a situation at St. Petersburg or near that city. I received several propositions and accepted the Assistant Managership of the Riga District of Traction on the Riga-Orel Railroad.

I lived at Riga and carried out my duties until the autumn of 1899, when Professor Berlow, of the Riga Polytechnic Institute, invited me to take a position as an assistant professor and candidate for a professorship, which I accepted. I filled that office until 1901, when I had to leave on account of a special order from the highest authority. An official document came from the Minister of the Interior, saying that I. S. Prokhanoff could not be left as an assistant professor of the Riga Polytechnic Institute, as he was considered to be a leader of "Stundism." All branches of the Evangelical movement were so styled by the Government.

The Director of the Institute invited me to his office and engaged me in a long conversation, in which he expressed his surprise and regret. Professor Berloff said that if he were in my place he would simply make a declaration that he would accept the Greek Orthodox confession and would then be allowed to continue as a professor. But to this proposal I had to say "No" very decidedly, adding that not even the loss of my life would make me give up my faith in Christ and His Gospel.

During the Christmas vacation of 1900-1901 I visited Tiflis and made a proposal to the daughter of Mr. I. N. Kazakoff, Miss Anne Ivanova Kazakova. The proposal was accepted and I became a happy bridegroom. This action was taken after much prayer. I had asked God that He would give me not a rich and not a handsome wife; I did not even make education an indispensable condition. I wanted to receive from God just a companion of life who would be a good Christian of humble character and with a devoted heart. And God gave me for a wife not only a good Christian but one possessing an angelic character, very handsome, rich and well educated. She could speak English, French and German, and beside all this was a talented musician.

We were married on August 31, 1901, and went directly to St. Petersburg, where I became associated with the Westinghouse Electric Company, as a mechanical engineer on the Board. The general manager of the company was Mr. W. E. Smith, a man who possessed a very enterprising spirit, although without any special educational advantages. I had made his acquaintance six years before, as I have previously noted.

# CHAPTER XVI

## 1901 — 1903

# Beginning of Practical Work

*"He will fulfill the desire of them that fear Him."*
Ps. 145 : 19.

AFTER my conversion, as I have said, I made a program for my life's work, including the acquiring of an engineering education and also of a theological education, planning to support myself by my own labor and establishing my double work, spiritual and engineering, in the city of St. Petersburg. As a goal I had the great missionary vision before my spiritual sight of the coming spiritual awakening of the Russian nation.

The real religious condition of the Russian people at that time was most distressing. The Gospel was not preached to the Orthodox people, and the clergy jealously endeavored to forbid any priest to preach the Word of God. One or two priests who attempted to start something like preaching were severely punished. The whole of Russia represented a spiritual cemetery, a "valley of dry bones." — Ezek. 37:1-14.

## The Source of Fresh Optimism

This picture could inspire only pessimism and despair, but I was full of optimism and hope. Why? Because I saw the further picture, i.e., the great resurrection of multitudes of dead bodies. I said: "This must happen to the Russian people."

The vision of multitudes of the Russian people rising from the dead has always been before my spiritual sight, inspiring me with joy and with an ambition to labor toward that great purpose. That the Russian people will spiritually rise became my profound faith.

Whatever hardships and sorrows met me on my way, I saw before me the rising masses of the Russian people and

joy anew filled my heart. "The Russian people will rise;
there will be a sublime Easter of spiritual regeneration and
reformation" continued to be the shining light of my life,
urging me on in both small and large matters. This conviction came from the optimism of faith, and became the source
of fresh optimism.

The year 1901 was the time when some of the most important parts of my life program began to be realized. On
my graduation in 1893 from the Institute of Technology at
St. Petersburg, I acquired the means of earning my living
as a technical engineer, thus being able to labor spiritually
without burdening any church or religious organization with
my support.

Through my work at the Polytechnic Institute at Riga I
deepened my engineering knowledge. I spent more than
three years abroad studying theology in the best institutions
of the Protestant world, and thereby equipped myself with
the necessary Biblical knowledge.

## St. Petersburg Again My Center of Activity

At last I returned to St. Petersburg, apparently able to
realize the ideal with which I was inspired in the days of my
conversion, i.e., a double life work, religious (spiritual) and
engineering. Surely He fulfills the desire of them that fear
Him.

My time was distributed as follows: The whole day, from
9 to 5, I was engaged in engineering work in the Westinghouse offices, and all the evenings until very late and holi-
days as well were devoted to religious work, attending meetings, preaching in the churches, writing letters, composing
hymns, etc.

The Westinghouse Electric Company decided to project
an electric railway system for the city of St. Petersburg, and
I actively participated in the undertaking.

In the spiritual work I continued maintaining a very wide
correspondence, also taking an active part in all kinds of
meetings. My expectations, which in 1888 might have seemed
to be too optimistic, were fully realized in 1901. The prayer

about my return to Russia, sent forth to the Lord in 1896 at Bristol, was fulfilled now at St. Petersburg.

During this time I accomplished a work very important to the whole Evangelical movement. Under the conditions of that time it was impossible to print in Russia any religious publications except those in the Orthodox spirit. This explained why there were at that time almost no hymn books existing among the Evangelical Christians. Some attempts to supply hymn books had been made, but they could not satisfy the need. In most cases our brethren used handwritten hymns. By 1901, in spite of all the persecution and effort to stamp it out, the Evangelical movement in Russia became noticeably strong. In many parts of Russia frequent secret meetings were held, and the need of hymn books was felt more and more.

## The Government Prints My Gospel Hymns

I decided to attempt the publishing of a hymn book, called "The Gusli" (harps), comprising hymns which were used in these secret meetings, with some more which had been composed or translated by me. When the Government did not permit the publishing of any religious matter except those things which were of strictly Greek Orthodox origin, how was I to get this book printed?

The horizon was gloomy and there was no hope from the human standpoint. Many friends said: "Don't try; it is impossible." But I felt a bright assurance that it would be possible to accomplish the printing of the Hymnal in spite of all the prohibitory laws and control by the Government and the State Church.

Guided by an inward impulse, I went to the Director of the Printing Bureau of the Ministry of the Interior, showed the manuscript to him and asked for an estimate on the printing of 20,000 copies of the hymn book. This printing establishment, although it belonged to the Government, accepted outside orders, because it was managed on a commercial basis.

After a few days, when I returned to see the Director,

he handed me his estimate. I did not bargain, saying that the only thing I desired was to print the whole quantity as quickly as possible. At the end of our conversation he said:

"All right, we will push the job. *As to the approval of the censors, you will not have to trouble yourself. We will get that!*"

When I heard this I was extremely glad. Here I had been worrying over the censors and trying for some time to cross that bridge, and now I found the bridge was not there, at least, not for me. It was just what I desired.

I pushed the matter in every possible way, and within two or three months the whole edition of 20,000 copies of "The Gusli" were delivered to us. Lest there should be a reversal of the censor's ruling from Orthodox Church sources when they discovered this new Evangelical publication, causing us to lose the entire printing, I ordered that the books should be sent without delay to all the congregations and groups of believers throughout Russia.

The Christians outside of Russia, who have not known for centuries any interdiction against the publishing of religious literature, cannot fully understand the joy that was spread among the believers over the whole country when they received these hymn books. They could scarcely believe the evidence of their own eyes, but immediately began the use of the books in their secret meetings.

The police made their raids as usual on the meetings, arresting the preachers and searching the buildings. In their searches they seized some copies of "The Gusli," which they were about to confiscate, when they discovered on the title page, according to the regulations, the inscription:

"Printed in the Printing Establishment of the Ministry of Interior, St. Petersburg, Fontanka No."

It was the usual thing that by order of the Ministry of the Interior the police agents had to seize all kinds of printed matter discovered in the meetings of the sectarians. But when the police agents found these hymn books had been printed by the Ministry of the Interior they were simply dumbfounded.

## Confiscation Order Came Too Late

Of course, the puzzled police agents sent their reports to the Ministry of the Interior. As the reports multiplied, the Ministry ordered the edition of the hymn books to be confiscated. But it was too late; all the books had been distributed!

Visitors at some of our meetings, seeing the hymn books, with the address of the printer, and desiring to purchase one or more copies, began to write letters to the Printing Establishment, approximately as follows:

> Printing Establishment of the Ministry Interior.
> Dear Brethren:
> Enclosing a money order for ——————— roubles, I would ask you to send me one copy of "The Gusli" printed by you for the Evangelical Christians. We inform you that the book is very edifying and spiritual.

Was not all this a real miracle? The Ministry of the Interior, which had absolute power to destroy all our printed works, produced a hymn book very much needed by the persecuted Evangelical Christians! It was a miracle. But from this very fact one can understand how difficult it was to do even such a simple thing as the printing of a hymn book. What a task! What a risk! What a feat! Nevertheless, God gave sufficient faith and energy to accomplish such things.

Although the books were printed with the permission of the censor, and by the Ministry of the Interior, in view of the importance of the hymn book as Evangelical Christian propaganda, the Ministry could have arrested me as the author and publisher. They might very soon have decided to take such action, but here something unexpected happened.

## A Sudden Journey to America

The General Manager of the Westinghouse Electric Company invited me to his office one morning and informed me that the company had decided to send five engineers to their American works for training in American methods, and that *I was included*, and therefore should at once prepare for the journey!

## IN THE CAULDRON OF RUSSIA

In April, 1902, my wife left St. Petersburg for Tiflis (Caucasus) to be with her parents, and I left for America with my companions, Mr. F. H. Park, the engineer of the Westinghouse Air Brake Company; Mr. Choglokoff, a Russian engineer; Mr. Shatilovich, an engineer from Finland, and Mr. Veitch, an engineer from Scotland.

I will not describe in detail the whole journey, our visit to England, our arrival and stay in America, but I must mention that my first impression of New York City, with its Statue of Liberty, its skyscrapers, etc., was beyond any description.

We had a certain schedule, based on the desire of our chiefs that we should visit the main places of engineering interest. At New York we inspected the great skyscrapers, the underground railways, the Brooklyn Bridge and various power plants. At St. Louis we saw various plants and the premises of the World's Fair, which was at that time in the stage of preparation. At Niagara Falls we saw with great interest the unique hydro-electric plant which supplied electricity to Buffalo and other places. At Chicago we saw various plants and the celebrated Stock Yards, a striking example of mechanization.

At Pittsburgh we saw enormous iron furnaces and steel manufacturing plants with the fires that made the city at night "hades with the lid off." There also we entered and examined the Westinghouse Electric Manufacturing Company, Westinghouse Engine Plant, Westinghouse Switch and Signal Company, and the Westinghouse Air Brake Company. Naturally all these works produced upon us a wonderful impression of the energy of the American people. Both the plants and the output manufactured by the Westinghouse companies were very complex and at the same time very simple, bearing the imprint of a genius. These great plants were created by the energy of one man, George Westinghouse, who was a real genius in the world of mechanical inventions, one of the most notable and celebrated inventors of his time.

As my specialty was mechanical engineering, I was instructed to study the foundry methods in the Westinghouse Electric Manufacturing plant at East Pittsburgh and in the Westinghouse Air Brake plant at Wilmerding, Pa. I lived at Wilkinsburg, and made daily trips to the plants.

## The Engineer Makes His Report

After thoroughly investigating the foundry work at these plants, I wrote an extensive report, which I later submitted to my Board at St. Petersburg. On the basis of this report, after my return to Russia, I received instructions to investigate the methods employed at the foundry of the St. Petersburg Westinghouse Works, which I did to the full satisfaction of my Board.

After the completion of my studies of the Westinghouse Works, I received instructions to visit the Crane Company, at Chicago. Mr. Charles Crane showed me through the plants and enabled me to accumulate the information for our St. Petersburg Board.

During my stay in Chicago I had a remarkable experience. Mr. Charles Crane was a great lover of Russian history, literature, the arts and sciences. In his house one could see Russian paintings and even icons. One morning Mr. Crane said to me that Prof. P. N. Milukoff was in Chicago and would be present that evening at a reception arranged by Dr. Harper, at the University of Chicago. Mr. Crane invited me to be present, and to this I gladly consented. I had heard of Prof. Milukoff, but had never met him.

At that time he was a professor at the University of Sofia, Bulgaria. Prior to that he had been a professor at St. Petersburg University, but was dismissed on account of his participation in a students' strike. Having left Russia, he found refuge in Bulgaria. He had been invited to deliver a series of lectures on the history of Russian Law.

At the reception Mr. Crane introduced me to Prof. Milukoff. Later in the evening we left the University together and took the same train. As Russians usually do, we began to discuss various political and social questions. I remember that, among other things, Mr. Milukoff said:

"Russia needs a good revolution." I did not contradict that statement, but said:—

"Russia needs also a good reformation."

Three years later I met Mr. Milukoff again at St. Petersburg, at the State Duma, where he was the leader of the Constitutional Democratic party. I supplied him with materials concerning the legal position of the religious societies and our Evangelical congregations. The purpose was to influence the Duma to abolish some of the old laws and to promulgate new laws more favorable to the rights of religious societies in Russia.

Since that time I have met Mr. Milukoff several times in the Duma, and I saw him at Petrograd even after the revolution, when he was Minister of Foreign Affairs in the Kerensky Government.

The correctness of my statement to Mr. Milukoff only confirms me in the rightness of my general idea and encourages me as to its realization.

I remember the thousands of Doukhobors who emigrated from the Caucasus to escape the persecutions, finding refuge in Canada, and also the thousands of Molokans who emigrated from Russia to California. And I have also met in America some Russian Evangelical Christian brethren who found refuge here from the persecutions in their own country.

From this it can be easily understood that America as a country of liberty proved to be a refuge for all Russians persecuted for their political or religious views or activities in the homeland during the old regime and in the present time.

During that first journey to America my impressions were extremely deep. Later on I expressed these emotions in a poem, which reads:

### AMERICA

*"Happy is the people whose God is Jehovah."*
*Psalms 144 : 15.*

My weary voyage almost ended,
    I saw, one morning clear and bright,

126

# ENGINEERING AND EVANGELISM

Across the waves, a mighty statue
  Upbearing still the torch of light.
New York before me!  How the buildings
  Towered up until they touched the sky!
Midway in air hung mighty bridges —
  I hailed the sight with joyous cry.

America! my heart repeated,
  And all my sorrow fled at last;
There swept upon me in that moment
  The hopes and longings of the past.
America!  To darkened races
  The symbol of a life reborn;
To sufferers in all the ages
  The dawning of a radiant morn.

America!  The light of heaven
  Upon you clearly ever falls;
But one star shines more fair than others —
  To perfect liberty it calls.
You free the soul from every fetter —
  You forge no chains for men to wear;
And in your wondrous open spaces
  We find release from dungeon air.

No inquisition tries the faithful,
  No ancient bond can hold them fast;
Your ruins hold no bones of martyrs
  Who died for Christ in ages past.
No ancient hierarchy can rule you,
  No mitred priest nor royal crown;
You hold one law for all believers,
  From ancient days still handed down.

When, persecuted in their homeland,
  Men fled to you from Europe's shore,
You granted them your strong protection
  And made them free forever more.
And those who stood with me in battle
  Shoulder to shoulder, side by side,
Have found here homes in which they greet me,
  With doors of welcome opened wide.

Imperfect though some choose to call you,
  All things you can by faith subdue;
From this is born creative genius
  To make your fairest dreams come true.
The elements must do your bidding,
  Both fire and water, earth and air,
And nations who have sought to crush you
  Are proud if they your glory share.

127

# IN THE CAULDRON OF RUSSIA

For those who fled from persecution
  To seek your shores in days of old
Brought in their hands the Bible only,
  A gift more precious far than gold.
As by this Book their lives were ordered,
  So let it guide your steps aright,
And you shall be to all the nations
  A beacon of far reaching light!

I. S. PROKHANOFF.

July 29, 1928, Hamilton, Ontario, Canada.

# CHAPTER XVII

## 1903 — 1905

## Signs of Better Times

THE BEGINNING OF SPRING IN THE STATE LIFE OF RUSSIA

*"The Morning cometh."*
*Is. 21 : 12.*

THESE years brought to Russia changes of immeasurable importance, very favorable for the Evangelical movement. Toward the beginning of 1903 a certain nervous, agitated state of mind could be observed throughout Russia. There were riots among students and workmen. The liberation movement began among the people. Under the influence of this growing trouble, Emperor Nicholas issued a special manifesto on Feb. 26, 1903, in which, referring to these troubles, among other things, he conferred the principle of freedom of confession of faith and fulfillment of rituals to all the denominations and religions.

Although everything was oppressed, there was something in the general psychological condition of the people that caused the Russian newspapers to write about the "coming spring" in the political life of Russia. The trouble, i.e., the liberation movement, was still growing, and it resulted in great changes, which were largely influenced by the Russo-Japanese War (Jan. 27, 1904, to August 25, 1905).

The defeat of Russia in the war with Japan weakened the Czar's Government and strengthened the progressive movement among the people. As a result, the work of the Evangelical groups began to grow and consequently my spiritual work was increased. Under the influence of the failure of the war, the people from the lower to the upper classes began to feel that the old order of things in the State, the autocracy which was the cause of the powerlessness of Russia in all branches of life, could not exist further, and therefore, changes must take place.

The Czar and the Government also recognized this fact. They began to seek a strong man for leadership in political affairs, and they found him in the person of S. U. Witte. He was appointed to be the President of the Council of Ministers and occupied that office until 1906.

S. U. Witte proved to be a statesman of a very high type. The transition of Russia from the autocratic to the parliamentary form of government is connected with his name. On August 26, 1904, the Czar appointed Prince Sviatopolk-Mirsky to be the Minister of the Interior. Taking his office, the new Minister declared that the Government would take a new attitude in its policy, i.e., the course of "confidence toward the people."

## A Move Toward Toleration

Sviatopolk-Mirsky did not succeed in introducing any important reforms and resigned on Jan. 22, 1905. During his short ministry, however, he did something important for the religious question. He announced that he wanted to have as much information as possible regarding the present condition of various religious societies, denominations and churches.

Other brethren and myself felt that we should give the Government all the information we could. I wrote an extensive paper on the Evangelical movement. We telegraphed to the South, from where two delegates, Ivanoff and Kushneroff, came to St. Petersburg with documents regarding the persecutions there, the imprisonments and exiles.

One must remember that at that time the old laws with regard to the religious life still existed, forbidding separation from the Greek Catholic Church, punishing severely proselytizing, forbidding any religious meetings among the Russians except the services of the Greek Orthodox Church, the formation of any other religious societies or congregations among the Greek Catholic population, etc. It was impossible at that time to print any religious literature in the non-Greek Catholic spirit. All the Evangelical meetings were secret or unofficial, and in all the provinces and places of exile there were hundreds of those who suffered for their religion.

As I saw our condition then, the whole of Russia represented one vast prison. On the basis of the material which I had and that which was brought by the brethren from the South, I wrote "The Report to the Ministry of the Interior concerning the legal condition of Evangelical Christians, Baptists and others in Russia."

The report was read by me in the Commission of our brethren, was approved and tendered to the Ministry of the Interior. Some months after that we received a copy of the report printed in the printing establishment of the Ministry of the Interior, as a part of the materials gathered by the Ministry of the Interior. Later on we saw that our principal suggestions about necessary changes in the religious laws were accepted by the Government in its decrees of April 17, 1905, concerning the strengthening of the principle of tolerance in Russia.

## The First Protestant Christian (Evangelical) Association of Young People

Knowing how important it was for the Evangelical movement to have the younger generation properly educated, I paid special attention to this question, which was a part of my general program. On account of the prevailing severe laws, it was impossible at that time to have open meetings for the young people. The small meetings, which took place in a secret manner, were accompanied with great risk, and there was then no organized group of our Christian young people.

When possible I took part in their secret meetings, and finally I decided to undertake with them the organization of the first association of the Christian youth in connection with the St. Petersburg congregation. We appointed an organization meeting at the lodging of one young brother in a suburb of St. Petersburg. It was on the now celebrated day, January 9, 1905.

I expressed to the young men gathered there the general basis of the Christian Young People's Association and described the glorious future of the Christian movement among the young people in Russia, if the work was begun in a proper manner. I said that according to the progress of events in Russia great changes should take place, that religious liberty would be proclaimed in the near future for all organizations, that we would have a Union of the Evangelical Churches and afterward we would form the Union of the Young People's Associations, that their Union would have all-Russian conferences and we would have for it our own magazines, Bible courses, and other activities.

I spoke concerning all these things in the secret meeting, in which we could expect any moment that the police would enter and arrest all of us. It was a speech of pure optimism of faith amidst conditions of pessimism.

The young men heard my words with glowing eyes and flaming hearts. Of course, we passed the resolution to form that first association, and soon after that statutes were written and accepted for their guidance.

Later on all my predictions were fulfilled in an amazing way, and my optimism was justified. After the proclamation of the Toleration Act, on April 17 of the same year, 1905, the first national conference of our Christian young people took place at Moscow. The Union of Christian Young People was formed, and I was elected the first President.

Soon after this I founded the organ of the Union, the first periodical for the Christian young people in Russia. Two of our young men were sent to England by me for a short course in practical instruction in the methods of work in the missions, and soon after that we had two missionaries chosen especially for work among the young people. Other routine work was undertaken, as is usual in similar organizations.

This All-Russian Union of the Christian Young People was called the "Small Union," as compared with the Union of the Evangelical Churches, which we called the "Big Union."

During the above described secret young people's meeting, as we were quietly discussing questions pertaining to the formation of the Union, suddenly we heard the booming of canon. I asked all to be quiet and we continued our meeting, but we were quite well aware what it was.

A revolt of workmen under the leadership of a very well-known priest, Gapon, was taking place. With ikons and singing religious hymns, a great number of workmen began to move toward the Winter Palace, where the Czar lived. They desired, as their leaders afterward declared, simply to see their father, the Czar. But when they approached the palace, the booming of guns began and shooting was started by the soldiers and cossacks. There were many, many people killed that day. It was disclosed afterward that the Priest Gapon was one of the provocators. The workmen were his victims. However, it produced a kind of reaction in the circles of the Czar and his Government.

When the workmen and the revolutionary leaders learned of the double-dealing role of the Priest Gapon they decided to murder him, and fulfilled their purpose in a lonely summer house in the neighborhood of St. Petersburg.

### The Clergy of the Established Church

The activities of the Priest Gapon give a picture of the moral condition of the Greek Catholic clergy under the Czar. The Union of Church and State in Russia deprived the Church of its liberty, enslaved it and demoralized it. The members of the clergy of the Greek Orthodox Church, beginning with the simple deacon in a village church and ending with the highest Metropolitan, were not so much ministers of the Church as officials of the State. All of the priests were ordered by the Government to reveal the secrets of the confessions of the people, especially if they had something to do with politics, and to report about everything which was not favorable to the Government.

The Procurator of the Holy Synod, K. P. Pobedonostzeff, founded a certain missionary institution, all the missionaries of which had as their chief purpose to point out all the most active leaders of the Protestant Christian movement in Russia and of all the sects, and to report all about them to the authorities, that they might be exiled. One of the usual methods of these Missionaries and Priests was the arrangement of religious debates. In most cases the Evangelical preachers who took part in those debates were exiled shortly afterward.

It is sad, but a true fact that ninety-nine per cent of all the prisoners and exiles among the Evangelical Christians and other free religious organizations in Russia suffered as the result of the reports of those deceiving missionaries and priests.

Not with censure, or as one sitting in judgment, but with deepest sorrow, I observed conditions of this kind and became more and more convinced that the union of Church and State in Russia was not only unscriptural, but most detrimental for the Church and even for the State. The Church was enslaved and the clergy occupied with politics and thus were taken away from their direct duties of the spiritual education of the people. *The State was thus preparing the atheistic and materialistic elements which later destroyed both the Church and the State.*

It became increasingly apparent therefore that for the recovery of the Christian religious life in Russia *the separation of the Church from the State should be the first step.* To aid in the realization of this reform was one of the paragraphs of my program.

### Decree and Manifesto Regarding Religious Liberty

There were Greek Orthodox bishops and archbishops who also saw the necessity of this reform, but they were few and powerless. Beside this, when talking about this reform they had in view more the rights and supremacy of the Greek Orthodox clergy than the enormous spiritual work of regeneration of the Church and the spiritual education of the people which should be carried out and for which the freedom was essential. However, the sense of the necessity of a certain change in the position of the Church began to grow.

As the result of the failure of the war with Japan, which lasted until August 25, 1905, the revolutionary movement at that time embraced all classes of the people. The strongest degree of the revolutionary movement manifested itself among the soldiers of the army returning from the Far East through Siberia. Some cities in Siberia even declared themselves to be republics.

At St. Petersburg and Moscow there were big demonstrations of the people. Among the workmen of St. Petersburg a revolutionary organization was formed called "The Council of Workmen's Deputies", which began to publish their demands. Under the influence of all these events and following the advice of S. U. Witte, President of the Council of Ministers, the Czar issued an Act of Toleration, on April 17, 1905.

It was a great blessing for the Protestant religious organizations, but it was insufficient for the whole people, who expected something more. Delegates of the best social workers from the province of Tver submitted to the Czar a petition for further reforms. From other provinces similar petitions followed.

The Government hastened to conclude peace with Japan, the treaty being signed by Count S. U. Witte at Portsmouth in America in August, 1905. But the liberation movement grew and grew, and the result was the issue of the celebrated Manifesto of October 17, 1905. In this manifesto toleration was changed to freedom of conscience and the autocracy was changed into a parliamentary form of government. Freedom of the press, of meetings, organization of societies and freedom of political activities were proclaimed.

## Rejoicing in Our Liberty

The declaration of this manifesto was followed by great demonstrations and festivities over the whole vast territory of the country. What joy it was for the Evangelical Christians and all the Protestant Christian groups in Russia, who had been so bitterly persecuted during many years and who now heard about liberty for the work of preaching the Gospel. We at once arranged special prayer meetings, in some of which I delivered addresses and sermons pointing out that these new manifestos of liberty were the result of aspirations of those who had suffered and prayed with the optimism of faith for many years. This was the joy of reaping after many years of sowing with tears.

I also pictured the great possibilities opened before all the believers to preach the Gospel, to create new churches, to organize them, to start our Evangelical periodicals, and to establish our religious schools and the Bible Seminary. I drew a program for this great undertaking and started at once to realize it with regard to evangelization, publication and Biblical education. Our secret labors under the persecution schooled us well for the enlargement of our work.

As the religious meetings became quite free, I encouraged the brethren in the provinces to use this new opportunity to open as many meetings as possible to spread the Gospel throughout the country. Soon I began to receive from all parts of the country reports about the numerous and crowded meetings in the towns and villages over the whole vast territory of Russia.

The evangelization work began to develop in all directions. Some of our exiled and imprisoned brethren were liberated and returned to their homes and their churches. What joy it was for their fellow-believers!

### Contact with S. U. Witte

But many of them still remained in their places of exile, because the local authorities had not received special orders from the highest authorities and did not fully understand the new laws published. The central Government, having published the general new laws which brought about these reforms, forgot to issue special decrees about the liberation of all who were deprived of their liberty for religious reasons.

I received some letters from our exiled brethren, who asked me to plead for their liberation. I wrote a petition to the Prime Minister, Count S. U. Witte, from the Council of the St. Petersburg Evangelical Church, and received a permit to present it to the Count in his palace. Together with Brother Dolgapoloff, an elder of the church, I went to his palace. I saw Count S. U. Witte for the first time, and was strongly impressed by his stature and the quickness of his movements. He rapidly perused our papers and said: "What you write, gentlemen, is very important. To-night I will tell the Minister of the Interior to issue a special order." He fulfilled his promise, and in a few days we read a circular order of the Minister of the Interior about the liberation of all who were imprisoned and exiled for religious reasons. Many more Christians were thus liberated and returned to their homes, to the increased joy of the believers.

## The First Protestant Christian Periodical in Russia

The next clause in my program was the open publication of an evangelical spiritual magazine, for the undertaking of which my former secret efforts were a considerable schooling. Such a publication in Russia could not have been undertaken openly before the manifesto of October 17, 1905.

To understand this, one must remember that before this time no Protestant Christian hymn book, other books or periodicals could be printed, and they were not printed and did not exist, with the exception of the quite remarkable publication of our hymn book by the Ministry of the Interior.

Immediately after the issue of this new manifesto I began to take the necessary steps, and wrote an application to the Minister of the Interior. In November of that year I had an official permit for the publishing of the first Protestant Christian (Evangelical) monthly magazine, which was entitled "Christianin" (the Christian).

What joy I experienced when I walked out of the office of the official who gave me the precious permit. Arriving at home, I gathered the members of my family and those brethren who were within reach, and we gave our thanks in prayer to the Lord for this realization of the expectation of our faith.

In the same month of November I issued a lithographic test number of this magazine and sent it to various centers of our religious activities. The impression was most encouraging.

On January 1, 1906, the first printed number of the magazine was issued. It was published continuously, with an interruption caused by the revolution and civil war, until the end of 1928, that is, for twenty-two years, and until it was stopped by the atheists.

Three main principles were laid as the basis of this periodical:

1. The revelation to the Russian people of the substance of Christianity; the living Christ, *nothing save Christ.* "I determined not to know anything among you save Jesus Christ and Him crucified." — 1 Cor. 2:2.

This great truth was lost by the leaders of the Greek Orthodox Church and lost for the people, who were separated from Christ by the hierachy of their clergy, by numerous rituals and by the hosts of saints who were proclaimed to be their mediators between them and God. "The Christian" was to be a call to the millions of the Russian people to come directly to Christ as the only mediator between men and God, by demolishing all kinds of walls and partitions and declaring that fellowship with God through Christ was the substance of Christianity.

2. The evangelization of the Russian people and "the building up of a spiritual house out of the lively stones", on the basis of the Gospel — a new Gospel (Evangelical) Church — by "striving together for the faith of the Gospel." Phil. 1:27. The Russian people called themselves Christians in the highest sense, although they really did not know the Gospel and its main truth, salvation by faith and grace, and lived in continual slavish fear under the law of Moses, trying to gain salvation by their own works. They knew nothing about conversion, the new birth or sanctification. They knew the Church only as a system of rituals and traditions and had yet to hear about the Church of "lively stones." "The Christian's" objective was to bring the people by evangelization to the reformation, or rather to the transformation of spiritual regeneration. Our slogan for the magazine included three Rs: *"Revival, Regeneration, Reformation."*

3. *The unification of all the branches of living Christian-*

138

*ity* on the principles of freedom and brotherly love.  The slogan was:

In essential things unity.

In secondary things freedom.

In all things charity.

During its existence "The Christian" was faithful to its slogans, and even now it is considered to be the best of all the Russian Protestant publications.  It was never influenced or carried away by politics or by any controversy.  It never criticised or censured any Christian group or any religious worker.

The magazine spread everywhere the ideal of Christ and his sacrifice, promoting unity, freedom and charity and the great optimism of faith, the faith of the Gospel.  No count can be made of the letters which I received from the readers of "The Christian", informing me about the edification, the conversions and various blessings received through the magazine.

**The First Protestant Christian (Evangelical) Bible Course**

The next paragraph of my program was also realized, that of Bible education in its primary stage for our Evangelical workers.  In the city of St. Petersburg I arranged the so-called two-months Gospel courses for the young preachers of St. Petersburg and other places.  Four brethren came from Samara and other cities of Russia to attend these courses.  Along with the general educational studies we gave lectures on theological subjects.

The lectures and studies took place in the palace of Princess Lieven, who belonged to the Church of Evangelical Christians and who through all the dark years of persecution permitted the believers to have religious meetings in her palace somewhat in secret manner.  We could not secure a permit to open a permanent school until 1913.  In that year, as I will describe later, we opened a regular Bible College, which as a matter of fact was the germ of the first Protestant theological school for Russians in Russia in their own language.  It functioned until 1928, when it was closed by the atheists, along with the magazine.

# CHAPTER XVIII

## (1906-1911)

## The Extension of the Work

### *"The Word of God Grew."* — Acts 12:24

THE year 1906 is remarkable for another important fact: the beginning of a parliamentary regime in Russia by calling together the Gosudarstvennia Duma, the first Russian Parliament, on April 27, 1906. As is known, this Duma existed only a few months, and on July 8 of the same year it was dissolved.

The second Duma was called together on February 20, 1907, and was dismissed on June 3, 1907. The third Duma was called on November 7, 1907, and existed until 1911. In 1912 the fourth Duma was elected, which existed until 1917, when the revolution began.

The first Dumas were too radical in their demands on the government. The third Duma was elected on the basis of a special election law created by Stolipen, the Prime Minister after Count S. U. Witte. Owing to that law it could exist longer simply because in the Duma was created a majority which came to an agreement with Stolipen on the basis of realizing the manifesto of October 17, 1905. The party of this majority was called the October party, and it was also predominant in the fourth Duma. In spite of many defects, all the Dumas defended the rights of the people and rendered great services to the people by educating them in matters of politics.

In the year the first Duma met another event of great importance to the believers occurred, an additional decree being published which gave the right to all those who separated from the Greek Orthodox Church to organize congregations and churches and to develop their activities. In the next year a special conference was called at St. Petersburg, made up of representatives of Evangelical Christians and Baptists. This conference discussed the new law and gave its comments to the Government, with the request that some changes be made.

But on the whole, that law of October 17, 1906 (different from the manifesto of October 17, 1905) was satisfactory, and on the basis of it the congregations could develop their work with success.

It will not be out of place to say a few words on how the Duma proved to be useful to our cause of spreading the Gospel.

## Struggle for Religious Liberty

Notwithstanding the fact that fundamental laws were issued, guaranteeing freedom of conscience to all religious societies and denominations in Russia, still there were difficulties in various provinces of Russia, where the local authorities were not acquainted with the laws and committed all kinds of violations of them. I received many complaints from our brethren, who wrote that in such a place the police did not give permission for a meeting, and in another place they closed meetings. In all these cases I always applied to the Department of Religious Affairs of the Ministry of the Interior for correction of the faults of the local authorities, and in most cases received satisfaction. Special orders were sent to the local authorities and the cause for complaint was removed.

But sometimes the officials of the Department of Religious affairs could not satisfy our requests, and in such cases the Duma was of great usefulness to us. In the Duma was a special Commission on Religious Cults. The President of that Commission, Kamensky, was very sympathetic toward the Evangelical movement and all sections of Protestant Christianity in Russia. In almost all cases he applied to the Minister of the Interior personally with a request to give such and such orders to the local authorities.

Very often I applied to P. N. Milukoff with the request to plead for us, and usually he and his fellow-members of the party helped us considerably. From my youth I was in

sympathy with the most radical ideas of freedom, brotherhood, justice and equality, but being a Christian I could not
and did not belong to any political party.

## Contact With the Political Parties

I approved of all that was done in these parties which was
in accord with the principles of Christianity, and equally
disapproved of all that was contrary to the precepts or the
general spirit of the teaching of Jesus. Therefore, in the
matter of religion and all our difficulties and persecution I
applied to all the parties in the Duma to help us. It is to
be regretted that the extreme parties (the left and the right)
were not eager to aid us because of their general opposition
to religion, the left to all Christianity, and the right as to the
narrow Orthodox Church. But the moderate parties, October
party and Constitutional Democrats, aided us considerably.

There were, for instance, various defects in the decrees
issued concerning freedom of conscience. The children of
the Orthodox Church, up to a certain age could not join any
Protestant Christian congregation. Of course, these inconvenient laws could be changed only in the legislative manner,
through the Duma. In connection with these matters I had
to visit the President of the Commission on Religious Cults
in the Duma, to present to him papers written on various
laws inconvenient to our congregations. That Commission
worked out a systematic collection of laws with regard to
religious life in Russia, but the Duma was so occupied with
the political questions and internal struggle that these laws
never were finally passed.

Complaints from all parts concerning violations of the
laws of religious liberty multiplied and accumulated. The
explanation of laws and the correspondence regarding this
question became more and more difficult. Therefore, in order
to help our congregations and individual brethren in defend-
ing their rights when they were infringed upon by the local
authorities, and to give them guidance on the necessary steps
to receive permits, etc., I composed a book, "Law and Religion". This was a collection of the laws issued by the

Government with regard to religious liberty, together with my comments and interpretation. This book proved to be a great success.

With this volume in their possession, our brethren immediately began to feel that the laws were on their side and defended themselves in a wonderful manner. They would show my book to the local authorities, referring to certain paragraphs and clauses bearing on the case in point. The authorities, in many instances, not knowing the laws themselves, were surprised and compelled to agree with our brethren, and not infrequently the authorities wrote asking us to send them a copy of the book.

In this way the book of laws published by me became a guide and handbook not only for the Evangelical Christians and other Protestant Christians, but also for the authorities themselves. Even Kamensky, the President of the Commission on Religious Cults of the State Duma, was pleasantly surprised when I presented him with my book, and said: "Oh, this is what we want for our work!"

## Enlargement of My Publishing Work

I started the publishing of "The Christian" alone, contributing to it many articles on questions of practical and dogmatic Christianity. It became a messenger of spiritual life to the Evangelical Christians of Russia. Along with this periodical I began also to publish small tracts and booklets bearing on the practical and spiritual needs of our growing membership in all parts of Russia.

Also at this time I was able to realize another paragraph of my program, regarding hymn writing. With great difficulties and at considerable risk, as I have already written, I had published my first hymn book, "The Gusli".

Now when the freedom came I used it for printing my hymns according to my inspiration and general ideas. While highly appreciating the translation of western hymns, I thought that the Russian Evangelical Christianity should produce hymns according to the character of the Russian people and their tastes.

## IN THE CAULDRON OF RUSSIA

I decided to give monthly to my subscribers one hymn as a supplement to my magazine, "The Christian," with my own words and the music of competent composers. For the musical part of the work I invited Mr. K. P. Inkis, a believing Latvian, who was then a student at the St. Petersburg Musical Conservatory. He was instructed by me to select foreign melodies for some of my hymns and to create new ones in the Russian style for the majority of them. I also decided that each melody should be written in two ways, i.e., in the Italian notation and in the way of figures. The second system was adopted together with the first, because of its simplicity, for the brethren who lived in the villages.

### Growth of Christian Choirs in Russia

In this way every monthly issue of my magazine contained one original hymn, with my text and with a melody selected or composed by Mr. Inkis and written in two note systems. These hymns produced a great sensation among the Christian believers and were many times the stimulus which caused the multiplication and growth of choirs and orchestras in our churches and made for the development of spiritual music among our congregations.

The Russian people are naturally very musical. The Russian Orthodox Church music is excellent, and the Russian secular music is also very rich. But in neither style of music which existed could be expressed the feelings of the Evangelical Christians. The Greek Orthodox music was beautiful, but sorrowful, which was quite natural because their religion was purely pessimistic. They preached that no man can attain salvation here on earth, that God is the Judge of the universe, that there is no direct way to Him and that every man desiring to come to God must apply to a priest or to a certain saint. This religion kept the people in a state of fear, like slaves. Therefore the music of this Church could not be otherwise than sad and mournful. There was nothing in the Greek Orthodox religion about conversion, new birth or regeneration, and I felt it would not meet our needs.

The Council of the All-Russian Evangelical Christian Union at Leningrad in the Winter   (See page 150)

Faculty and Student Body of the Evangelical Christian Bible College in Leningrad    (See page 166)

On the other hand, the popular music of the people was also sorrowful. It could not have been otherwise. The people, kept for centuries in slavery by the autocratic power, lived continually in fear and trembling. On the whole the Russian music has been mostly pessimistic or in a minor key.

But the music of the Evangelical Christian movement could not be mournful like the popular music, nor sad like the music of the Greek Orthodox Church. Every Evangelical Christian passes from darkness to light through his conversion and experiences indescribable joy and happiness. All his life is lighted by the bright rays of salvation in Jesus Christ. So I decided to make sure that the Evangelical Christian music in Russia, in contrast, must be capable of expressing the highest joy that can exist on the earth, the joy which the heavens share (Luke 15:7, 23).

Our music must be of such a character as to contain the joy of the Gospel, a joy overwhelming and overcoming the sadness of the former Russian music, like the rays of bright sunshine penetrating through a rain cloud, like optimism dispersing pessimism.

## Songs of Victorious Faith

Since this conception of the Russian Christian Gospel song and music came to me, I acted accordingly. All my hymns express the victorious faith of the Gospel, picturing the passing over the seas and overthrowing mountains.

I explained my ideas to Mr. K. P. Inkis and other Russian composers from among my fellow-workers and did everything possible to inspire them with this new kind of spiritual music. Gradually such melodies were created and now the number is ever increasing. We may speak now of a new Russian Evangelical Church music and singing. After being accustomed to the sad religious and secular music for so long, the Russian Christians and even those who clung to the Orthodox Church and some who denied all religion began to sing some of our most popular joyous songs. Thus the sectarians and even the Orthodox sang the Gospel songs in Russia from pure love of the tunes, if not of the words, and undoubtedly many have thus come to the true light who were for the time beyond reach of the preached Word or who refused to read the Scripture.

The number of my hymns was gradually increasing, and I was compelled to make collections of them in various hymn books. Toward the year of writing this autobiography no less than ten hymn books have been printed, for use by our congregations, for our young people, the women and children, and still there are two books which I have composed yet to be printed. These are listed below and indicate how the Holy Spirit has blessed this part of my program:

ALREADY PUBLISHED

| | | |
|---|---|---|
| 1. | Gusli (harps) | 507 |
| 2. | Christian's Songs | 100 |
| 3. | Timbrels | 100 |
| 4. | Cymbals | 100 |
| 5. | Life's Dawn | 100 |
| 6. | David's Pipe | 100 |
| 7. | The Songs of the Primitive Christians | 101 |
| 8. | New Songs | 75 |
| 9. | Anna's Songs | 30 |
| 10. | Depth Songs | 20 |

NOT YET PUBLISHED

| | | |
|---|---|---|
| 10. | Depth Songs | 40 |
| 11. | Union's Songs | 110 |
| 12. | Songs to God | 60 |

| | |
|---|---|
| Total number of hymns | 1443 |
| Hymns by other authors | 406 |

| | |
|---|---|
| Produced by I. S. Prokhanoff | 1037 |
| Translated | 413 |

| | |
|---|---|
| Written by I. S. Prokhanoff | 624 |

Every book in the above list was produced for a special purpose, and has found its place in the congregational or group meetings.

1. *Gusli* is a general hymnal for meetings.
2. *Christian's Songs* is mostly the translation of foreign hymns with beautiful melodies.
3. *Timbrels* is a book containing original hymns written by myself at different moments of my spiritual experiences. Many of them were printed as supplements to "The Christian".

4. *Cymbals* comprises more hymns translated from the English for their sweet melodies.

5. *Life's Dawn* contains hymns for children.

6. *David's Pipe* is especially for the young people. It has a striking appeal to them because I wrote all the hymns while in prison following our young people's national conference at Tver.

7. *The Songs of the Primitive Christians* was written by me from the standpoint of the primitive Christians.

8. *New Songs* is a special arrangement of hymns with beautiful melodies.

9. *Anna's Songs* comprises hymns for the women, written in memory of my wife, who died in 1919.

10. *Depth Songs* relates to subjects of the Christian life or the deep things, and was written while I was in another prison at Moscow.

11. *Union's Songs* contains hymns written by me for the various branches of the Evangelical Christian Union in Russia, according to their districts and provinces. These hymns express, beside spiritual experiences, also characteristic features of the local life of believers. They all have the local color. Their music will also have a local character according to the provinces. Evangelical Christian Armenians will have hymns according to their national characteristics in text and music; so also the Georgians, Ossets, Tartars, etc.

12. *Songs to God.* These songs describe the attributes of God and the relation of the human soul to Him.

These twelve books when complete will express the main needs, experiences and aspirations of Evangelical Christians in Russia and are already creating a new style of music, — the Gospel music.

The development of the spiritual music has a very great importance for the evangelization of Russia. The Russian people are fond of music. A large number of conversions have taken place through hearing the Evangelical hymns. A peasant hears a certain hymn in the village, learns it, and becoming interested in the Bible, begins to attend meetings and is converted.

Many have been converted through reading the hymns and others under the influence of singing the hymns in the churches. Yes, the music and song is a great means, perhaps next to the Scripture, for spreading the Gospel among the people. It has certainly been an important factor in the progress of the Russian Evangelical movement.

In this connection I have always given special attention to the development of the music services in our churches. Almost every denomination has its own views with regard to the place and service of music in their churches. The Greek Catholic Church uses only singing in the churches and does not permit the organ. The Roman Catholic Church uses both vocal and instrumental music. Neither of these churches in Russia would allow the playing of orchestras or pianos.

During this period of time I published our first book containing the notes to "The Gusli", and later three large volumes containing the notes to all the twelve hymnals.

## The First Evangelical Christian Publishing Association

The work of publishing the magazine, "The Christian", tracts and hymns was growing more and more taxing, so that I was entirely unable to manage it all personally, with the other parts of my work as President of the Union, not forgetting that I was still engaged in the engineering work which brought my daily bread. I began to think about creating an organization for the publishing of Evangelical literature, and this was accomplished in 1908.

In the south of Russia there were settlements of Mennonites, a very old Christian group originating in Holland in the seventeeth century by a converted Roman Catholic priest named Menno Simons. They became very numerous in Holland and emigrated partly to Germany, but mostly to Poland. In the end of the eighteenth century, under Catherine II, they were allowed to migrate to Southern Russia, where they founded flourishing colonies.

Toward the close of the nineteenth century a new group was formed among them, the "Brudergemeinde" (brothers' Church), which resembled the Evangelical Christians very much. One group of them in one of the colonies had a small publishing enterprise which issued a German Christian paper, "Friedenstimme" (The Voice of Peace). Their leader, Heinrich Brown, became interested in my work, and came once to St. Petersburg. In the course of our conversation I proposed that we should form an All-Russian publishing company for producing and spreading Russian literature, that they should manage all the financial part of the work and I would undertake the literary labor.

Brown and his companions consented to my proposal, and in 1908 the first Russian Protestant Christian (Evangelical) Publishing Association was formed, under the name of "The Rainbow". I proposed the name as a symbol of our activities, — a quiet, peaceful labor after the deluge and storm of the revolution (1905). Very soon we opened the first Evangelical Christian book store in the city of St. Petersburg, which became a center of the new religious publishing interests among the Protestant Christians.

This combination proved to be a great success. The Mennonites had their printing plant in their colony in the South of Russia, where they could print very cheaply. The literature was spread through our magazine and book store, by mail and messenger.

My Mennonite companions were occupied with all the financial and other practical matters and I was quite free to do my literary work. "The Rainbow" was able to publish many tracts and books on religious topics. Its calendar, "The Family Friend", became very popular.

## The First Convention and the Founding of The All-Russian Evangelical Christian Union

As described above, one center of the wide publishing work was founded in St. Petersburg. After this, according to my program, I directed my attention to the question of organizing the whole Evangelical movement. At that time the Evangelical churches and groups in Russia were not united with each other in any way, and besides there was a lack of organization inside the individual churches. In many cases the groups had more confusion than order, and even the St. Petersburg Evangelical Church was not an exception.

I felt that to start a proper organization work there should be a unification of all the churches and groups and there should be a specially organized center. I wrote letters to the

most important places, such as Odessa, Sevastopol and elsewhere, explaining my idea, and when I saw that it was accepted favorably, and that in one place even a movement
toward unity was shown, I began to work energetically in
that direction. I commenced this heavy undertaking by
printing in 1908 a special program for organization of the
St. Petersburg Church.

The program was accepted by an overwhelming majority
of votes and a very energetic work was begun in all the
activities belonging to a well-organized church, in the preaching, in visiting the members, in the work among the women,
among the young people, children, etc. According to the
new constitution of the church, I was elected President of
the Council of the Church and also president of the general
meetings of the Church, which duty I fulfilled since that time
for twenty years, and until my departure from Russia in 1928.

To make the organization complete and national in its
scope, I immediately proposed that the St. Petersburg
church should come in contact with other groups of Evangelical Christians in Russia, as I already had the consent of
the leading brethren in the south of Russia. I worked out
a program for the "All-Russian Conference of Evangelical
Christians", to be called in St. Petersburg, and sent it to
other Evangelical groups in Russia.

## Organization of the Union

We fixed the time of opening for the Conference for
December 25 to January 7, 1909, in St. Petersburg, and soon
obtained permission from the Government, though they were
afraid that there would be too noisy a demonstration and
therefore gave their consent only a few days before the opening of the Conference, and thus we were unable to properly
invite the delegates from the provinces. Nevertheless the
Conference was a great success. It lasted two weeks. The
first week was devoted chiefly to business questions, the organization of the churches and the organization of the All-
Russian Evangelical Christian Union. After one session of
the Conference in a large meeting the unification of the

Evangelical churches in Russia was declared under the name of *"The All-Russian Evangelical Christian Union"*.

What joy, what a jubilant feeling it produced upon all present in the meeting! In my solemn sermon I explained that this founding of the All-Russian Evangelical Christian Union is the realization of one of the most important clauses of my program and of years of longing and expectation of many servants of God in Russia, and a very important historical event. It was one of the rewards for our many years of persecution.

When I invited the meeting to pray and give thanks, one general cry of gratitude to God was heard. The Union when founded was as a grain of mustard seed, but since that time, as one can see from the following chapters, it has grown into a mighty tree of spiritual life among the Russian people. I was elected President of the Union, which office I filled for more than twenty-two years, having been unanimously re-elected every year.

I left Russia in 1928, but I continued to be President of the Union for three years more, until 1931, when on account of my long absence and the inconveniences connected with it, in August, 1931, I was unanimously elected the Honorary President of the Union.

It was my hope to have our All-Russian Evangelical Conferences every year, but unfortunately it was impossible. First of all, seeing the great success with which they were attended, the Government refused to permit further conferences after 1912, probably supposing that our success would soon be capitalized by us for political purposes. That, of course, could never happen in our Union, which was purely spiritual in its origin, purposes and labors, and had no desire for political activity in any form.

After the beginning of the great war in the year 1914 very heavy restrictions were laid against all religious activities by the Government. No conferences were permitted. We could renew our conferences only after the revolution. The result was that from 1909 to 1928, the year of my departure from Russia, we had only ten conferences, which, of course, was not our fault, for we would have carried them on annually had we been permitted to do so.

In these conferences many important decisions were made. I cannot here describe all of them, but I will mention some of the more important ones.

## Organized Mission Work

In the first conference we laid the foundation for the organization of mission work. We elected one young missionary to begin his work at once, and another to begin his work when we had more means. Very soon I sent one of them on a journey to the Far East, through the whole of Siberia. Many groups of Christians in that territory called themselves Evangelical Christians or by similar names, but they were unorganized and not united together. They had not been visited by anybody from Europe and lived a very imperfect religious life.

The missionary journey of our brother Persianoff had for its purpose a spiritual revival among these Christians and the proper organization of their work. It produced a great impression upon all the churches and groups visited, like a visit from one of God's messengers, and our missionary field was thus immensely enlarged.

## Skeptical About Our Missionary Support

I put the work of our missionaries on the basis of faith from the very beginning. The optimism of faith helped us greatly. When we elected our first missionary, Brother Persianoff, with a salary of 400 roubles a year, some of the brethren expressed their doubts as to whether we would be able to pay the sum. I delivered an inspired address, in which I developed the principle of faith. I said:

"Brethren: We have now only one missionary, but the days will come when we shall have more than five hundred missionaries!" I saw great surprise on the faces of the brethren, but afterward my prediction was fulfilled in a greater number than I had mentioned. When I left Russia in 1928 we had more than the five hundred at work in the districts of our Union, in Russia and Siberia.

As the missionary and evangelistic work grew new provincial sections of our Union were opened. Russia was divided into seventy provinces, (Gubernias), and gradually we had our sections and labor organized in all of them. The basic unit was the congregation, the church. We had the principle that every church should be entirely autonomous and free. But at the same time I promoted the spirit of unity and advised that wherever there were five groups or churches they should form a local association of churches for missionary, publishing and spiritual educational work. In each province there should be a center, uniting all these local associations into Provincial Unions of Evangelical churches. Until 1926 we had seventy such provincial branches of the Union, but on account of administrative changes effected by the Soviet Government we have now fifty Provincial Evangelical Christian Unions, all of which belong to the All-Russian Evangelical Christian Union.

## Over Six Hundred Missionaries at Work

Each provincial union has its own Provincial Council, yearly conferences, and being strictly autonomous in its inner life, is united with the All-Russian Union only in the main branches of the general work. Every Provincial Union used to have before the persecution was begun in 1929 not less than ten missionaries supported especially for their work in the provinces. Beside that, the Council of the All-Russian Evangelical Christian Union supported toward 1928 up to 100 missionaries, so that we had not less than six hundred missionaries laboring all over Russia and Siberia.

Of course, I do not include in this number the regular permanent workers in the churches, ministers, preachers, deacons, etc., whose number is very large. There are actually thousands of churches and groups. In every church or group there are not less than two preachers, so that the total number of workers who preach the Gospel in Russia is equal to several thousand.

Of course, the condition of our missions in 1928 surpassed the prediction which I made in 1908. Such is the optimism of faith. Perhaps I should here explain two other principles which I laid as bases of our missions and which have proved to be effective aids in the growth of the Evangelical Church.

## The Universality of Mission Work

We had, of course, our elected brethren for the missionary work, missionaries, ministers, preachers, etc. But I adopted and laid emphasis on the slogan, "Every Evangelical Christian must be a missionary (Numbers 11:29), and we began to educate the members of our church to be personal messengers of the Gospel. In some groups a rule was adopted that every member must give his testimony about Jesus Christ and his salvation to at least one person (sinner). It produced a wonderful effect.

We had a sister who worked as a cook in St. Petersburg, for example. When she died we learned that several persons were converted through her first testimony. She was an example of an exemplary missionary.

## Evangelization of Russia by Spiritual Conquest

From the very beginning of our organization I declared a slogan: "From city to city, from town to town, from village to village, from man to man." I used to say to our workers: "You must have a good map of your province, first of all to mark all those places where there are groups of Evangelical Christians. Then you must say to yourself, as a general says: We must conquer for Christ all those places in our province in which the Gospel has not yet been preached. First of all, you must begin your work in all the towns of the Uezd (county); then to start the preaching of the Gospel in one village, in another village, making your towns the center of the spiritual work. Faith, prayer and work must be applied with full devotion."

This method brought considerable results. Very soon we had powerful provincial unions, with many groups and congregations in new places over the whole territory where the Gospel had never been heard before. In 1928 we had fifty such unions, in Odessa, Vladivostok, Central Siberia,

Turkestan, Archangel, etc. Actually we began to spiritually conquer the whole of Russia, and would have covered the whole territory but for the interference of atheism.

### Confession of Faith

At that time I thought very much about the necessity to create a strong basis for the unity of the whole movement. All of us recognized the New Testament as our only guide in our faith and our spiritual life, and have remained true to it until now, but for our practical work we needed to have a certain expression of the main bases of our faith.

It was necessary for those persons who desired to become more acquainted with our doctrines. I wrote "The Confession of Faith of Evangelical Christians," and the statutes of our Union, and submitted them to the Second Conference, in 1910. Unanimously they were accepted and approved, and since that time we have had use of them according to necessities.

### Religious and Spiritual Education

One of the most important subjects in all our conferences was the question of spiritual and religious education of our people. In all the programs of our conferences I always put this question just next to the question of missions. I knew that in this matter there were two irregularities. The churches without missions usually were dying. On the other hand churches which were occupied with missions and which neglected their own spiritual education could not make any spiritual progress (Mat.. 23:15). The Greek Orthodox Church had neither mission work nor spiritual education of the people, and thus it was doubly dead.

From the very beginning, I combined the missionary and spiritual education work, and even stated very often that before beginning a mission work at a certain place it would be necessary to make certain of the spiritual education of those who would be connected with it or those who would be converted after it was organized.

In every church we arranged edification meetings, Bible and prayer meetings. We also paid special attention to the proper spiritual education of the children. *Every church had a Sunday School.* In those places where it was impossible in consequence of persecutions to have Sunday Schools, the children were taught the Bible in their homes secretly. In many churches the parents received instruction in the Scripture and ably fulfilled at home the work of Sunday School teachers for their children.

We made the effort to organize a young men's association in every church even where there were five or six young men, and so also for the young women. These circles had a kind of autonomy. The young people elected their workers, approved of their programs, etc. In this way they acquired an experience and knowledge which fitted them for future work in the churches and in the Union, while they were doing missionary work among the people of their own age. Every circle was divided into several groups, for prayer, missions, visiting (poor, sick and prisoners), literary and musical groups). The young people in those groups were kept very busy in spiritual work. With these arrangements they were able to prepare for us in the churches good missionary workers. We have at the present time in Russia some outstanding workers who obtained their first training in the young people's circles.

I also was deeply interested in the question of spiritual education of women and the development of work among them. I wrote a booklet, "The work of women in the churches," in which I explained and proved that women can render a great service in the churches. Accordingly special meetings were arranged in connection with every church, and first of all in St. Petersburg. The meetings were started with very meagre funds in 1909. The Women's Circle had special edification meetings, under their own guidance, where they talked about their specific needs. They also had missionary work meetings in which they sewed various articles of linen and clothing, prepared toys, etc. All these products were sold and the income was devoted to missionary purposes. These women's meetings proved to be of very great value in our church.

Since 1912 this Women's Circle produced sufficient means for the support of four missionaries of our Union. They gave to the Church Council several thousand roubles for the building of a prayer house. They opened two shops for the sale of their products in the city of St. Petersburg.

In the beginning of the new regime, when all such shops and stores were confiscated, the total cost of only one store was stated at 50,000 roubles, which was a large sum at that time.

When the number of women's circles throughout Russia had considerably increased, a special Conference on Women's Work was called, in which more than one hundred women delegates participated.

## Small Beginnings and Great Developments

I began to organize the work of the Council which we had created. Until that time I had worked alone, without any aids or regular assistants, though some help occasionally came from willing members. I had, however, personally maintained all the wide correspondence with the churches in all parts of the country, did the bookkeeping, edited the monthly magazine, "The Christian", wrote hymns, and published hymn books and tracts. I was everything, — President, Secretary and bookkeeper.

I remember how we started the organization of the work at St. Petersburg, buying the first typewriter and inviting a brother to give part of his time in a small room. But as the work grew we were compelled to extend our office. At the time of my departure from St. Petersburg in 1928 we occupied a whole story of the building and had twenty-seven workers who were engaged in the various branches of the work of the Union, and the task was so great that it was frequently impossible to manage it. In this sense also the Evangelical Christian Union proved to be a grain of mustard seed which grew to be a tree.

I decided to publish a weekly paper, and the first issue of "The Morning Star" was printed on January 1, 1910. The paper was a great success from the very beginning, and soon spread all over the vast territory of the country. It began at once to invite the cooperation of all who were striving for a free Christian Church in Russia.

During this year I found myself to be the editor of quite a series of magazines and papers: 1. The monthly, "The Christian", as the organ of the spiritual life of the Evangelical movement. 2. "The Brotherly Leaflet", also monthly, especially for congregations and churches and their needs. 3. "The Young Vineyard", for young people, monthly organ of the All-Russian Union of Christian Young People. 4. The monthly magazine for children, "Children's Library". 5. The monthly periodical for spiritual music and song, "The New Melody", for choirs and singers, devoted especially to the development of the Evangelical spiritual music. 6. "The Morning Star", a weekly Evangelical light projector upon all questions of life in my country.

## Large Audiences Hear the Gospel

On Sundays I usually preached in the large Terishevsky Hall, in the center of the city, one of the finest halls in St. Petersburg, which could hold upwards of 1000 people. It was filled with hearers from all classes at nearly every meeting. A great many conversions took place, and many who were intelligent and educated began to think about religion and a personal faith in God in a manner entirely different from that which they had been following under the old Greek Orthodox Church.

To promote unity and brotherly love among the believers, I also arranged at this time united meetings at another large hall, called "Nobel's People's House," where not only the members of my own church, but also those of other groups in St. Petersburg participated. Those united meetings were very solemn and edifying.

With the necessary writing of special articles for the publications mentioned above, editing all the material for each issue, presiding at the regular weekly meetings (very often several times a week) of the Church Council, the meetings of both the large and small Unions, preaching in regular meetings both morning and night on Sunday, the wide correspondence with workers in various parts of Russia, as well as my duties as a mechanical engineer of the Westinghouse Air Brake Company — all this kept me very busy in those days. I usually worked until 2 o'clock in the morning and had far too little time for rest, but the urge and necessity of the Evangelical work impelled me, and surely the strength of the Lord was provided to meet my needs. Hard as I labored, I felt bright, strong and cheerful, and my mind was continually full of new ideas and projects vital and necessary to all branches of my work. The daily habit of doing all things according to a written program was most valuable at this period of my life and labors.

## My Family Life

Besides the above mentioned work I had to pay special attention to my family life. I had an ideal wife and two fine boys. My wife took part in some of the women's meetings, but at the same time was an ideal mother. Her highest pleasure was to be always with her boys. She accompanied them to school, she met them when they were coming home from their studies. She prayed with them and taught them the Bible.

As to myself, I planned to give them the highest possible education. They were made pupils of one of the best schools in St. Petersburg, the High School of the German Reformed Church, where they learned the German language. I desired them to know also French and especially English. The former language was taught to the boys by a lady, but as to the English language I engaged in London a special Christian governess and brouht her to St. Petersburg. She lived in our house and taught my sons. Thus they grew up with a good knowledge of all three languages, beside the Russian.

As to my older son, who showed a special gift for languages, I made all arrangements that he should also learn Latin, Greek and Hebrew. He studied them very well, so that he can now not only read but knows by heart portions of the Old and New Testaments in the original languages.

159

This knowledge fitted both boys for very successful studies in the St. Petersburg University, from which both were later graduated. Besides that, they were both teachers in the Bible College which I founded later on.

I lived with my family at St. Petersburg, but my father and mother resided in the city of Vladikavkas, in the Caucasus. Sometimes they visited us at St. Petersburg, and these were very happy days for all of us.

But in 1919 my father began to suffer from an illness which became so serious that in 1910 I was compelled to make a trip to Vladikavkas, where I found him in the condition of complete physical exhaustion. I had a long conversation with him, we read the Word of God and prayed together and parted with tears.

I loved and highly esteemed my father. From the general standpoint he was a man of outstanding qualities. His father died when he was a boy. His mother belonged to the old sect of Molokans and suffered persecution and imprisonment, and his aunt also. To escape these persecutions, being twenty years old, he decided to emigrate, with his young wife, mother and aunt, to the Caucasus. With a single horse cart they made the journey from Saratoff to Vladikavkas, about 1500 miles, which traveling was very dangerous.

## A Picture of Russian Life in 1867

At that time the Caucasus was as much separated from other parts of Russia as America from Europe. On arrival at Vladikavkas my father and mother began to work very hard, his mother and aunt helping them by cultivating the garden. The result was that my father became well-to-do, having a flour mill and land. He became a member of the City Council. He attended very diligently the meetings of the old sect of the Molokans and was an esteemed member of the community.

Near the middle of the year 1876 my father heard the Gospel message delivered by a visiting brother from Tiflis, believed and joined the local congregation of Brethren. Later

**Typical Group of the Children of Russian Christians**   (See page 156)

**Last All-Russian Evangelical Christian Conference at Leningrad** (See page 151)

on, in 1894, he was exiled, as I have written, together with two other brethern, from Vladikavkas to Guerusi, a small Armenian village in the mountains of Transcaucasia, a natural prison. There were many other exiles sent there for the faith's sake, whom I met during my five day visit to my father at Guerusi.

I described my visit to that place of exile in a previous chapter. During all the time when I was with my father, whether at home with his family, in public or in exile, I admired him for his humbleness, gentleness and wisdom, and especially for his Christian character. Very often I thank God for such a father.

It can be easily understood what a blow it was to my heart to see him so seriously ill, and after three months to hear that he had passed away. I found my consolation in the Word of God and in the thought that, although my father had physically died, the good seed that he sowed in the hearts of his children will never die, but bear its fruit in the future.

In one respect perhaps my father was more fortunate than my mother and all of us. He did not experience the horrors of the World War, the Russian civil war and the terrors of the present time.

My mother lived twenty-two years longer after my father's death, till ninety years of age, and passed away at Moscow only on August 5, 1932. Under the present regime she lost all her property and became absolutely poor. I helped her with all my power; nevertheless she suffered greatly from many hardships.

During the last three years she suffered from a very serious illness, but no one heard any complaint or murmuring from her. Her life was an example for all of us.

After the death of my father, I gave up all my hereditary right to my youngest brother Vassily, who proved to have commercial talents. He developed the flour mill, built baking factories, hotels, purchased large tracts of oil land in the Caucasus and became a very wealthy man, but lost everything in the Revolution.

## IN THE CAULDRON OF RUSSIA

From the very beginning of the present regime in the Caucasus my brother with his wife and four sons fled the Caucasus to Constantinople, in Turkey, and from there to Bulgaria and thence to Paris. They had most dramatic experiences and were rescued from death many times by the Grace of God.

———•◆•———

# CHAPTER XIX

## 1911-1917

# The Great Development of the Work
### Beginning of the New Persecution

*"Thou, Lord, hast holpen me."* — *Ps. 86:17.*

FROM the very beginning of my work I felt that one reason for the defects of the religious life of the Russian people was their ignorance with regard to the basis of Christianity as given in the Bible, and especially in the New Testament.

The Holy Synod of the Greek Orthodox Church had the exclusive right to print the Scriptures in Russia, but they printed them unwillingly, as a matter of necessity. Two Bible Societies labored to spread the Scriptures in Russia, the British and Foreign Bible Society and the Russian Bible Society, both of which, as is known, were supported by free will offerings.

In 1907 the British and Foreign Bible Society succeeded in obtaining permission from the Holy Synod for the printing of a good edition of the Bible without the Apocrypha. But it was a small issue and was soon out of print, swallowed up by the great hunger of the Russian people for the Word of God.

### The Contact with the Holy Synod

Thinking the matter over, I wrote a special application to the Holy Synod, showing the necessity for a very wide spreading of the Bible and asking permission to print a Bible of portable or pocket size without the Apocrypha. I asked the other members of our Council to sign this application with me.

In reply to this application I received a church paper in which was printed an open letter to me written by Archbishop Antonius Khrapovitsky, a member of the Holy Synod.

In his letter to me, the Archbishop argued that the Evangelical Christians were heretics, that they were infected with protestantism and rejected the holy tradition. But his reply did not even make mention of my request for the printing of Bibles.

On receipt of such a reply as this, I felt a great inspiration, and immediately I wrote a very extensive answer, in which I showed why we, the Evangelical Christians, do not accept the holy tradition, but accept the Scripture in its canonical consistency as the only guidance in the matter of our faith and life. At the same time I explained the fault of the Greek Orthodox Church and the Roman Catholic Church in giving so much attention to the holy tradition and neglecting the Scripture, with the result that they overlook the cardinal truths of the teaching of Jesus Christ. I showed that all the drawbacks and evils which were so abundant in the Greek Catholic Church were due to this fault.

### Orthodox Antagonism to Scripture Distribution

I referred also to the fact that the Archbishop's silence on the question of printing the Bibles without Apocrypha was a token of their unwillingness to spread the printed Word of God. I explained that, however pompous may be their services and rituals, and however ancient their temples, if the people know not the Word of God and do not live according to it, there can be no real spiritual life among the Russian people. I quoted the very well-known passage from Rev. 3:1-3, about the Church which seemed to be alive but in reality was dead, especially emphasizing the call of the Lord to "Remember . . . and repent!" (vs. 3).

### A Warning to the Greek Orthodox Church

I said that the Church, instead of being dead, should come to a revival state, and asserted that to become alive repentance of the whole Church is necessary, especially of its spiritual leaders. I also explained that if the clergy of the Greek Orthodox Church would not repent they could not escape the judgment of God and that this judgment would be very severe. As the prophets of old warned the Hebrews, so these words of my letter to the Holy Synod were a remarkable prophecy *fulfilled within seven years,* when the decree compelling the separation of the Church from the State was issued and when an unparalleled persecution of the Greek Orthodox Clergy and the Church began. Under that decree a great many Orthodox clergymen were exiled to the extreme north of Russia, many starved to death and many were shot.

In 1910 and 1911 the differences between the Duma and the Czar began to grow, and this resulted in various restrictions which the Government began to introduce in every branch of Russian life. Of course, these restrictions touched the religious life. On October 4, 1910, a special decree was issued by the Minister of the Interior, compelling restriction of all religious meetings. Following soon after was a decree of the Government withdrawing permission for our All-Russian Conferences, after the one which took place in 1912.

The Government introduced a censorship over all the religious press outside the Orthodox Greek Church, with the priests as censors. For one article published in my weekly, "The Morning Star", in 1912, I was tried in a law court and sentenced to pay a fine.

From many places in Russia I began to receive letters written by our brethren, describing serious difficulties with their meetings and various other troubles. The winds of persecution began to blow, reminding us again of our old times of suffering.

## Activities of the Orthodox Clergy

The rapid development of the Evangelical movement in Russia greatly alarmed the Greek Orthodox clergy. They could not produce any similar influence upon the people to counterbalance the power of our work, and therefore they again had recourse to secret political influence for producing measures with which to attempt to destroy the movement. They created a plan to capture the czar morally. For this purpose they found a suitable man in the person of G. E. Rasputin, a character well known in Russian history.

Rasputin mobilized all classes of the Russian people against the Czar and the monarchy and made the revolution a matter of necessity. The destruction of the Greek Catholic Church followed naturally, its clergy through Rasputin having incurred upon themselves this terrible calamity.

If the Church had known what would be the result of their acting through Rasputin, they would, of course, never have adopted this method of persecuting the sectarians.

It could be proved that the activity of Rasputin was one of the chief causes of the increase of these persecutions.. In any case, it created such a state of spirit among the masses of the people that the revolution became inevitable.

For those who believe in one invisible hand that directs all events in the world it is clear that the really unparalleled calamity which later befell the Greek Orthodox Church was a punishment from God for the many sins of the clergy, among others the sin of elevating Rasputin for the wicked purpose of wiping out the religious liberty granted by the Czar.

Some of the members of the Greek Orthodox clergy have recognized this fact, but others have not. Nevertheless it is true and quite clear for every unprejudiced mind. *"Be not deceived. God is not mocked. For whatsoever a man soweth, that shall he also reap."* — Gal. 6:7.

## The Founding of the First Russian Protestant Christian Theological School at St. Petersburg

The time of the "reign" of Rasputin was a very dark period. In all branches of Russian life a kind of pressure was felt. Even the Duma constantly expected to be dissolved, and nobody knew what might happen. In the religious life of the Evangelical Christians and other independent organizations this heavy pressure was especially noticeable. The horizon was gloomy and everybody was deeply pessimistic, feeling that some calamity was about to be visited in our country.

## A NEW PERSECUTION BEGINS

The influence of this pessimism had no effect on my program, and at this very period another important deed for the Evangelical movement was accomplished, i.e., the founding of the First Russian Protestant Christian Theological School at St. Petersburg.

Almost from the first months after the proclamation of the manifesto of October 17, 1905, I began to take steps to fulfill this next step in my program, to obtain permission from the authorities for a Bible School. But my applications were refused every time they were presented. The last time I received a refusal from the Procurator of the St. Petersburg District of Education, Count Musin-Pushkin. He spoke to me in a harsh manner, saying that such a school would undermine the established Greek Orthodox Church.

When leaving his office I quietly prayed, and immediately I received in my heart a joy and an assurance that permission would be given after all. I went very shortly to the highest officials of the Ministry of Public Instruction and fully explained the matter to them. One of the officials even showed a personal interest in the matter, and declared that my application was based on the manifesto and all the new laws with regard to religious activities, *and therefore could not be refused.*

A special letter was written from the Ministry of Public Instruction to the Procurator of the St. Petersburg District of Education, and in the beginning of 1913 I received an official permit for the St. Petersburg Bible Courses for Evangelical Christians. After the long effort I had made to secure this result it is scarcely possible to describe my joy and gratitude to the Lord, which I endeavored to express in the meetings with brothers and sisters as I told them of this blessed gift of my Master. Thus a most important part of my program was fulfilled.

One must remember that before that time there was not even one Russian Protestant Christian school. We had many good preachers, but they had not received theological education, and thus we had no men or women qualified to become teachers in this Bible School.

This created a serious difficulty, but after some efforts a satisfactory arrangement was made. Being the principal of the Bible School, I took up personally the teaching of Interpretation of the New Testament, Dogmatics, Apologetics, Homiletics; A. A. Reimer, a Mennonite preacher from the Southern German colonies, Interpretation of the Old Testament, and Church History, and K. G. Inkis, Church Music.

## Many Nationalities in the School

There were nineteen students, of whom 5 were Letts, 1 Mennonite, 1 Georgian, 1 Osset from the Caucasus, 1 Ukrainan, 1 Belorune. The constituents of this first Bible School were characteristic of the peoples comprising the whole Evangelical movement, which at that time numbered among its members some of the numerous nationalities inhabiting our vast country. To reach all these tribes we required native converts to train in our school.

Here in America I met Mr. K., who was for a year a student in our Bible College. Afterward he studied in an English preachers' college and in two American Bible colleges. He said to me:—

"I have been in quite a few colleges, but I have not found any with such a wide and deep program as that of St. Petersburg Bible College."

The time from September, 1913, to July, 1914, was perhaps one of the busiest periods in my activities at St. Petersburg. The preaching in one of the best halls in the city, participation in the business meetings of the church and its Council, of which I was the president; the editing of the six periodicals, writing new articles and hymns, attending to matters of the book store, lecturing in the Bible College, and a very wide correspondence all kept me very busy.

Very often I was compelled to work through the night, and the morning found me still at my study table. Of course, I had almost no time for recreation or for change of any kind from my daily routine. Nevertheless, I felt bright, energetic and happy, and the people saw me ever smiling.

## A NEW PERSECUTION BEGINS

### Beginning of the Great War

In August, 1914, the great war started and life and every-thing in Russia changed completely. One of the first meas-ures of the Government was to issue heavy restrictions for all societies and meetings, both secular and religious. Our enemies availed themselves of the war conditions to begin a fresh persecution.

The Clerical leaders began to write in the newspapers that the Evangelical Christians, having a faith different from the Greek Orthodox Church, were not reliable people and therefore politically dangerous. Of course, it was untrue. Nevertheless their persecution of us was thus justified in the minds of many Orthodox Russians who did not know the truth.

Here are the sad results: We had to give up our Bible School. Our periodicals, "The Christian" and "The Morn-ing Star", were closed by the Government, and all our Evan-gelical meetings at St. Petersburg were forbidden.

The same thing happened throughout Russia. In many places not only the Evangelical congregations were closed, but their preachers and ministers were arrested and exiled to Siberia.

Most of the exiles were transported to Narim, a district in the central part of Siberia known for its cold and severe climate. In the time of the old regime it was the place for the exile of political offenders, many of whom died there.

### Indicted for Founding the Union

They soon found an excuse for persecuting me personally. I was indicted by the Law Court of St. Petersburg as the founder of the Revolutionary Union called "All-Russian Evangelical Christian Union". This was announced in large type in the newspapers, and I expected every day to be arrested.

The condition of our affairs became very gloomy, but at the same time the Lord helped through faith and its optimism. As a matter of fact, our Union was a purely religious institution. We had nothing whatever to do with politics and were the most law-abiding subjects of our Government. The accusation against me seemed like pure nonsense to everybody.

Something unexpected happened to distract attention from my indictment and give the Czar's Government other things to think about. On December 16, 1916, Rasputin was murdered, and following this other important political events occurred. There was great unrest among the people and in the army, and everybody felt that a storm was approaching.

These troubles explain why I never received any summons from the Law Court. They were too busy with other things. The immediate effect of the elimination of Rasputin was that all actions instigated by him or the Clerical party in the Law Courts lost their importance. It was an indirect proof of the fact that the general persecution, and also the one against me personally, were the result of the activities of the Clerical party. One must remember that at the time described the war was raging. In Russia there was a universal conscription. My age was such, however, that I could not be called into the war, and so I was enabled to remain at St. Petersburg, administering to the needs of the people. This was from God.

The Bible School, periodicals and all our meeting places having been previously closed on orders from the Government, only our book store, "The Rainbow", was still open. Being all the time in St. Petersburg, I used to meet the believers in the book store. I also visited them in their homes and comforted them with God's Word. We also arranged in various places in the city secret meetings, mostly in private lodgings, in which I took part, as in the old early days of the persecution. Oh! how sweet was the Christian fellowship in those secret meetings.

# CHAPTER XX

## 1917-1922

# My Work During this Period

*"In all things approving ourselves as the Ministers of God . . . in labors, in watchings."* 2 Cor. 6: 4, 5.

I SHALL not describe the beginning of the revolution and its development. The facts are very well known. I was in St. Petersburg all through those terrible scenes. The house in which I lived was near the building of the Ministry of the Interior. I saw the motor cars and trucks with armed workmen attacking the building and arresting the dignitaries. I saw how the workmen arrested the generals on the streets, took from them their arms and transported them to prison.

I saw multitudes of people filling the streets and moving slowly too and fro. I heard shooting everywhere. I saw dead bodies of soldiers and private persons on the streets.

I saw regiments of infantry, cavalry and artillery marching to the Tavrichesky Palace, where the Duma was housed. I heard there Rodzianka, Gutchkoff, Milukoff and others delivering their addresses to the troops. I remember the great enthusiasm of the people, who appreciated this revolution especially because there was little bloodshed.

However, I remembered the history of the French and other revolutions, and very often I expressed the opinion that, although beginning peacefully enough, the revolution would yet come to great bloodshed and terror, because the extreme left parties would yet take their chance and must triumph for some time.

If the revolution does not pass through the left extremity, it will not be well rooted. To bring a real liberty the revolution must pass through the abyss of insanity and overcome it. But this was not spoken in any spirit of pessimism on my part, nor with any sense of despair. Just to the contrary.

171

I only pictured a natural process, which, although connected with suffering, must precede the establishment in Russia of real Republican freedom.

The events developed according to my prediction. After the Prime Ministers Lvoff and Kerensky, there must have come Lenin as the Prime Minister. It was a matter of psychological necessity.

## "No Politics; Only the Gospel"

Although I was witnessing the development of the revolution and its extraordinary political events, my mind was occupied not with politics, but exclusively with our religious matters. Together with my fellow-workers we declared at one of our conferenences the slogan: "No politics, only the Gospel."

We considered that the Gospel was the best of spiritual medicine for all kinds of spiritual diseases and that our duty was to heal with an equal faithfulness bolshevicks and menshevicks and the men and women of all political tenets.

According to the Gospel principle, the Evangelical Christians were willing to welcome everything just, helpful for freedom and the well being of the people, but we could not take part in any political party because their methods, based on hatred and violence, must be by their very nature quite opposite to the Christian method founded on love and charity. We declared our standing to the authorities and were loyal to our decision.

On two occasions I took part in political events, but only in the interest of the Evangelical cause. The first was the Moscow State Conference, so called, summoned by Kerensky on August 18, 1917. As the President of the All-Russian Evangelical Christian Union I received an invitation to attend that conference and to take part in it.

I was given ten minutes for my address. I made an appeal to the Conference to become inspired with faith, and declared that then the mountains of difficulties would be thrown into the abyss.

The second political event in which I was interested and

took part was the election campaign for the State Organization Parliament or Congress.

In many circles our program had produced a very strong impression as something new and extraordinary. In the election for the St. Petersburg district, from which four delegates were to be chosen, we announced our policy and named our candidate. We knew that our candidate could not be elected, but we did all this in order to make known our program and our aspirations. It was our best opportunity to advertise our program and we used it to full capacity. The result was quite satisfactory.

In the election which followed the most votes were secured by the so-called cadets (Constitutional Democratic party) and the bolshevicks. Our group (Christian democratic) with its nominated candidate — I. S. Prokhanoff — received more votes than the Social Democratic party (menshevki) with their candidate, Plekhanoff. Under these conditions the result was better than we had expected.

### Freedom of Conscience Allowed Again

We enjoyed again the freedom of conscience under the new regime, and without delay I renewed my work at St. Petersburg. First of all I again began to publish "The Christian" and "The Morning Star". On account of the revolutionary conditions of the country, the printing establishments were in disorder and could not perform the required work. So we were compelled to print our papers in a reduced form and on very poor paper.

I also began again my meetings in Tenishevsky Hall. All other meetings were renewed, and we endeavored to arrange large public meetings in the biggest halls and buildings. One of these meetings is to be remembered. It was held in the Circus of Chiniselli, with upward of 3000 people present, and was a great success.

We had our regular meeting in the morning at the Tenishevsky Hall, and after that we marched in procession from that hall to the building of the Circus. On some corners we stopped, and myself and others delivered short addresses to the crowds. While marching we were all singing. Great crowds of people joined us, so that when we came to the Circus it was overfilled.

There was prayer and singing. Two or three brethren delivered short addresses. My sermon at the end took about forty minutes. I spoke on the subject: "The Spiritual Revolution." My idea was that for the political revolution to succeed in the State it is necessary for every man and woman to undergo a spiritual revolution, to overthrow sin and give the first place to God in every heart.

When after my sermon I invited the people to prayer, all knelt and there was an immense cry, a groaning and moaning of the people. Among those who knelt I saw simple peasants and workmen, as well as officers, officials, soldiers, and fine ladies and gentlemen. All were crying to God.

After that we secured for our meetings the huge building of the Marine Menage (horse drill hall), which was capable of holding upwards of 10,000 people. Half an hour or more before the beginning of the meeting we used to make a procession, with singing, praying and the delivery of short addresses from the buildings of St. Isaac's and the Kazan Cathedrals. Crowds of people followed us as we returned to the meeting at the Marine Menage. Those were grand meetings.

It was really a marvelous evangelization work. Without exaggeration, thousands of the people heard the Gospel message in those meetings. This was the time of unlimited freedom. One thought, "Liberty, Freedom!" filled our hearts with great enthusiasm, and I saw before me an immense, endless field for God's harvest.

## Separation of the Greek Orthodox Church from the State

On October 25, 1917, the second revolution took place, which I considered as a natural sequence in the political drama. At that time Lenin's party did not call themselves communists, but simply "The Social Democrats-bolshevicks". They began calling themselves communists only in the spring of 1918. One must know the origin of the word "bolsheviks". In 1903 there was a conference of the Russian Social Democrats, in which part of the participants took a smaller (menshy) program and began to be called "mensheviki" (moderate socialists). The other part, with Lenin at their head, accepted a larger (bolshy) program, and therefore were called "bolsheviki".

At first they did not insist on their atheistic doctrines. They declared their opposition to the reactionary section of the Greek Orthodox Church, but generally speaking in the beginning they showed a friendly spirit to the Evangelical movement and various other religious organizations and sects originating among the people, which were persecuted under the Czar's regime. In their papers and speeches the leaders of the bolshevicks sometimes recalled the fact that in the places of exile Stundists and Evangelical Christians found themselves together with the Social Democrats.

In the general policy of the bolshevicks toward the religious organizations they gave full freedom to all, with the exception of those groups and members of the clergy who were infected with political opposition to the new regime. One of the first steps of the Soviet Government was the decree of *the separation of the Church from the State.*

With the promulgation of this decree the Greek Catholic Church in Russia lost its financial support from the State and all the privileges and monopolies by which it had existed and flourished since the time of Peter the Great. Thus the State made a most important move toward economy, but for the Church it was a very hard blow.

Millions of roubles were taken away from the Church and it was deprived of the means to conduct the work of the Holy Synod, academies and other Church machinery. The majority of the Greek Orthodox clergy were very discontented with the disestablishment, but the enlightened members of the clergy understood this reform in the right way and approved of it.

For other Russian religious groups beside the Orthodox Church the separation of the Church from the State was also a great advantage. All the persecutions of the independent

175

Russian religious groups used to come from the clergy of the privileged Church, through the military or secret police arm of the government. It could not have been otherwise, because the granting of a monopoly of religion to one Church and depriving other churches and religious groups of equal rights is in itself a latent persecution. In this way the dis-establishment of the Church is significant as being in reality the first basis of religious liberty.

### Religious Liberty According to the Laws of the Soviet Government

For many readers it will be a somewhat new idea to learn that in the first months of the bolshevick government there were issued many decrees and laws securing religious liberty for the citizens of the Soviet Republics. The above mentioned decree on the separation of the Church from the State contains clear, unambiguous paragraphs forbidding any kind of persecution for religious reasons and granting a real freedom of conscience. The Constitution of the U. S. S. R. contains the Thirteenth Paragraph, saying:

*"Freedom of religious and anti-religious propaganda is guaranteed for every citizen of the Republic."*

Some minor decrees to the same effect were issued, which strengthened the principle of religious liberty. In practical every-day life we Evangelical Christians saw facts confirming the generally favorable attitude of the Government toward the religious questions. As an instance of this propitious condition I may cite an incident connected with our Evangelical Church at Kazan. The religious meetings there were closed by the local authorities. I telegraphed to Lenin at Moscow, and we received from Mr. Bonch-Bruevich, General Secretary of his office, a telegram to the effect that Lenin had ordered the Commissary of the Interior to open the meetings and to punish those who were guilty of closing them. In similar cases the same orders came from Moscow.

In some places, when our missionary or preacher showed a certificate given by our Union Council at Petrograd, he received immediately help for the work, with the use of the largest possible hall and a permit to print the bills to be used on the streets for advertising the meetings.

The general conviction of the believers in Russia today is that if Lenin had lived there would not have been such a terrible persecution of the Christians by the atheists in the country of the soviets.

Yet I knew that these favorable laws would have power only for a certain time and that they would then be followed by restrictions at least, and therefore I decided to use this temporary religious liberty by laboring to our utmost capacity for preaching the Gospel, to which intensive program I invited all my fellow-workers.

I felt the necessity of using every possible bit of energy for the work before the closing in of the dark clouds with a new storm. Thus great emphasis was laid on every branch of our work, that we might accomplish as much of our labor for the Lord as possible while there was yet time. It was appropriate to sing as we labored:

*"Work, for the night is coming!"*

# CHAPTER XXI

## Calamities of this Period

*"If it had not been the Lord Who was on our side . . .
then the waters had overwhelmed us . . . the stream had
gone over our soul . . . Blessed be the Lord who hath
not given us as a prey to their teeth."    Ps. 124:1-5.*

NO greater time of calamity has ever visited our country
than the years 1917 to 1922. These calamities came
first of all as the result of the world war beginning in 1914,
with the killing of millions of people, leaving destitute families, other millions wounded and disabled for work, and the
general exhaustion of food and clothing supplies.

Gradually the scarcity of food, inflation of money and
other hardships began to be felt by the whole people of
Russia. The revolution and the civil war only added to this
calamity in an appalling measure.

In 1920-21 there was a great failure of crops, which resulted in the unparalleled famine. The horrors of this famine will be described fully in due time. The number of victims would have been simply appalling if at that time help
had not come from the generous American people through
the American Relief Association, the "ARA". I cannot describe what joy we felt as we received these food parcels.
Without any exaggeration I can say that the ARA saved
millions of lives from starvation. The Russian people who
passed through those days will never forget that brotherly
help from the American people.

Many died from starvation. Among the first whom I
remember was Prof. Gesechus, who was my professor in
younger years. He simply died from the lack of food in his
apartment in Leningrad. The number of such deaths was
large. Many died from being poisoned by the food in the
public dining rooms. The newspapers of the time were full
of such awful facts.

There were hundreds and thousands of such poor souls who had no power of faith to overcome the horror of those days. All the newspapers were full of items of suicide.

At that time I felt it was my duty to serve the suffering brethren and sisters. Very often I was called to the sick from typhus and cholera and visited them, read the Word of God and prayed. Though continually exhausted from lack of food, and probably in most favorable condition for infection at every turn, and being frequently touched by persons ill with both typhus and cholera, I was not infected by any of those brothers and sisters whom I visited. Very often I remembered the words of Ps. 91:6-7: "Thou shalt not be afraid . . . for the pestilence that walketh in darkness . . . A thousand shall fall at thy side . . . but it shall not come nigh thee." Truly it was so for me! Yes, those were terrible years. The whole of Russia represented one vast cemetery, for there was death throughout all our land.

The Evangelical movement did not decrease, however, but as a grain of mustard seed increased in a wonderful way.

## The Terror

To the calamities described above I must now add also the Terror! The political struggle of various parties against the ruling party became very bitter and sharp. Being desirous of defeating their enemies, the bolshevicks began to develop an appalling reign of terror. Petrograd and Moscow were divided into sections and a special revolutionary tribunal was formed in every one of them. Also in every small village and town throughout all Russia these revolutionary tribunals were set up.

Hundreds of people were brought before these officials day and night. A few were liberated again; others were sent to prison, but many were shot immediately. The shooting of the arrested people sometimes took place in the court yards where the tribunals met; sometimes they were taken outside the cities in companies of from 100 to 200. People were taken to the so-called Petropavlovsky Fortress and shot there at about 1 to 2 o'clock at night. The inhabitants of the houses on adjacent streets were usually awakened in the night by the sounds of firing, and shuddered as they knew the reason and in constant fear lest they might be next to face the firing squads.

Detachments of soldiers usually walked on the streets from house to house, arresting all whom they regarded as suspicious from their standpoint, bringing them to the tribunals, where they were shot. Without any exaggeration, it may be stated that during these three years beginning with January, 1918, and ending February, 1922, the ruling party was chiefly engaged in acts of terror.

Their aim was to annihilate physically the leaders of the bourgeoisie, capitalism and all men of influence who might be in sympathy with the old regime. It is very well known that thousands of officers of the army were taken one night from St. Petersburg and drowned in the Finnish Gulf on the way to Cronstadt. During this time there were trials of the Greek Orthodox clergy and a number of them were shot. A number of aristocrats and grand dukes were killed in the same manner. At last the Czar and his family were shot at Ekaterinburg in the Ural district. At that terrible time every morning we read in the newspapers long lists of those who had been shot during the previous night.

### Many Innocent People Slain

According to the official figures, which were published from 1917 to 1922 in the Soviet press from day to day, a total of about 1,800,000 executions took place, including 28 archbishops, 1400 priests and 8800 doctors. Sometimes groups of people, as for instance 5000 sailors, rioters of Cronstadt, were shot at one time.

Since that time and up to now the above figures should be doubled. Besides that, one must remember that many cases were not published, so that the total figures should be still greater.

No one was sure when they went to bed at night whether they would be allowed to sleep the whole night through or would be taken to be shot. One day a report was spread that all the priests, pastors, preachers and active religious workers would be shot.

One evening a brother came to my house and said that I. S. Prokhanoff was sentenced to be shot. I awaited a visit of the executioners during weeks, but they have never come. Another day many informed one another that on such a night all the business and commercial men of the city would be shot. Nobody knew anything definite and everybody could expect the very worst to happen.

Many people could not stand these days and nights of terror and lost their reason. The lunatic asylums were more than filled with these victims.

## My Share in the Calamities: The Death of My Wife

The condition of affairs in Petrograd had become so unbearably terrible that many members of our Petrograd Evangelical Church left the capital for the country villages. Many preachers and religious leaders also left the city. I received invitations from some groups of our brethren in the south of Russia to leave Petrograd and to come and live with them because the food conditions there were somewhat better and the terror not so great. Some of the elders of our church also proposed that I should leave the city and go to the south of Russia.

To all this urging I replied: "You know that if a ship is going to perish the captain will not leave until the last man is saved. I cannot leave Petrograd until all our suffering members have gone to safe places."

I decided to send my family to the South, but myself to remain in Petrograd. On May 13, 1919, my wife and my two boys — Yaroslav, 17 years old, and Vsevolod, 15 years old — together with Mrs. Milkereit, a lady member of our Church, departed for the South. Their goal was the city of Tiflis, in the Transcaucasus, where the parents of my wife lived and where food conditions were better than in the other provinces of Russia.

They wrote to me from Moscow about their experiences there, telling me that they could not have purchased any tickets but for the fact that they received a special paper through some friends from a high official in the Government. Then a letter came from Kharkoff, about June 10, and after that time I heard nothing at all from them or about them until October of the same year. It was a continual strain on me, the thought that my wife and sons might all have perished, but there was no way to discover what had occurred. I continued my daily ministrations to our remaining members, but my heart was not light.

On the night of July 30, 1919, after midnight, I had a terrible dream, which I can never forget. I saw my wife dying as clearly as in reality, and I kissed her face and wept bitterly. I awoke and found I was perspiring and trembling. I knelt before my bed and prayed, not knowing what the dream meant.

In the morning when I arose and told my dream to the girl servant, she said that she also saw my wife dying in the presence of Mrs. Milkereit, her companion. This put me in a still greater condition of anxiety, but I could not hear anything from or about my family. The reason was that when arriving near the city of Melitopol on their journey south, my family found themselves in the territory occupied by the "White Army," under the command of General Denikin. The army of General Denikin was marching to the North, and soon was near Moscow, in the city of Orel, not over 200 miles away. On account of this condition of civil war, little or no news was coming from the South to the North. In October of the same year a brother arrived at Petrograd from a southern city. He came at his own risk, for the purpose of spiritual fellowship with the Petrograd Christian believers.

## Definite News Comes at Last

This brother said to me: "I heard that your wife passed away." He could give me no particulars, so that I was unable to determine whether it was the truth or a misleading rumor. But in December of the same year I received a postcard from Brother Sh., from Melitopol, saying: "Your wife died at Vladikavkas (my home city in the Caucasus) on the night of July 30." This was the night on which I had the terrible dream of her death.

Afterward I learned the particulars regarding the death of my wife. When she came to the southern province, bordering on the Crimea, she could not go further because the railroads were either occupied with military transport or were in disorder. In that Province there were colonies of German Mennonites who immigrated there about 140 years ago from Poland and Germany. The new section of the Mennonite Brotherhood were kindred to us in doctrine and in preaching. My good friends and companions of "The Rainbow" lived there.

My family was invited to live among them. My eldest son, Yaroslav, was infected with typhus and was near to death, but God preserved his life. When in the end of July the railroad traffic was opened, my family departed through Rostoff on Don for the Caucasus. On the very day of their arrival at the city of Vladikavkas my wife fell ill with Asiatic cholera, which is the most dangerous form. All possible measures were taken, but nothing availed, and my wife died toward three or four o'clock in the morning. She was buried in that city, in the grave of the Prokhanoff family.

Fortunately at Vladikavkas, my own native town, my brother Vassily still lived, and my sons found refuge in his home. Mrs. Milkereit was a mother to them, but in a few weeks she died also. After a few months the mother of my wife arrived at Vladikavkas from Tiflis and took my boys to Tiflis, where they stayed for a considerable time. I did not hear from them until Easter, 1920.

## My Sons Return to Petrograd

They finally wrote to me that they were alive and would like to return to Petrograd, but they could not on account of the civil war conditions. Toward 1921 their desire to return to Petrograd became irresistible, and they made heroic efforts in that direction, in which they were successful by June of that year. But at that time I was imprisoned at the town of Tver as described further on in this narrative. You may be able to imagine something of the terrible days and nights which I was compelled to undergo, humanly speaking. I was deprived of my liberty and did not know what might happen to me, and my sons were far away. But in this time of tribulation the optimism of faith still aided me.

Every day I repeated to myself those glorious words of Christian wisdom: "All things work together for good to them that love God" Rom. 8:28. I believed and prayed on.

Finally God brought me consolation in my two sons, whom He helped to return to Petrograd. The elder son decided first to depart for his home and father. He told a touching story of his traveling. At that time the railway traffic was in great disorder. Brigands and all kinds of robbers were everywhere, and food was scarce. He was very often in danger of death. But after all his trials and hardships he reached Petrograd, in torn clothing and wornout shoes, and came at last to the door of our apartment, which I had occupied since the departure of my family to the Caucasus the year before.

## My Son Receives Disheartening News

With a trembling heart he stood at that door, hoping in a few minutes more to see his father. He rang the bell. A servant whom he did not know opened the door, and he asked:

"Is my father at home?"

She said:—

"No; your father is in prison at Tver." It was a city not far from Moscow, which he had passed through on his way to find me. You can imagine all the sorrow that came rushing in where before he had the joyous thought of again seeing me at the end of his weary journey and hardships. But he was able to write to me. I answered his letter and so at length he became more quiet and resigned to his unfortunate condition.

Several weeks after that my younger son left Tiflis. He did not know where I was until he arrived at Moscow. When he was told by the believers that I was at the Tver hard labor camp he hastened to Tver to see me. One can imagine something of what this young boy felt, after the sad loss of his mother and his long absence from his father, to see me through the grating of the hard labor camp gates. Poor boy! They both suffered bitterly during those years of the whole nation's tribulation.

Seeing their sufferings, I forgot all about my own sorrows and thought and prayed for my boys. Such is the father's heart! The Lord gave me a good comfort. These sufferings drew my sons nearer to God. When I returned to Petrograd from the prison camp and resumed my work, I had a great joy in seeing their zeal for the work of God.

## My Work During This Period

These years of great calamities and tribulation created really very difficult conditions for the work. In my lodgings, I had no fuel, and therefore all five rooms were in a frozen condition, and only the kitchen was a little heated. I slept in a room in which the windows were frozen, clad in my felt boots, and wearing a fur coat and a fur hat. My food was very scarce. My best was the dry bread which brethren from various parts of Russia sent to me. I drank carrot tea, having no genuine tea. This was for my breakfast; the same for luncheon and the same for dinner.

Every day I could expect to be arrested and taken away again, or else to become infected with some disease, as thousands of others were. Nevertheless I did not discontinue my work even for one day. I did not miss a single meeting where I was expected to speak.

On account of my half-starved condition I was like a skeleton and very weak, being scarcely able to walk. Twice I fell on the streets. Twice in the meetings while preaching I swooned from weakness. But the optimism of faith never left me. I did not cease preaching the Word of God, comforting God's people, and calling on sinners to repent. I continued visiting the people ill with typhus and cholera. I also endeavored to help our starving brethren in Petrograd and Moscow by practical methods.

## IN THE CAULDRON OF RUSSIA

I wrote to various places in Russia to our brethren in the country, to farmers who had a little bread. Some of these sent me by parcel post so-called "suchari," dry bread or rough biscuits. These dry biscuits are not attractive in ordinary times, but then they seemed to be a delicacy. What I received I divided among the starving workers of the Church.

### Efforts to Obtain Food From Abroad

I also used every possible effort to get as much help from the American Relief Association as I could, in the way of food parcels through our friends abroad. Without any exaggeration, I may say that in this way a great many Christian believers and workers were saved from starvation and death. My aim was to preserve the lives of the active workers in the Church.

As the Government had not yet issued any special interdiction against the Christian literature, I applied to some Western Christian organizations to supply us with the Russian Scriptures. Through them I was enabled to bring to Petrograd about 50,000 copies of Bibles and New Testaments and to send them to various places throughout Russia to our groups and congregations. After that time, however, the importation of the Scriptures from abroad was forbidden.

I was at all times in correspondence with the groups and churches and tried to satisfy their spiritual needs by sending missionaries and preachers to them from other places. By doing this we promoted the mission work. Besides, in spite of all the unspeakable difficulties, I tried to arrange the Conferences. In 1918 we had a conference at Moscow.

In 1919 we had our conference at Petrograd. Just at this time General Udenich and his army surrounded Petrograd and seemed to be about to capture it. We heard the cannon volleys on all sides. In Petrograd there was a so-called "siege law". It was forbidden to anybody to walk on the streets after six o'clock. But we desired to accomplish the whole work of the conference, and therefore we continued our sessions also at night, and after we had finished slept on the benches in the meeting hall. It was the "Conference under Cannon Volleys and Bombs". In 1920 we had a joint Conference together with the Russian Baptists at Moscow.

Overcoming almost endless difficulties, with all the printing establishments closed or in disorder, I succeeded in publishing several copies of our paper, "The Morning Star".

In the beginning the Soviet Government issued various laws with regard to the land. The general regulation was that the Government would give the land not to individuals, but to associations and collectives.

## Organizing For Land Holding

Our peasant brethren applied to me for advice and assistance. I wrote a draft of the necessary statutes for such collectives, which we called "Vseobshina." Our associations adopted these statutes and the Government permitted them to have land and to use it on the same basis as the other collectives.

In the Province of Tver and elsewhere a number of such labor associations were formed under the New Testament name, "Gethsemane," "Bethel" and similar titles. These Evangelical land associations acquired the highest reputation in the sight of the Soviet officials. To give the brethren guidance in legal matters, I published a booklet, "Republic and Religion," containing all the new laws issued with regard to religion. In case of various charges of violation of these laws, our brethren began to visit the Soviet authorities with this booklet in their hands.

In some places the Soviet officials asked for this booklet, and after a certain time they began to publish their own book containing the laws of the Republic concerning religious activities.

Of course, the correspondence with our church concerning spiritual questions, preaching, etc., was going on in an increasing way. The whole work occupied all my time. With the scarcity of food, cold and all kinds of dangers, I worked every day up to 1 or 2 o'clock at night and felt happy and joyful in the Lord in spite of the tribulation.

I was so engrossed in this enormous work that I did not notice that I had become emaciated and exhausted. But when the second swooning happened to me in a meeting the doctor was called, and he found that I was too exhausted to continue my labors. He also stated that if I lost any more weight from starvation I would probably die! He advised, therefore, that I must go to some place where there was good food and where I could have a rest.

Our labor association "Gethsemane", in the Province of Tver, wrote an invitation to me, asking that I come to their place and spend a month with them. It was in the winter time.

# CHAPTER XXII

## My First Imprisonment and Work Among the Young People

*"The Word of God is not bound." — I Tim. 2:9.*

### 1921

I have always taken it as a rule for my guidance not to reduce work, but to continue it and to expand even in the face of hindrances and calamities. This rule had a very definite bearing on my work among the Christian young people. As already stated, the Christian Young People's Association was founded at St. Petersburg in 1905, and I predicted a great development for it.

Following our own organization I was in communication with the young people all over Russia in our Evangelical Christian groups and congregations, and in 1906 at Moscow there was held the first All-Russian Conference of Christian Young People, at which the Smaller Union was founded. In that Conference I was elected President of the Union in my absence.

Soon after that I began publishing a special magazine for the Russian Christian young people, the first in Russia in the Protestant Christian spirit, "The Young Vineyard". This periodical was the organ of information, edification and a means of training our young people in the organized Christian life. After that several other conferences were held, and always with great blessings.

In the beginning of 1921 I was asked whether we were going to have our Young People's Conference in that year or not. You will remember that the general conditions were not at all propitious for such an undertaking, but I said:

"Of course we are going to have it!"

"Will you be there?" I was asked.

"Yes, if God wills, I intend to be there," was my reply.

Date for the Conference was fixed, May 5; programs were written, and letters of invitation were sent over the country. This Conference proved to be a time of triumph of the optimism of my faith, though but for the leadership of the Holy Spirit to interpret what happened and to capitalize our troubles and viewed from the entirely human viewpoint it seemed as though we suffered the greatest calamity possible, for the entire Conference ended within prison walls and all delegates were in durance for a long time.

## Meeting Where Food Was to Be Had

It was the time of greatest trouble and hardship. Everywhere there was a shortage of food, especially in the larger cities like Petrograd and Moscow. For that reason we chose the smaller city of Tver as the place for holding the conference. We hoped that our Evangelical village groups in the Tver province would be able to supply us with some bread and potatoes during the Conference.

Secondly, it was a very hard time for transportation. Just in those days travel on tramways and railroads was declared to be quite free of charge. On the tramways there were only motormen, but no conductors; on the railway trains there were only engine drivers, but there were no conductors. There was, as might be supposed, a shortage of cars in running condition, so those in use were filled to more than capacity, what with everybody wanting to get to almost any place except where they were and able to do so at no cost for railroad fare.

As a result of this condition, when I arrived at the Nicolaevskaia Station half an hour before the train was scheduled to leave, all the cars were comfortably filled. All the glass in the car windows was missing, having been broken out by hoodlums. People entered not only by way of the doors, but also through the windows. It was with great difficulty that I was able to secure a seat for myself, though in my weakened condition it was quite a necessity. Soon the cars were overfilled. All the passages were packed with people; passengers were riding on the bumpers, and even on the roofs of all the cars. Some boys even crawled under the cars and found places on the rattling trucks. It was known that accidents happened on every train, passengers falling from their precarious perches and from the roofs, usually losing their lives.

The atmosphere in the train was so stiffling that I could scarcely breathe. What would it have been with glass in the windows! Almost all the passengers looked sad and gloomy.

## Singing a Welcome to Their Leader

When our train finally approached the city of Tver I heard singing, and soon I saw on the platform a crowd of young people engaged in a burst of song. They were the delegates to the Young People's Conference and members of the local Evangelical churches. They had come to the station to meet their president and escort him to the place of meeting.

Although they were very poorly clad and many of them lacking anything like proper food in quantity or quality, they looked cheerful and even full of joy. The station was at a distance of about two miles from the city, and as we walked along to the place of our Conference there was singing all the way. This scene was in violent contrast with the surroundings and the times, where everything was dark and gloomy, but thus God deals with His own. We have joy and peace in our hearts in spite of calamities and hardships, knowing that "He doeth all things well."

Sixty young people had arrived from other places to attend the Conference, coming from different parts of European Russia — from the Caucasus, Crimea, from the Volga Provinces, Ukraina, etc. Considering the times and the great difficulty of transportation, the attendance was remarkably good.

We opened our sessions as usual, choosing the presiding officer (myself) and vice presidents and secretaries. The first day the sessions passed quickly and quietly, without any especially outstanding incidents. We discussed the items on our program for the day and decided various questions.

On the second day of the Conference, however, about 2 o'clock in the afternoon, while I was delivering an address, we heard a noise in the street. Soon our room was entered by armed men in quite a company. They were of three kinds, soldiers, police and officials from the Cheka, those terrible political police. We were in peaceful religious gathering, but thus the soldiers came for our Lord, even while He was praying.

One of those Cheka officials pointed his revolver squarely at me and said: *"Do not move!"*

## A Whole Conference Goes to Prison

Then they began to search us, looking through all our Conference papers and minutes, gathering them up as they went about. They also searched all corners of that and the adjoining rooms. Then the same official said:

"Now you must all go with us!"

Not asking for any permission, which I felt sure would be refused anyway, I said:

"We will pray!" All present arose to their feet and I prayed, in the midst of our dear group of young people, now fully surrounded by soldiers, police and the Cheka. One can easily imagine what a lasting impression this prayer made on our hearts, especially when remembered with all that followed.

It happened that in this session of the Conference not all the delegates were present, some committees being absent, but there were about 47 delegates, including seven young ladies. All of us came out to the street, where a crowd of awe-stricken people stood watching what was happening and wondering at the arrest of the Evangelical young people. We were put into rows like a small company of soldiers, and then surrounded with the three kinds of guards (you can see how dangerous we were!) — the militiamen with drawn sabers, the red soldiers with their guns and the Cheka officials with their revolvers drawn and ready for immediate action!

Sixth Young People's Evangelical Christian Conference at Tver.  (See opposite page)
All in the Group were Arrested and Imprisoned

I. S. Prokhanoff with his Fellow Prisoners at Tver on the Day of Their Liberation    (See page 198)

MY FIRST IMPRISONMENT

## Prisoners On The March

Then the command was given: "March"!

Just at this moment all of us began to sing a very popular hymn: "We are marching to the battle, with Jesus Christ"! We were not forbidden to sing. Possibly some of our captors were secretly enjoying the music, and especially the novelty of having captured a group who were so unafraid that they raised their voices in praise!

After this first hymn we began another, then a second, and so on, singing all the way to our place of confinement. A great many people were attracted by the singing, and stood on the sidewalks looking at us with wondering eyes. We heard their voices calling out to each other:

"These are Evangelicals arrested!"

We came at last to the headquarters of the Cheka, a three-story building, and according to the usual arrangement of these institutions were placed in the prison department in the basement. This consisted of two large rooms for the male prisoners, and a smaller one for the women. When we entered our rooms we saw a young man lying on one of the wooden platforms, and we knew at once that he was not a prisoner, but was placed there for spying purposes, being one of the agents of the Cheka, planted to make observations and report on our behaviour and conversation. He certainly had much to report!

## We Resume Conference Sessions

Those wooden platforms, by the way, are to be found in all the places of imprisonment, and are the substitutes for beds. On them we were to sleep for some time to come.

I suddenly felt a strong inflow of joy, and exclaimed:

"Brothers and sisters! All come here!"

When all had gathered around me, I said: "We are now in a place where the Apostle Paul and Silas were. They prayed and sang praises to God. (Acts 16:25.) Let us sing praises."

All sang a hymn of glory to God, with a great inspiration. After that I said: "Let us pray. Let us thank God for the

193

great honor which He bestows upon us, in allowing us to be placed where His Apostles were. Ask Him to bless our stay here to His glory. Ask Him to bless the chiefs of this institution, and the guards, and especially all the prisoners."

It is unnecessary to add that the prayers which followed were full of warmth and deeply spiritual, cheering all our hearts with overflowing joy. After that, examining our quarters, I said:

"Here are spacious rooms. We can continue the sessions of our Conference." Unanimously we decided to resume the interrupted meeting of the afternoon, and without delay the presiding officer, vice presidents and secretaries took their places and the routine business of the session began.

During the next two days we finished all our work in the greatest detail, according to our program, though when we planned it the place of meeting was certainly not chosen in a prison. The minutes were all carefully written, read and approved. Everything was done with as much orderliness and neatness and despatch as though we were still in the conference room and had spent our nights peacefully sleeping in the quarters provided for us by the Christian brethren in Tver, instead of by the Cheka. Needless to say, that in the story of the Christian Church this fact of a Young People's Conference in prison is unparalleled in the history of persecutions.

I felt continually a great triumphant joy, and so also did my fellow-prisoners. My young people were singing almost all the time, and how our hearts were knit closer and closer together in these days of our imprisonment.

### Christian Prisoners Are "Noisy"

However, on the second day the chief of the Cheka came to our cell. He was a short fellow, somewhat lame, and of a stubby, rather uncouth appearance. He said:

"We have had all kinds of prisoners here, but we have never had such noisy fellows as you are! You sing all the time. You disturb us in our work. The people gather in the streets around the building. We cannot allow you to continue this noise any longer!"

## MY FIRST IMPRISONMENT

We argued with him, saying: "If we are deprived of the possibility of singing at liberty we must have the right to sing in prison where there is no liberty." But he would not listen to us. Finally, after some negotiations, a compromise was reached. We were allowed to have our meetings for prayer and singing twice a day, two hours in the morning and two hours in the evening. Possibly it was a provision of the Lord for our welfare, for in our enthusiasm and joy we were likely to burn ourselves out in praise at high pressure.

We now had our meetings in the court yard, and we availed ourselves of this opportunity to its utmost capacity. We sang, read the Word of God, and prayed. The red soldiers, militiamen and even the officials of the Cheka who were in this institution came and listened to us. We even saw some of them, red soldiers at that and supposed to be atheists, trying to learn the hymns of praise to God and making an effort to sing with us. It only illustrates how our Evangelical hymns have been taken up even by non-Christians, who thus aided in proclaiming the Gospel over Russia.

We saw men and women on the roofs of adjacent houses, where they had climbed to see who were daring to sing in the presence of the terrible Cheka. Many people gathered in the street outside to listen to our singing. Was there ever such a testimony! It was so unusual, it was wonderful! Who could ever forget it! We used to come out of our basement cells into the court yard in rows of two in a solemn procession, like the processional of a large choir in the cathedral, and two by two we marched back again to our cells, singing as we came and went. Usually when we were returning to our prison cells we sang one verse of a hymn previously composed by me: "In the Town of Antioch".

"In the towers and in the caves;
In catacombs of different lands,
The world could see the fine examples
Of steadfast primitive Christians."

While in this prison of the Cheka I composed a poem relating the story of a soldier of the Cheka, guarding the prisoners and becoming impressed by their joyful singing, in

195

which he learned to join. You will find a translation of the poem at the end of this chapter.

The guards of the prison had great sympathy for us, and no wonder, for we were young and at the threshold of life, clean and upright, and not at all like the hardened criminals which they were used to guarding. In their pity they permitted us to receive visits from our friends, who brought us our letters, food and books, and also permitted us to send letters to our friends and families. Imagine the fathers and mothers of some of the delegates receiving word that those who had left their homes in pursuit of further education in the Word of God, and to plan for the enlargement of the work among Russian young people, were now in prison for the Gospel's sake.

## Cheka Chief Gets Rid of Us

The chief of the Cheka did not relish such joyous prisoners, and endeavored from the beginning to hurry the procedure of our trial and to get rid of us in some manner or other. After three weeks of imprisonment every one of the prisoners was called upstairs into the hearing room of the Cheka, where it was declared that the trial body of the Cheka had considered our case and had passed a resolution that the twelve oldest were sentenced to hard labor at the Suzdal Monastery, in Yaroslav Province. Of course, that included me. This monastery fortress was very old, and under the old regime the highest members of the Greek Orthodox clergy when guilty of wrong doing and of heresies were confined in this monastery and died there. Many "staroobriadzi" or "old believers" bishops died in that monastery in confinement.*

According to the resolution which was read in our hearing, the rest of the prisoners, thirty-five in number, were to be

_____
* In the seventeenth century the Patriarch Nikon corrected the old Slavonic Church books, which caused a Dissent in the Greek Orthodox Church. The Dissenters began to be called "Staroobriadzi" or "Old Believers". They had the same creed and differed from the rest of the Orthodox Church only in that they accepted the old Church books, while the Orthodox Church began to use the new corrected books.

sent to their homes after giving a written promise that they would remain there until a Law Court trial over their cases could take place in regular order. Soon every one of our young fellow prisoners left the place and departed to their homes. With every one of them I parted with a prayer. Some of them I never saw again, but I am assured even now that their days and nights in prison were well invested in training their minds and hearts for future service for the Master. What testimonies these young people could and did give in after days and years!

## THE PRISON

Outside the prison chamber
   The guard walks slowly by.
A song of glad thanksgiving
   Is loudly sung on high.

The people passing swiftly
   Can hear its clarion call;
They marvel: why this gladness
   Inside a prison wall?

Who sings, within, such praises?
   They wonder, as they stare;
But, "Brethren of the Gospel,"
   That is the name they bear.

Says one who pauses, showing
   That *his* face, too, is bright:
"These are their songs of rapture
   To Christ, Who is their Light.

"They sing in fullest measures
   When heavy falls the rod;
No prison bars or shackles
   Restrain the truth of God."

In vain the guard is waiting;
   This song will never cease
Till God's own will and pleasure
   Shall be fulfilled in peace.

The distant plains of Russia
   Shall now receive the Word;
Her forests and her mountains
   The joyful sound have heard.

# IN THE MONASTERY PRISON

Through all the lands and nations
  God's Word shall conqueror be,
And bring souls out of prison
  To rapturous life and free.

See where, beside the prison,
  Men stand to hear the song;
And many, taking Jesus,
  Forsake their life of wrong.

The guard, most deeply stirred now,
  Has laid his musket by;
He listens — grasps the meaning —
  His doubts all fade and die.

His eyes grow clearer, brighter,
  He gazes up the street,
While his soft humming echoes
  The prisoners' music sweet.

More fully now he gathers
  The meaning of the song;
For he has found his freedom
  From sin, and shame, and wrong.

      I. S. PROKHANOFF,
        In Tver Hard Labor Camp (1921)

# CHAPTER XXIII

## The Old Monastery Prison

*"Love your enemies, and pray for them that perse-*
*cute you."*        *Matt. 5 : 44.*

IT was declared further in the resolution that the twelve
oldest prisoners who were to remain behind would be taken
temporarily from the Cheka building to the hard labor camp
which was in the ancient monastery at Tver, called "Otrosky
Monastery". What prisons these old monasteries did make!
This one was situated directly on the shore of the Volga
River and one could see from some portions of it very picturesque scenery.

But the historical reputation of this monastery was anything but cheering to those compelled to enter its gates under
sentence. In the olden times of the Czar's regime it was a
place of confinement for the highest clerical offenders.
Among others the celebrated Patriarch Philip was confined
there for courageously objecting to some cruel things done
by the Czar.

We were shown his dark cell there, possibly to chill our
spirits. On the command of John the Terrible, his terrible
executioner, Maluta Skuratoff, murdered the Patriarch Philip
in his cell at that monastery. The Soviet authorities transformed this monastery into the hard labor camp.

On a certain morning we were called out and told that
we were to be transported to this place. We marched as
formerly, surrounded by armed militiamen and red soldiers
and led by one Cheka official. Within the monastery we
were taken to the old church building, which was transformed
into a real prison. All the Greek Orthodox Church buildings
have three departments, the hall, the altar and the sacristy.

Some of us were placed in the hall and some in the altar
room. Here every prisoner was provided with a kind of bed,

consisting of plain hard wooden boards laid on wooden supports. When we entered the hall we learned that there were only a few prisoners in this place, comparatively, yet altogether in this camp at the time there were more than 500 under arrest.

### Prison Regime Not Rigorous

After we had laid our things in their proper places I said: "Brethren, this holy place requires holy men. Let us pray that these old walls, which in past centuries saw many things, may now see for the first time the followers of the Gospel under the wonderful influence of the Holy Spirit". We then prayed and sang praises unto the Lord.

The chief of the hard labor camp said to us that his mother was somewhere a member of the Evangelical Church. He treated us very mildly, allowing our brethren and friends to bring food and other things to us.

Very soon the chief of the camp gave three of our brethren work in his office. Two brethren were sent to work in the offices outside of the labor camp. With the consent of the chief, the prisoners elected our Brother B. to be their "Starosta", or official representative. The regime within the prison was not severe. Sometimes we were taken to the public bath house in the city, accompanied by a guard without any arms.

Two or three of our brethren worked in the fields and in kitchen gardens of the camp. Some of them were employed in building a house. As to myself, I was ordered to keep our court yard clean and with others to clean the toilets, which were, as usual in the Russian places of imprisonment, in a terrible condition.

I said to my companions: "Here we are, Christians, in the midst of about five hundred prisoners. God has given us a great field. Let us work!"

We began to have meetings every evening. A great many prisoners used to attend the service. They listened very attentively, and some of them began to sing and pray with us. The authorities found that it was too much of a religious gathering, too large in size, and so they made the restriction that only those prisoners confined in the church building could attend our meetings. The prisoners in the other buildings were forbidden to visit our building or to take part in our meetings.

But God found a way for our testimony to every one of them. Toward evening, after our day's work was ended, all the prisoners had from one to two hours for exercise, walking freely within the prison walls. There we had our opportunity to speak to every one individually about Christ in personal conversation.

### Bible School in the Prison

God gave us then remarkable manifestations of His Spirit, in the visions He sent to our Brother B., which I endeavored with prayer to interpret. Most of his dreams were fulfilled. For instance, he saw the Priest V. trying to accomplish the wreck of a train and perishing under it. The dream pictured what actually happened to that priest afterward.

Usually all the prisoners were free from work of any kind after six o'clock. Once I said: "Dear Brethren, we have sufficient time to begin here Bible courses." Everybody rejoiced, and we started. At our request we were all transferred into the back room of the church, the sacristy, where we were entirely by ourselves. We prayed, read the Bible and sang very much.

I began to deliver lectures on homiletics, church history and the interpretation of the Bible. We had the most interesting and helpful time. Of course, this fact of arranging a Bible School within prison walls is no doubt quite unique in the history of religious persecutions. All this time I was in a condition of real joy and happiness. I had an inspiration to write poems. Poetry flowed from my pen like a living stream. During the time of my confinement I wrote a whole book of special hymns, dedicated to the young people, the "Pipe of David", consisting of one hundred hymns. Afterward this book was printed, and a book of musical notes was also printed to accompany the songs, and at the present time many of those hymns are sung by our people throughout the vast territory of Russia. Needless to say, the singing has an added depth and meaning when the young people re-member the story of our imprisonment in the midst of the Young People's Conference at Tver.

One must not forget that, though we were daily worship-ping our Lord, we were in the midst of terrors. In that hard labor camp we were surrounded by all kinds of criminals, some of them murderers, robbers and thieves. Many of them were shot for their crimes. Our little group was an oasis of joy in the midst of sorrow, crime and suffering. The days were passing quickly for the group of believers, because of our attitude toward God.

## My Son Visits the Monastery

During this time I had a most dramatic experience. One day a guard from the gate came to me and said: "Your son is at the gate and wants to see you." I did not know which son it was. When I went to the gate there I saw Vsevolod, my younger boy, who was at that time seventeen years old. Oh! what a joy it was to see him once more! We greeted one another through the grating of the gate, and quite un-expectedly I began to weep, though not for myself, but about this young man, who had recently lost his mother and now beheld his father through the grating of a prison wall.

As soon as I had recovered somewhat, I asked the chief of the prison for permission to bring my son to our cell. He was permitted to enter, and partook of a meal with us. We had a very comforting talk together, in which I explained some of the beautiful things that were happening in our re-ligious experience there, and he departed in a far better mental condition than when he approached my prison house. Vsevolod went at once to St. Petersburg, to our apartment there, where he found his older brother Yaroslav.

I should add that he carried with him a piece of good news, which also lightened his heart and gave him a good message to carry to Yaroslav. We had but recently learned that we were about to be liberated from our prison. And surely the lad deserved this added bit of comfort for all his suffering.

IN THE MONASTERY PRISON

We made the discovery that our arrest was connived by a very remarkable person, V. He was both a priest of the Greek Catholic Church and at the same time a member of the Cheka, those terrible revoultionary political police who executed multitudes of people.

### False Witness of an Orthodox Priest

On the one hand, he hated the Evangelical Christians, disliking violently anything connected with the popular free Protestant Christian movement. On the other, he was in a position to do us no inconsiderable amount of harm by his false witness and lying.

He reported that I. S. Prokhanoff, under the pretext of his religious activities, was conducting a secret counter-revolutionary work, which he was developing among the young people. In proof of his assertions, this Young People's Conference at Tver was cited by the priest V. as especially dangerous, because young delegates had arrived from all parts of Russia. As a result our arrest took place as I have described.

When we learned the reason for our arrest, and understood fully from the human standpoint the cause of all that was happening to us, I wrote a detailed explanation about my own work and the purpose and program of this Young People's Conference, bringing indisputable evidence that there was no politics whatever in our activities, and proving that we were just what we purported to be, thoroughly religious people.

We also took pains to mention that under the old regime the Greek Orthodox clergy were wont to accuse us of revolutionary tendencies and acts, and that now one of the representatives of the same old State Church had accused us of these counter-revolutionary aims and that it was solely at his instigation that we were arrested and accused.

At the same time our churches from all over Russia, and especially those at Kieff, sent a delegation to Moscow, with documents proving the non-political character of my activities. The services of Brother Shenderovsky in this case were precious beyond any description.

203

After all the evidence in our case had been considered by the Board of the Central Executive Committee of deputies, workmen and peasants, the Board was convinced that we were not harboring any revolutionary elements in our work and passed a resolution to set us free.

## Our Release Ordered from Moscow

In the early morning of July 16, three and a half months after the time of our arrest at Tver, I saw from the window of my cell, through a grating the very familiar figure of Brother Shenderovsky and also Brother Motorin coming rapidly in the direction of our camp, the former waving to me with papers in his hand.

It was clear to me that he was bringing a document which would mean our liberation, and I told my fellow-prisoners. Everybody rejoiced. The formality of presenting the document to the chief, giving out orders for our liberation, was completed very quickly, and we at last became free.

Before leaving the camp we arranged a prayer meeting at our usual place. Our lately made friends, the other prisoners, all wept bitterly. One of them took my hand, kissed me and said:

"The last rays of light go away from us!"

Oh, how hard it was to part with these souls, to whom we had been given the privilege of bringing the message of salvation in Jesus Christ. We asked for permission to have a picture taken of all of us just within the wall of the camp. This photograph will remain as a souvenir of those memorable days.

Taking up our beds, pillows and other things, and having said farewell to the prisoners and also to the soldiers and our guards, we left the prison camp through the gates and journeyed in the direction of the city.

## The Priest Replaces Us in Prison

Just at the moment of our liberation we learned that at the very time of our release from prison the priest V., who caused our imprisonment, was arrested and put into one of the Moscow prisons. We immediately elected a small delegation of brethren, who went to the office of the local authorities and presented the following statement:

"Although V. was guilty of our arrest by his false charges, nevertheless we forgive him in the Name of Him who forgave us, and would ask about his liberation."

To this petition we received a verbal reply approximately as follows:

"It is very good on your part that you ask about this, but it will also be good if he stays a little bit in jail." We heard later that he was kept in prison for the exact length of time for which we were confined.

We could not help seeing that the same thing happened to the priest V. as was recorded about the wicked Haman, that great enemy of Mordacai and the Jews, who was hanged on the gallows which he prepared for Mordacai. Under these circumstances our liberation took on quite the character of a triumph, though we were truly sorry for V.'s imprisonment.

The local congregation of Evangelical Christians insisted that we should remain with them for a week at least. Special meetings were arranged in the hall of the local congregation; also a solemn meeting at the local Lutheran Church, and we even called together a small Conference of Young People from the churches of the district.

The meetings were crowded with people, and all the addresses brought new spiritual fire to the hearts of our people. Believers were encouraged, sinners repented and the Gospel was preached. The farewell meeting which was arranged by the local church was a kind of love feast and commemorated our joy.

When after these meetings I came, together with Brothers S. and V., to the railroad station to take a train to Petrograd, I was told that the price of a ticket was *five million roubles!* You will remember that on my outward journey, when going to Tver to attend that conference, a ticket cost nothing. And now, five million roubles! Such a change!

Generally speaking at that time conditions were so fluctuating and changeable that one could expect almost anything to happen. I was soon sitting in the train and moving off toward Petrograd, however. I saw the pale faces, ragged clothing, indescribable dirt in the cars. I heard the swearing words of drunken men who had not bread enough, but who had their "moonshine". I said: "The Gospel will remedy all the evils from which the Russian people are suffering. Let us spread the Gospel with multiplied energy!"

The whole experience recorded in this chapter served to the glory of God and to the advancement of His Kingdom throughout Russia, for it was published abroad and handed on from mouth to mouth until it became known everywhere, a testimony to the power of God to keep His own in times of danger, persecution, suffering and imprisonment for Christ's sake. Truly the Word of God is not bound! He at all times and in all places accomplishes His purposes.

Now for the poem written about our prison experience, which is a true record of what happened during that remarkable period:

# CHAPTER XXIV

## Renewing Spiritual Activities
### 1922-23

*"Laboring night and day."* — *I Thes. 2:9.*

ON my return from the Tver hard labor camp to Petro-grad, I called together the Council of the All-Russian Evangelical Christian Union. We had a thanksgiving prayer meeting for the spiritual victory wrought in our be-half. After describing our arrest and imprisonment and its glorious ending, I emphasized what we had accomplished in prison, ending with the appeal that (as we were now free) we must double, triple and multiply our energy to do the work of God in Russia. Of course, I laid out a special program, and we began at once vigorously to press a new Gospel campaign throughout the city.

First, we found some new private halls at different points in Petrograd; secondly, we examined the buildings of the Lutheran and Reformed Churches. Many of them were un-occupied because their German, Swedish, French and other parishioners had left Russia.

These empty, neglected buildings were being destroyed by moisture, and naturally the small church committees in charge of them were always glad to turn them over to the Evangelical Christians on very liberal terms. We secured for our meetings the buildings of the Swedish Lutheran Church, the French Reformed Church, two German Lutheran churches and others.

I usually preached in the building of the Swedish Lutheran Church and in the French Reformed Church. Both were near the Kazan Cathedral, in the very center of the city. By 1922 we had a dozen places of worship within the city and a num-ber in the suburbs. In every church the Gospel was preached with great enthusiasm and abundant results.

We continued our efforts to obtain food from abroad through the American Relief Association and to send it to the districts where our workers and churches were most in need of it. We would gladly have renewed the publication of "The Christian" and "The Morning Star," but could not realize this part of our program on account of the printing plants in Russia being in a condition of great disorder.

## Resuming Work in the Bible School

We succeeded in obtaining a permit for the reopening of our Bible School, and classes began again in October, 1922. My fellow-workers in the school of 1913 — A. A. Reimer and K. P. Inkis — having died from disease as the victims of the revolution, I found new teachers for the school among my nearest fellow-workers. I taught dogmatics, Introduction to the Bible, Exegesis of the New Testament and Homiletics, while seven other teachers including my two sons, carried the remainder of the usual subjects.

As to my older son, I assisted him to learn in the proper manner the ancient languages, Latin, Greek and Hebrew. He studied them almost to perfection, writing in Latin the translations of his botanical books, and being able to recite from memory whole pages of the Greek New Testament and of the Hebrew Old Testament. All this was a fine preparation for a professorship in the Theological School, and his achievements in these branches of human knowledge were ample proof that the Lord heard my prayers. Now it can be readily understood that in reopening the Bible School it was only natural that my older son, Yaroslav, was appointed a teacher in the Greek of the New Testament, the Hebrew of the Old Testament and also in Church History.

As to my younger son, Vsevolod, he showed great ability in financial and economic matters. He chose the teaching of the "Constitution of the Republic," called "Politgramata," a subject made obligatory for all schools in Russia. Both sons were successful as teachers and very much loved by the students.

208

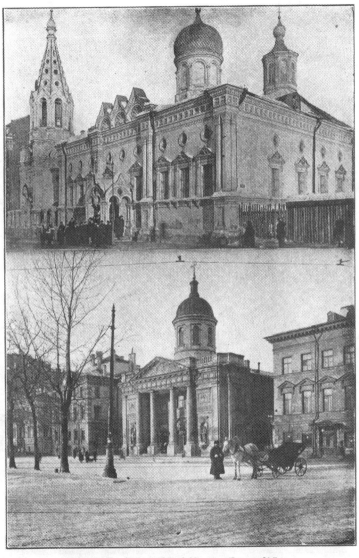

1.  Temple of Peter and Paul, Moscow.—(See page 214)
2.  St. Catherine's Lutheran Church, Leningrad.—(See page 207)

I. S. Prokhanoff and the Council of the All-Russian Evangelical Christian Union at Leningrad    (See page 157)

My younger son had a remarkable poetical gift, writing poems which had always a deep philosophical sense. He had also an extraordinary gift for organization, and would have been of great service to the Evangelical movement, which he idealized. Unfortunately he passed away on July 23, 1926.

I was informed by cablegram of the death of my son while I was in Chicago, Ill., in the interests of the cause of God in Russia. Every father will easily understand what a terrible blow it was to my heart. After prayerful fellowship with God I found spiritual power to cable to my family in Leningrad the words of Job 1:21: "The Lord gave and the Lord hath taken; blessed be the name of the Lord."

———•———

# CHAPTER XXV

## Second Contact with the Greek Orthodox Church
### 1922-23

*"A great company of the priests were obedient unto the faith."* Acts 6:7.

IN 1922 a great change took place in the governing system of the Greek Orthodox Church. The Patriarch Tikhon, the head of the Church, was dethroned as the result of a campaign started by the Russian Government. Being in great difficulty on account of the famine, and in need of finances to feed the starving population of Russia, the Soviet Government issued a decree to the effect that all the silver, all the gold, and all the precious stones which were stored in the churches, temples and monasteries, having come to them originally as gifts from the people, should be given to the State Treasury, for the purpose of feeding the famished people.

At that time there was a progressive group of priests, who called themselves "Obnovlenzi" (renewers) and were in opposition to the Patriarch. The Government made use of them, encouraging violent action. They came to the Patriarch and demanded that he should give over his administrative power, which he did, though still retaining his title of Patriarch. This group of priests then formed the so-called "Supreme Council of the Greek Orthodox Church" and began to govern the Church in a spirit agreeable to the Government.

Other divisions of the Greek Orthodox Church were soon formed among the clergy and people:

1. The "Living Church," at the head of which was Protojerey Krasnitzky.

2. The "Ancient Apostolic Church," with Protojerey Vvedensky at its head.

3. The "Church of Regeneration," under the leadership of Metropolitan Antonine.

These groups differed very little doctrinally from one another or from the old Greek Orthodox Church. They were even afraid to mention the word "reform." They were apparently aiming at something which was not clear to themselves. I felt that it was an opportune time to say a living word to the leaders of these progressive sections within the Greek Orthodox Church, and so I wrote a special appeal, entitled, "The Gospel Call." In this appeal I developed three main thoughts:

## My Appeal to Greek Orthodox Leaders

In the first place, I said that the Evangelical Christians forgave their Greek Orthodox persecutors for all their offences in the Name of Him who forgave us.

Second, I said that now the time had come for the Orthodox clergy to begin a national Gospel (New Testament) Reformation. I laid down the New Testament principles on which the reformation should be carried out.

Third, I mentioned that the Evangelical Christians intended to arrange special prayer meetings at Moscow and Leningrad to pray for the help of God to carry out this Reformation, and that we wanted to invite the representatives of the various sections of the Greek Orthodox Church to those meetings.

This appeal was printed in the quantity of 100,000 copies and was sent all over Russia, to the clergy and other leaders of the Orthodox Church. It produced a great effect. My friends wrote to me at Petrograd, saying that at Moscow there was great excitement and that many priests wanted to see me. I went to Moscow immediately.

The first priest whom I visited had an ancient church in the very center of Moscow. When I entered his house, he greeted me most cordially, and showed me a paper containing the main principles laid down in "The Gospel Call," and signed by one hundred men. The priest said:—

"I am forming a new religious community on the prin-

211

ciples of your "Gospel Call," and have already a hundred friends who join me."

Then he showed me a document signed by Patriarch Tikhon, containing his abdication. In conclusion he invited me and two brethren who were with me to take service in his church that evening. The services in the Greek Ortho- dox Churches are brilliant; everything glitters with gold, silver and precious stones. When we entered the church the priest greeted us as brethren in Christ and gave us hon- orable seats. The two brethren who were with me delivered short addresses. After that I preached a sermon on the text: "Repent and believe in the Gospel."

After explaining the repentance which Christ spoke of, and also the repentance which was practiced in the Greek Orthodox Church, with the participation of the priests, I said in conclusion:—

"Now the days have come when all the Russian people must repent of their centuries of sins, and their spiritual leaders must set an example for them." When I finished my sermon, the priest said: "Let us pray." He knelt before the altar and began to pray approximately like this:

"Lord, forgive me as a simple sinner and as the sinner- shepherd of these immortal souls with regard to whom I was so neglectful."

### Visiting the Metropolitan in Moscow

After that I visited the Metropolitan Antonine in his cell in the Novospassky Monastery at Moscow. He showed us his copy of our "Gospel Call," on which we saw marks in lead pencil. He said: "I agree with almost everything that is stated in your 'Gospel Call,' but this program can- not be realized in the Greek Orthodox Church at present."

Then he turned to his bookshelves, picked up a book and said to me: "This is the book from which I am taking drops of living water every day."

When I looked at the book, I saw that it was "The Gusli," the hymn book composed and published by me for the use of our Evangelical congregations. At the conclusion of our conversation I proposed that we should pray together, to which he consented.

One of the brethren who accompanied me wept with tears of joy. Surely there was a reason for his tears. It is certain that in a thousand years never such a thing happened as that a Metropolitan of the Greek Orthodox Church would pray in his own words with outsiders, yet here he prayed with the representatives of the people's Evangelical movement.

I invited the Metropolitan Antonine and other priests to attend our prayer meeting, which was fixed for November 2nd, at the Hall of our Moscow Congregation. On this date two solemn prayer meetings of the Evangelical Christians were held, one in Moscow and the other in the Leningrad church in which our meetings usually took place.

These meetings produced a deep and lasting impression upon public opinion in both capitals, and as the news gradually drifted into the vast country a spiritual impulse was given to many of the Orthodox priests and their people and even a better understanding between Orthodox and Evangelical members of the churches. From that time the attitude of all sections of the Greek Orthodox Church changed altogether toward us, and for the first time the priests understood the motives and plans of this "dissenting" group.

## Metropolitan Endorses Our Labors

At one city there was an anti-religious debate before a large gathering, to which the Metropolitan Antonine was invited. In the meeting somebody asked the Metropolitan which church or religious organization, in his opinion, embodied in the nearest way the teaching of Christ. The Metropolitan's reply was:—

"I know one group of Christians; they are called Evangelical Christians. *They restore the primitive Christianity of Christ and the Apostles.*"

Since that time, in many places, the priests invited our Evangelical preachers to preach in their churches, even turning their buildings over to the Evangelical Christians for their meetings, since the latter in few cases were able so soon to create houses of worship for themselves.

Metropolitan Antonine died in 1926. Some time before his death he told his priests to give the Temple of Peter and Paul, in which he held his services in Moscow, to the local Moscow Church of Evangelical Christians. Since that time the Evangelical meetings have been held in that Temple. In 1927 and 1928 I frequently went from Leningrad to Moscow and preached where for years the Metropolitan had gone through with the old ritualistic service. Every time I preached in that Temple a large crowd was in attendance, and when the people were requested to pray a universal cry to God was heard.

The new groups formed in the Greek Orthodox Church endeavored to start their own organizations by arranging congresses, conferences and special meetings. On March 15, 1923, the "Congress of the Ancient Apostolic Church" was called at Moscow. I received an invitation from the Committee of Organization, which I accepted. They informed me that they had allotted me an hour for my address.

## Preaching to Orthodox Church Dignitaries

On arriving at the forenoon session of the Congress I learned that I had been chosen as the first speaker. The Chairman announced that I. S. Prokhanoff, President of the All-Russian Evangelical Christian Union, would be the first speaker of the session. As I approached the platform, Bishop Vvdensky, the Chairman, shook hands and I turned to speak. On the platform were also bishops, archbishops and professors of the theological academies, and I saw before me a great audience of monks, priests, bishops, archbishops and leading laymen of the Greek Orthodox Church.

I assured them that I came in the name of the whole Evangelical Christian movement, not to criticise them, but to help them overcome their difficulties by sharing with them our spiritual experience.

As I ended my address, I said: "If the Chairman permits, I would like to invite all present to prayer. All the monks, priests, bishops and archbishops arose in their places, and I prayed fervently for Russia, for the Russian people and the Greek Orthodox Church, asking the Lord to send a spiritual regeneration. I thanked God for the revival already begun in the Evangelical movement, and asked that it might bring the Russian people a new life.

As I finished my prayer a crowd of clergymen and laymen surrounded me and shook hands, and some of them asked: "Please give us a copy of your prayer!" It was a natural request, for the Orthodox clergymen and laymen are accustomed to pray only in the words of formal prayers established centuries ago. Many of them did not even know whether it was possible to pray in one's own words. They also asked where we held our meetings, about our literature, and many other questions. One could see that new thoughts and new resolves were filling their minds.

After my address and prayer, the Chairman announced an interval of recess, because, as he said: "We must recover from the unusually strong impressions which we have just experienced."

During this interval I made many new acquaintances. One of the professors from the Academy said: "It was a remarkable approach to the question." The session being resumed, the Priest E. read from his New Testament the second chapter of the Acts of the Apostles, and explained the construction of the Apostolic Church in the spirit of my declaration.

### One Dissenting Voice in the Crowd

That the audience were not entirely of one mind was to be expected, and even as the Priest E. finished his address a voice in the rear of the audience shouted:

"What do I see! A representative of the sectarian movement was allowed to speak in this congress of the Orthodox Church! What would our Holy Fathers (the saints of the Church) say if they became alive!"

Chairman Vvdensky quickly said: "I would ask him who has just spoken the words which most of us heard to rise."

But the man did not make himself known, and the Chairman continued:—

"I. S. Prokhanoff came to us on invitation and has said to us quite frankly and courageously what was in his heart, but here are people who have not the courage to express openly what they desire to say!"

The social and spiritual influence of our Union at this time gained its highest level, manifesting its spiritual power upon these new efforts of the progressive group of the Greek Orthodox Church, and also upon another movement, starting among the people outside the Church, called "Tresvenni-chestwo," a temperance effort.

The priests, bishops and archbishops of the Greek Orthodox Church having failed to give attention to the spiritual needs of their people, the laymen themselves began to build up a new life as they understood it. This movement was started by Ivan Churnikoff, of St. Petersburg.

One of the followers of Churikoff, named John Koloskoff, started the same movement in Moscow. He was also persecuted by the Orthodox clergy.

In the fall of 1922, when I was in Moscow and took part in the services of the Greek Orthodox Church, Brother John Koloskoff was very much impressed. Soon afterward he expressed his desire to join our Moscow Church with all his members. He was accepted, and after that he and his followers visited our Leningrad Church and were accepted into the Union.

I can never forget how trying were the years 1920, 1921 and 1922. It was a time of unparalleled famine for the whole Russian people. Food was absent or very scarce and of very deficient quality. Brother Koloskoff and some of our members opened dining halls in various sections of Moscow, in which they succeeded in feeding the people pretty decently. It was a good testimony of Evangelical Christian efficiency for outsiders.

# CHAPTER XXVI

## My Second Imprisonment
### 1922-23

*"The mystery of the Gospel, for which I am an ambassador in bonds."*　　　　　*Eph. 6:20.*

CHRIST said: "If they persecuted me, they will persecute you." — John 15:20. This law of the spiritual life found its application at this time. Some members of the Greek Orthodox clergy, even among those who were present in the Ancient Apostolic conference, seeing our moral success, became hostile to our Union. They sent some unfavorable reports to the Government, resulting first of all in a systematic and careful search of our houses and places of work.

In April, 1923, about 12 o'clock at night, while I was still sitting in my study engaged in writing, I heard a noise. The door was opened and I saw two men. They were officials of the Cheka, the political police of the revolution.

### Seeking Evidence to Incriminate Me

They showed their papers, in which they were authorized to make a search in my house. I was extremely kind and showed them willingly all my papers on the table and shelves. The chief official was asked:

"For what are you searching?"

"Counter-revolution," he said.

Evidently they found nothing of an incriminating nature, but after completing their search the chief said to me:

"We have to go out."

"Shall I return tonight?" I asked. "Yes," he replied.

When we came out on the street I saw a motor truck, into which we climbed and were driven to the offices of our Union. During the short journey the chief became quite talkative, and said: "You made a good propaganda of your ideas in the Greek Orthodox Church." Evidently he was at the meeting or it had been discussed in headquarters of the police.

On arriving at our offices I saw in the court yard a great number of militia, red soldiers and Cheka officials. They had searched the Bible School and even the store room where we had our wood and food supplies. My chief captor asked them:

"What is the result?" "Nothing special" was the reply.

Nevertheless, the officials in my presence very carefully renewed their examination, going through every room, searching all the closets, and came at length to my own office. I showed them all my papers, as I had done in my study, but they did not seem to be interested in them.

After the end of the search the chief said: "We found nothing and leave you at liberty." At that time many were arrested who never returned to their homes. As the searchers and their formidable looking escort left the premises, my fellow-workers gathered with me in my office for prayer, then we returned to our homes at about 3 o'clock in the morning.

In those days our Union offices occupied an entire floor in a large house. We had in the offices twenty-seven fellow-workers in various branches, Missions, Publishing Work and the Bible School. During the search one of the Cheka officials said: "It is a ministry of the Evangelicals."

We were quite sure there would be a continuation of the searchings, but nevertheless I did not reduce my work, even urging my fellow-workers to persevere with greater zeal. I continued preaching on Sundays in the large building of the Swedish Lutheran Church, lecturing in the Bible College, editing and publishing our monthly, "The Christian," and conducting a very wide correspondence.

Once when I returned from the Bible College to my quarters at about 10 o'clock in the evening, I found in my kitchen a red soldier. He said:

"I must telephone to my chief."

He soon returned, and in a quarter of an hour there came to our house a military officer and two aides, with revolvers and others arms. The older officer, holding a revolver pointed at my head, said:

"Here is a paper for you to sign."

## The Summons Comes: I Finish My Work

As I read it, I saw that it was an order from the Moscow Cheka that I should voluntarily come on the third day to Moscow, to the offices of the Main Cheka, at 2 o'clock in the afternoon.

Threatening me with their revolvers while I signed an acknowledgment of having received the document, the officers left the house. We prayed and gave all these matters into the hands of our Lord.

On the next forenoon and afternoon I had meetings of the Union Council, the Church Council, a meeting of the teachers of the Bible School, delivered lectures according to my regular program, and parted with everybody in prayer. These were solemn hours, for it was not at all certain that I would return. I was accompanied to Moscow by one of our secretaries, Brother D.

At Moscow we visited the meeting hall of our local Church, where I delivered a short address and prayed with those members of our Council of the Moscow Church who were present, and then my secretary and I departed to the office of the Cheka.

As we entered the building, Brother Marzinkovsky, a lecturer on Christian topics, was coming out. He informed us that a decree of banishment had been given to him, and on that day he was to receive his passport and leave Russia. We parted with deep feeling. My secretary and I had to wait a long time, until nearly all the officials of the Cheka had left the office. Then the chief of the religious division of the Cheka came, accompanied by two soldiers with drawn revolvers, and we were taken into prison.

In a certain room in the basement we had to give up all we had in our pockets, watches, knives, keys, etc., and were then brought into a shabby room or half-shed, with wooden partitions. In common parlance this room was called "a pig's stable." It was a rather small room, packed with prisoners, among whom there were several priests and five bishops.

Entering the cell, I said very loudly: "Peace be unto you!" Some in low voices murmured a kind of greeting, but the clerical prisoners were silent, having no word of greeting for an Evangelical, even within prison walls and with their future uncertain. After about an hour all the prisoners were removed from the cell with the exception of two young fellows (probably thieves) and ourselves. We two knelt and prayed, laid our heads on our overcoats and endeavored to fall asleep, not at all a difficult undertaking.

## We Enter the Inner Prison

On the next morning the soldiers of the Cheka came and took us to another room, slightly better, but also packed with prisoners. This we understood to be the "dog kennel." But on the next day thereafter we were taken to the so-called "inner prison," where the most dangerous political criminals were incarcerated.

What a coincidence! The Apostle Paul and Silas were also in "the inner prison." — Acts 16:24. There were no stocks for our feet and no earthquake happened. We were soon taken to a room of medium size, where we remained about one week. This was the place from which the prisoners were distributed, some to other prisons and some to death. Here we were in company with different kinds of criminals.

A bandit was brought in who had been captured at the point of his crime. Of course, later on he was shot. He was nervous, but did not seem to have any remorse or trouble with his conscience.

The first day of Easter we spent in the cell of the inner prison. The food was very poor. In the morning we were given boiling water and two pieces of sugar. At 12 o'clock we had a soup made of fish bones. At liberty nobody would eat such a soup, but it was that or nothing and hunger prevailed. At 6 o'clock we had a proso pudding, made from a common grain used largely in Russia instead of wheat.

That was all. There was no fat at all, so necessary in that climate. We suffered greatly from this food. But on the first day of Easter I was called to the office of the inner prison. When I entered the room I was given a pillow and a blanket, and also two Easter eggs and sweet "Easter bread," with the remark:

"All this is from your friends."

Brother D. and others received the same. One cannot describe the feelings which overflowed my heart. We both thanked the Lord for these so welcome gifts.

### Transferred to a "Permanent" Prison

After an interval of one week, General K., Brother D. and myself were transported from the inner prison to the Putirsky Prison. It was the central prison for the whole of Russia. There we were put in a cell with twenty-six other prisoners. It was a terrible time.

Just a few days after we entered this prison the Roman Catholic Priest Butkevich was shot. Among the prisoners in our cell were thieves, robbers, and murderers, but most of them were political "criminals". There were groups of Kossak officers who awaited their execution. There were also officers of the White Army. It may seem strange, but the majority of political prisoners were soviet officials, communists and non-party men.

One day all who were in the cell were ordered to leave it. We were led through long corridors, then all stopped, and I was ordered to remain at one cell, and the others, including my friend and brother, D., were taken further.

Only those who have had a friend in prison from whom they were caused to part can understand what it means. During our stay in the first cell we spoke every day about Jesus Christ to the prisoners. We obtained with great difficulty a New Testament, which we read ourselves and gave to other prisoners to read. A real spiritual atmosphere began to reign in the cell. The prisoners showed a special respect for me.

Both Brother D. and myself used to read portions of the Scripture and pray every morning and evening. This was the source of spiritual power for both of us and a testimony for the other prisoners.

### Spiritual Atmosphere Within Prison Walls

The first days of our stay in the cell very abusive talks and swearing prevailed among the prisoners. But after a few days their language began to be more polite, and within two weeks not even a bad word could be heard. A quiet and peaceful state of spirit prevailed. Even the prisoners who were under threat of execution began to smile.

As the cell became more and more quiet and orderly, the inspector of this section of the prison expressed his surprise, and soon came to an understanding as to the cause. Sometimes the other prisoners asked:

"Why are you always joyful?"

"Because we believe and feel that God is with us," was our reply.

During our stay in the first cell the following incident happened. As usual the prisoners of our cell were allowed a twenty-minute period of exercise. In the court yard of the prison there was a large pile of wood. Brother D. climbed one day to the top of the pile and sat down. I was standing in the court. Suddenly I heard him begin to sob and weep, saying to me:

"I have compassion on you, Brother Ivan Stepanovich! You are innocent. You have been working for the good of the people, and now you are here among the criminals! Why is this injustice permitted?"

I comforted him with an inner joy, saying: "First of all, this is the will of God, which is always good, whether we have something pleasant or unpleasant. Secondly, it is a great honor to be where Christ and the Apostles were centuries ago."

# MY SECOND IMPRISONMENT

When I entered my new cell, I was shown a bed and was told: "Take this bed. Here slept General P., who was shot yesterday!" I accepted the bed with an inner prayer. By the side of it was the bed of an officer who was tried together with General P., and who received a sentence of five years' imprisonment. He was from the Caucasus, like myself, and we spoke often of facts, incidents and places well known to both of us.

Soon after I was brought to the new cell we learned that to our prison, but not to our cell, a terrible criminal was brought. Living at Moscow, he had murdered forty-eight men and women, whom he used to invite to his house to buy or sell horses.

## Fellow-Prisoners Described

In my new cell the prisoners were of the same character as in the first cells, but among them there was one very peculiar man. He was about thirty years old. Every day about 5 o'clock he fell down unconscious, began to swear bitterly and to beat himself. Even four other prisoners could not control him. After five minutes of such conduct he used to come to his senses. He suffered from a kind of epilepsy which was the result of a contussion during the war, in one of the battles on the North Divina River. In his unconscious condition he often repeated the name of the river.

After a number of days one Tolstovez (a follower of Tolstoy) was brought to my cell. I began to talk with him on the Scripture. Another Tolstoist was brought to the adjacent cell. All the prisoners were allowed to have about twenty minutes for their daily walk in the court yard. During these walks I met the second Tolstoist and we had friendly talks together.

During these short intervals I also met one priest who from the beginning to the end spoke in despair about his wife and children at home. I tried to comfort him by quotations from the Old and New Testaments, but he seemed not to understand anything.

I spoke also to another priest. We walked one time past

a window in which he saw the face of another priest. He at once began to loudly shout:

"Wait, Living Churchman, we will get you yet!"

This priest belonged to the old section of the Orthodox Church; the other who was in the window belonged to the so-called "Living Church," supported by the Soviet Government. The priests of the Old Church felt that they were arrested on the basis of false reports of the Living Churchmen, and therefore this one was so irritated against the other.

There were many priests, bishops and archbishops in that prison, but I did not come in contact with them. They were in other groups, in other cells. It seemed to me that the authorities isolated me from the priests purposely. Perhaps they considered my perpetual optimism contagious.

## Surprise Meeting with a Friendly Priest

Once myself and some prisoners in my cell were ordered to come out of the cell to the court yard to be photographed. When I came to the court yard I was astonished to see there the Priest E., whose address followed mine at the Moscow Church Congress. He was to be photographed, and also my Brother D. As the priest was returning to his cell I had opportunity to speak a few words with him, and the same thing with my dear Brother D.

Only by experience does one learn how sweet it is to meet good friends in a prison. I remember also another incident which brought to me some moments of real joy. Permission was given for Brother D. and myself to receive food packages from outside, provided by our brethren. One sister, a member of the Moscow Church, made the decision, together with another sister, to bring one food package every week for every one of us. Those packages contained ordinary bread, butter, cheese, sausages, etc.

Of course, all this was very beneficial to our health, because the food in the prison was very poor. It was helpful not only for me, but also for the other prisoners who did not receive such presents, and with whom I shared these gifts.

But for us there was a special feature connected with these gifts.  They were signs of Christian love of our brethren and sisters who were outside the prison.  Through these gifts they visited us in prison.  In those days I understood not only by reason but by all my feelings and all my soul what it means for a prisoner to receive a token of love from outside.

Since that time I have always repeated with special sentiment the words of the Apostle: — "Remember them that are in bonds, as bound with them, and them which suffer adversity as being yourselves also in the body."—Hebrews 13:3.

———•———

# CHAPTER XXVII

## I Visit America Again
### 1923-1929

*"Forgetting those things which are behind and reaching forth unto those things which are before."*
Phil. 3:13.

MY liberation from prison was celebrated as a great festival by the Council of the Union and the churches at Leningrad, as well as by the churches throughout Russia. Prayer had been made continuously, and the Lord answered.

My slogan now was, "To work still more zealously," to compensate for the time lost in that imprisonment.

The optimism of faith was a real power for me, and even while I was in the terrible prison, with expectation that exile or something worse might be my fate at any moment, I planned and wrote out a program of the work which I would endeavor to accomplish as soon as I was liberated.

I must mention here a remarkable feature of our work during my imprisonment. I supposed that with my being taken away the government authorities or the Cheka would completely close our offices and put an end temporarily at least to our Evangelical Christian work. But while I was in the prison the Soviet Government did not close any meeting of our Petrograd Churches, did not stop the publication of our magazine, "The Christian," and did not interfere with our Bible School nor hinder our missionary work. On my return from prison to Leningrad I promptly resumed my labors in connection with these activities of the Church.

This period, from 1923 to 1929, proved to be the most fruitful with regard to the work of our Evangelical movement through the Union. The publication work, Bible education and missionary effort were facilitated by favorable laws passed by the Soviet Government.

## Famine for the Word of God

"The Christian" was now being spread in 15,000 copies monthly, an insufficient supply, but all we could print at the time, due to the shortage of paper, and especially the lack of funds. It was not forbidden to print the Scripture in Russia, but no person or organization was able to do so, on account of the lack of money to pay the costs. Toward 1924 the supply of Bibles was exhausted and a real famine of the Scripture began to be felt. Everywhere, especially after our meetings, the people asked for Bibles, but we could not supply them with a single copy. It was very sad, but we had none to give them.

In some places the peasants offered a cow or a sack of grain (at that time of great value) for one single Bible. This need for the Scripture was so keen that I began to think and pray about a trip to America to raise funds for printing the Bible.

After negotiations with some Christian friends in America, I was enabled to arrive at New York, on May 23, 1925, and stayed in America until November 11, 1926. I cannot describe this journey over the United States and Canada, which lasted for eighteen months. Really, I should write a special book upon the subject of my tour.

I can say briefly that during this time I visited the churches, conferences of all denominations, many colleges and other groups, delivering addresses and making many new acquaintances and friends. All the Protestant denominations gave a response to my appeals, and I was able to raise a considerable sum, about $100,000.

In agreement with the Union Council, the Tenth All-Russian Evangelical Christian Conference was fixed for November 25, 1926. I journeyed on the fastest boat and the swiftest trains and arrived in Leningrad on November 24, just on the eve of the Conference.

At the station I was welcomed by a large crowd of our

brethren from the local church and more than five hundred delegates who had arrived for the Conference from the Central Provinces, Ukraina, Siberia, the Far East, the Caucasus and other parts of our country. Needless to say, I received a tremendous welcome, both for myself and on account of the work which the Lord had enabled me to do during my absence.

The Conference lasted one week. During the day there were business sessions, and every evening we had crowded meetings at which the Gospel was preached to thousands of people. Great enthusiasm and inspiration prevailed throughout all the sessions and meetings. I made a report on my visit to America which lasted two hours, and was heard throughout with eager attention. A resolution of sincere gratitude was passed by the Conference to the American Fellow-Christians who helped the Russian people during the great famine, and who had now assisted in this time of spiritual famine.

## American Gifts Enlarge Our Work

After the close of this Conference I laid out a program for extensive publishing work. We endeavored to obtain all the necessary permits and started to print Bibles and Christian literature to spread over our vast country. The first edition of the Bible was already printed during my stay in America, from the funds I had raised, for the Scripture famine was too sore to await my return.

During the last month of 1926, the whole of 1927 and the first five months of 1928, we were able to print the following:

| | |
|---|---:|
| Bibles (including those printed during my stay in America) | 35,000 |
| New Testaments | 25,000 |
| Hymnals: "The Gospel Songs" | 25,000 |
| "Spiritual Songs" | 25,000 |
| The above with notes | 10,000 |
| Bible Concordance (a very much needed work) | 15,000 |
| The Gospel Adviser (a Church Calendar preserved and read over and over again by our people) | 40,000 |
| Total publications at this time | 175,000 |

228

There was a humorous side worth mentioning in producing such a great quantity of Scripture and literature, i.e., the atheistic printing establishments eagerly grasped the opportunity of doing our work. But after this publication, no further printing of the Scripture was permitted. From 1914 to this year, 1933, this was the sole Scripture printing allowed by the Government. Surely God disposed the hearts of the American Christians to help, and God also disposed the minds of the Soviet authorities and the managers of the Soviet atheistic printing establishments to give permission and to print the Scripture. He did what it was impossible for us to attain.

This was a gift from God and the American Christians to the Russian people in the time of famine for the Word. The deep significance of this production and scattering over Russia of the Word of God will be better understood and appreciated if one remembers that while there was a famine of Scripture, the whole of Russia was being flooded with atheistic literature all the time. It was as though evil forces held back the Bible and poured out all that atheism could devise to pervert the minds of the Russian people, and so one can easily understand the joy of the Russian Christians and their deep gratitude when the Word of God was again available.

During 1922 to 1929 more than 420 young preachers were graduated from our Bible College and sent to the wide field of evangelization in Russia. Undergoing many hardships, these young preachers are working now in the central parts of Russia, in Ukraina, Caucasus, Siberia, the Far East and Turkestan, sowing the seeds of the Gospel. What a great achievement for the Kingdom of God in Russia!

### Journeys in Russia

Being the President of the All-Russian Evangelical Christian Union, I was flooded with requests to visit personally every section of the country. As might have been expected, on my return from mysterious and fascinating America, these invitations multiplied and became more insistent, and it would have been physically impossible to satisfy even a small number of them, even if my entire time were spent in this visitation. However, I made as many journeys as possible, preaching and taking an active part in many of the Conferences.

Trains between Leningrad and Moscow were running pretty satisfactorily at that time. One could take a sleeper at 11.30 P.M. and find himself at Moscow the next morning at 10 o'clock. In visiting Moscow I usually preached either at a very ancient monastery called Sretensky, or at the Temple of Peter and Paul, the gift of the Metropolitan Antonine to our Evangelical Christian movement.

The meetings at both places were crowded. The Gospel message sounded powerfully in the old temples of the Greek Orthodox Church under the shadow of the walls of the ancient Kremlin, within which the Soviet Government was in active control of the affairs of our country.

The fact of these meetings held in such locations would indicate the reality of the Evangelical Reformation in the country of the Greek Orthodox Church, but the real Reformation is taking place in the hearts of hundreds of thousands of the Russian people, who begin to live new lives under the power of the Gospel.

## The Old and New Capitols of Ukraina

On the very insistent invitation of the Evangelical Christian congregations I visited the city of Kharkoff, the new capitol, and Kieff, the old capitol of Ukraina. I preached to crowded meetings arranged in rented theatres. In Kieff there was an enormous open-air meeting on the shore of the Dneiper River, not far from the spot where, many centuries ago, under Prince Vladimir, the first baptism of the Russian people unto Christianity took place.

## I Fulfill My Promise to Siberian Christians

Before the great war I had given my promise to the Siberian churches to visit them, but much as I desired to do so, the way never seemed to open for such a journey. It was only in August, 1927, that I could fufill my promise. On the way to Siberia, in the cities of Viatka, Perm, Tumen and other large places, crowds of Christian believers met me at the stations with a hearty welcome, bringing flowers, greetings and addresses.

The cities of Sverdlovsk (Ekaterinburg), Omsk and Novosibirsk (Novonikolaevsk) were visited. The latter city is the administrative center of Siberia. Here was the seat of the Council of the All-Siberian District of the All-Russian Evangelical Christian Union. The local church had a newly erected wooden meeting house. During my stay there the crowds that gathered for the meetings were so large that the court yard outside the church was used. Many conversions took place.

From Novosibirsk, accompanied by two fellow-workers, I went further to the south and visited the city of Byisk, and still further to the Altai Mountains and the town of Ulala, capitol of the Oisat Autonomus Region. The purpose of this further journey was connected with one important clause of my program.

In all the conferences which I visited I insisted on the necessity of bringing our Gospel principles from the hearts out into practical, every day life, and for this purpose sought to create "The Gospel Standard of Life" in their minds. I feared it would be impossible to realize such a standard of living in the old cities, with their many vices and irregularities and their fixed ways of doing things.

Perhaps some time the Holy Spirit will enable us to fully conquer and make over these cells of the old life, but in the beginning it seemed to me that a suitable place should be found where our ideal of a new life could be realized in the form of a standard city, with standard villages and standard agricultural and industrial enterprises.

I was hopeful that we might find such a favorable location for our plan in the Altai Mountains. The city, when it was founded, we intended to call "The City of the Sun" or "The City of the Gospel". At the confluence of two rivers, the Bya and the Catun, we planted a number of oak trees to mark the place of such a future city. This trip gave me very many important observations, useful for the future.

I am still of the opinion that Siberia, with its unlimited natural resources, may be a country in which the Evangelical Christians will create new forms of a better life for the Russian people and make that vast land a foremost country on the continent.

## To the Caucasus, Home of My Boyhood

In the Caucasus I visited first of all Piatigorsk, where the All-Caucasian Conference of Evangelical Christians took place. After the conference ended the churches in the cities of Kislovodsk, Vladikavkaz, Armavir and Kropotkin were visited. To these seven churches I wrote spiritual poems for their Christian inspiration.

At the Piatigorsk Conference itself and in all these cities, especially at Vladikavkas, among the Russian brethren were seen also the groups of brethren of other nationalities, the Ossets, Kabardinzi, Armenians, Georgians, Gypsies and others.

The power of the Gospel has produced its effect even upon these wild tribes. I saw there the robbers who repented and became new men, good Christians. A really extensive revival was developing among the Ossets, a people who were before that time in a half heathen state. They left off their swords, formerly a fixed part of their equipment, and now they carry Bibles and New Testaments, "The Sword of the Spirit," as their new weapon.

These Ossets live in a country in the center of which is the city of Vladikavkas, the place of my double birth, for here I was born and here I found Jesus Christ and was born again. Naturally I was anxious to visit this home city again, and it delighted me to find that the local Church of Evangelical Christians was prosperous in the Lord. In its meetings prayers in several languages were heard. Brethren of various nationalities there live in harmony, peace and joy. In many meetings in which I participated the repentance and conversion of sinners occurred.

I frequently heard prayers like these: "I have been a robber. My Lord, forgive me"; or, "I have been an atheist. Lord, accept me." I could say with no exaggeration that the work of the Lord in the Caucasus was prosperous.

## To the Province of Veronege, in Central European Russia

At the city of Voronege, the central seat of a large district of our Union, a large local Conference for spiritual fellowship, inspiration and education was called together. I was invited in a most insistent way to be present at this conference.

All these meetings took place in the building of a large Monastery Temple, which was at all times very crowded. The temple became the central meeting place for the Voronege Evangelical Christian Church.

The real result of all these journeys over Russia and Siberia, and my fellowship with our Evangelical Christian brethren, may be summed up in the following words:—

The newly formed district unions or councils, the conferences, the revivals, the crowded meetings, the repenting sinners, the beaming joyful faces of our Christian believers — all these and many other observations made during my long journeys have strengthened my conviction that the spiritual awakening of Russia is spreading immensely.

# CHAPTER XXVIII

### 1923 to 1929

## "Dry Bones Begin to Stir"

### Mission Work During this Period

*"Behold, I will cause breath to enter into you, and ye shall live."*  Ezek. 37 : 5.

I HAVE already mentioned that from the very formation of our Union I gave to our workers the slogan: "From city to city, from town to town, from village to village, from farm to farm, from man to man, day by day and hour by hour."

The laws of the Soviet Government concerning religious matters were now more or less favorable, and I endeavored to inspire my fellow-workers with a special zeal to preach the Gospel with multiplied energy, a work which was very successful during this period. By the great sufferings of the world war, civil war and the famine the hearts of the people were prepared for acceptance of the Gospel.

We ourselves were on fire with enthusiasm and strained all our energies to send missionaries to every possible corner of the vast country. The result was that the Gospel message was carried to all classes of the Russian people, workmen, peasants, the educated class, and even to the clergy of the old State Church.

*The workingmen* of Russia have been the chief class to whom atheism and materialism were preached. They were supposed to be the most susceptible to such teaching, but the Gospel message has found a ready response in their hearts and there has been a rich harvest of souls among them, particularly in the industrial districts of Russia. At the present time we have in many places quite large congregations composed entirely of workmen. How much they are interested may be illustrated by the following story.

Among the workmen employed in a factory in a certain town not far from Leningrad was an Evangelical Christian. He never lost an opportunity to speak often and openly of his faith. One day a fellow-workman said to him:

"We want to hear more about this Gospel."

"Very well," replied the Christian. "Come to our meetings."

"No," answered the other, "We have no time to attend your meetings. We want to hear you now."

### Workman Preaches in a Factory

So, in order that the workmen might all hear, the factory was shut down. The Christian brother climbed on top of one of the machines and began to preach the Gospel. He continued for nearly one hour. Then they started up the machinery and went back to work.

When the official papers of the Government got the story they expressed great indignation, saying that the Christian evangelists turn the factories into religious meeting places and hinder production. However, the essential thing is that the Russian workman is intensely interested in the message of the Gospel.

The same thing may be said of *the Russian peasants* as a class. They number around 100,000,000 and constitute the great majority of the Russian population.

Sometimes it has happened that I sent a missionary to a certain village district for two weeks, and after five or six weeks I received a letter from him telling me something like this:

"Brother Ivan Stepanovich: I am a captive of the Gospel. They take me from one village to another and I do not know where I will stop or when I will be able to return."

### The Gospel Displaces Theories of Atheism

The Gospel also brought a powerful influence to bear upon the *educated classes* of the Russian people. They have been under the domination of the materialistic and atheistic philosophies of Western Europe, but the rising tide of revolution has made them realize that the theories of atheism were not satisfying in the bitter throes of human antagonism and strife engendered by such beliefs. Hence they have naturally become interested in religious questions. Some of them in their conversions resembled that of Saul of Tarsus.

Encouraging results were achieved with the Cheremisi, Chuvashi, Mordva and others from the Finnish northland; also the Tartars, Ossets and more in the south. We had Evangelical churches formed of Georgians and Armenians in the Transcaucasus District.

## Congregations of Russian Christian Jews

Not less important results were recorded as the result of our ministry among the Russian Jews. It is not uncommon to hear of individual Jews being converted to Christ, but one does not hear of Jewish Christian congregations. It is only in Russia that they are to be found, in Odessa, Kieff and other places.

It is worthy of more than passing notice that a tremendous change has swept over the Mohammedans in Russia. Their fanaticism is proverbial. Before the revolution the person who dared to preach Christ among their people would forfeit his life, and also those who had listened to him. Today there is a difference. In some places in Russia the Mohammedans have invited the Evangelical preachers to speak in their mosques about Jesus Christ.

Observing the wonderful progress of the Gospel during these years, its triumphs among all classes of the Russian people, including the clergy and among all the nationalities and tribes of my country, it seemed to me that during this short but eventful period from 1923 to 1929 the Evangelical movement was transformed into a national Gospel Reformation. In every place I visited there were evidences of the wide spread of the Gospel, with groups of new converts being organized into Evangelical Christian Congregations. The Lord has given me great comfort and joy in thus being able to see in my own country the fulfillment of my program, and the answer to my prayers, even in the time when atheism seems to control the government.

From the very beginning of the Evangelical movement the practical side of Christianity has been emphasized. Faith, to be followed by good works, was the principle lying close to the leaders' hearts. In order to express this principle in the clearest possible way, I wrote a short statement about "The Gospel Standard of Life", which was accepted unanimously and enthusiastically adopted by the All-Russian Evangelical Christian Conference of 1926. Here are the main principles:

### The Gospel Standard of Life in Russia

1. The broad underlying principle that every Evangelical Christian in Russia should be an *example* to all in every sphere of his life (1 Tim. 4:12), not only in his personal behaviour, but in his conduct in family, social, business and educational life.

2. That his conduct must be based upon the precepts of Jesus Christ concerning his love for God and His Word, his neighbors and his enemies. The highest aim of his life should be to reproduce the character of Christ. Instead of the world's principle of action: "homo homini lupus est" (man is a wolf to another man), the true Christian should be actuated by the principle which Christ enunciated: "A man is a *brother* to another man."

3. The Gospel should bring its influence to bear upon Science. Evangelical Christians must acquire all the scientific knowledge possible, either for themselves or their children, or to take part in the development and extension of scientific achievements. There should not be among us even one illiterate man or woman. (This rule is already being enforced, those who join our ranks being taught to read and write if they cannot do so.) All members, both parents and children must try to secure the highest education commensurate with their means.

4. The Gospel must find expression in the development of the arts, such as literature, music, architecture, printing and sculpture.

5. The Gospel must influence man's practical life. Two features are especially important:

IN THE CAULDRON OF RUSSIA

To improve all branches of industry by inventing and applying newer methods of work. The Gospel must have its effect upon agricultural pursuits. That is to say, the Christian farmers and cattle owners should exercise themselves to grow the very best farm products and raise the healthiest cattle. The Gospel apples, the Gospel wheat, the Gospel fowls are to be the best as compared with any others.

6. The houses of the believers in the villages should be surrounded with beautiful landscaping. Terraces in the front and the kitchen garden in the rear to give a pleasing effect to the eye. Flowers in profusion should be grown inside and outside and near by should be built houses for the birds. Order and beauty everywhere, that is the Christian way.

7. It is imperative that the dwelling places of the Christian believers must be noted for their cleanliness; built according to the plans described above; painted with bright colors and ornamented within by the use of Scripture verses.

8. Marriage between Evangelical Christians should take place at an early date.

9. Continually abstaining from everything superfluous and injurious to the health. Alcohol, even in the milder forms of drink, must not be used. The younger generation in particular must be taught the pernicious effects of alcohol on the body.

10. Great care should be exercised with regard to our fellow-believers, to the end "that not any among them shall lack." (Acts 4:34.)

This experience is possible of attainment only by the indwelling Holy Spirit, daily reading of the Word of God and prayerful fellowship with Christ, who said: "Without me ye can do nothing." (John 15:15.) Also, the exercising of a strong faith, "by which all things are possible." (Mark 9:27.)

Not only the All-Russian Evangelical Christian Conference in Leningrad, but all the provincial conferences, about seventy, adopted the resolutions about the continuation in the development of this standard of life, using all the methods of the Church discipline.

238

## CHAPTER XXIX

## My New Journey Abroad

*"When they had eaten up the corn which they had brought . . . their father said unto them: Go again."*
Gen. 43:2.

TOWARD the end of my eighteen months stay in Russia, we decided that the development of the Evangelical movement was so large that special measures must be taken to meet its needs. It was clear that we must print more Bibles and New Testaments, as those printed were by far insufficient. Funds were needed for further support of our missionary program, and we were also in great need of a building for our Bible College.

It seemed necessary for me to visit America again. The Council of the Union began to plead before the authorities to get a permit for my journey. After eighteen months of effort the permit was received, in May, 1928. Within three days I left Leningrad in the direction of the Estonian town of Kingiseppe. Before departing on this uncertain journey I had meetings of the Council of the Church, the Council of the Union and a crowded solemn meeting in the Swedish Church, at which about 1500 people were present.

In all the meetings fervent prayers were sent forth to the Most High for blessings on my second journey, and I was asked to greet in the names of the Russian believers all the children of God whom I should meet in my travel. I intended to return soon, but the Lord extended my stay abroad. On the way from Leningrad to the Estonian frontier in my talks with two brethren, members of the Union Council who accompanied me to the border, I reminded them of the substance of my talks with my fellow-workers in the last farewell meetings.

I mentioned again to them the fact which they very well knew, the amazing development of the Evangelical move-

239

ment in Russia during the last fourteen years, and once more said: All that has happened can be defined by the words of the Apostle Paul: "All things work together for good to them that love God." (Rom. 8:28.)

The moment came when I had to leave the Leningrad train. My passport was taken by the officials of the G. P. U. (State Political Board) and my baggage was taken to the station to be inspected by the custom house officials. We prayed, thanking the Lord for great things he had done for the spreading of His Word; then we prayed for one another, that He might keep us as in the hollow of His hand, but especially we prayed for the vast country of Russia, that the Lord may consumate in it His work of spiritual regeneration and resurrection of the millions of human souls. According to the Russian Christian custom, we kissed each other on either cheek and parted.

After all the necessary formalities I was permitted to again enter the same train, which soon started. I gazed from the window and saw my brethren standing in the station, waving their handkerchiefs and shouting:

"God be with you!" Those words sounded in a special way at this station, where all the officials and soldiers were supposed to be atheists and where officially there was no God.

I replied also, in a loud voice: "God be with you." Whether men desire Him or not, He is ever near them, "Our God, the Father of all, is over all and through all . . ." (Eph. 4:6.)

Evangelical Christian District Conference in the Caucasus. Participated in by the Osetts (See page 232)

I. S. Prokhanoff with the Kiev District Council of Evangelical Christians    (See page 230)

# CHAPTER XXX

## Why Has the Evangelical Movement Had Such Success in Russia?

*"All things work together for good to them that love God."* —*Rom. 8 : 28.*

A S I look back, analyzing the events of the past fifteen years, I cannot but see that every incident, every hindrance, even persecutions and imprisonments, served definitely and positively for the growth of the Evangelical Christian Movement in Russia. Many of these events were sad, and even tragic, but nevertheless they added to the development of the Kingdom in my country. They happened only by the will of God. He planned that all these things should work for good.

1. How the World War worked for good.

Let us take the terrible World War with Germany. We cannot describe the suffering, misery and evil that it brought to the world at large. But at the same time it helped the spreading of the Gospel in a wonderful way.

The young Evangelicals taken to the army for service met there many other young men of all kinds of creeds and no creed, from all parts of Russia. As the Evangelicals usually read the Bible, sing and pray in their barracks, it attracted the attention of other soldiers. Our members became evangelists on the spot, reading to them the Scripture and explaining the way of salvation. This resulted in the conversion of many soldiers, who after the war returned to their villages, began to preach the Gospel there, and thus founded new groups and congregations of believers where the people had never heard anything about the Gospel.

About 2,000,000 Russian soldiers were taken as prisoners of war by Germany and Austria. This opportunity was seized by the Russian preachers and missionary societies to organize a wide work of evangelization among them. Meetings with preaching of the Word of God were arranged in every camp of the war prisoners. Having nothing to do, many soldiers came to these meetings who would not otherwise have heard the Gospel preached. A great many conversions took place, and even Bible classes were arranged for the training of the new Gospel workers. The new converts returned to their homes with the Gospel message also, like their brother soldiers who had not been in prison, resulting in the foundation of still more congregations of Evangelical Christians, even in remote parts of our country.

## Hearts Receptive to the Word of God

The soldiers in the war, and especially those in the prison camps, were in such a spiritual condition that their hearts were receptive to the Word of God. Such opportunities to preach to great multitudes of Russian young men could not have been brought about in any other way or time or in other circumstances so favorable as this. Surely the evil is transformed by God into good for those who love Him and whom He loves.

The Revolution and the civil war which followed the world war brought great suffering to the Russian people. Millions perished in that terrible time. But it was a very favorable period for spreading the Gospel, especially the period from 1917 to 1929.

2. All Calamities were also favorable.

The great calamities of the period from 1917 to 1922; the unparalleled famine in 1920-21, and the epidemics of typhus and cholera were times of ingathering for many souls. It is a law of human nature that if man lives under comfortable and satisfactory physical and mental conditions he is inclined to be neglectful of God. But in times of suffering or difficulty he begins to think about God, and to cry out and pray to Him. The sufferings of this period brought the Russian people to the consciousness that it is very hard to live without God, and the hearts of many instinctively began to draw nearer to Him and thus became ready to accept the Gospel message, so that they heard the Word with gladness and believed unto their own salvation.

3. Good was worked also within the Greek Orthodox Church by some changes which took place during this period, viz.:

a. The separation of the Church from the State.

A protected, supported State Church, self-satisfied and complacent, neglects the work of preaching the Gospel and is careless of its responsibility for the human souls. After the separation of the Greek Orthodox Church from the State it lost its former political power and this source of persecutions was eliminated. Only after this separation was a real religious liberty possible, and only then did the priests of the church awake to their responsibility toward the members of their congregations.

b. The elemination of some myths.

### Worship of Dead Saints

Very often when the people heard the preaching of the Gospel and were willing to accept it, under the influence of the stories of their priests they used to say:

"All this is very good, but you have not what our Orthodox Church has, 'the holy relics of saints.'" The Greek Orthodox Church and also the Roman Catholic Church taught that the bodies of their saints are not corruptible and so remain for centuries perfectly preserved in their coffins.

Every Orthodox Church had holy relics of some kind. There were big monasteries which contained numbers of such holy relics of dead bodies of saints, before which by tens of thousands the people used to come from all parts of the country to worship.

The priests fostered the idea among the people that they could receive healing, blessing and even forgiveness of sins by such acts of worship. Really it was a kind of fetishism, or idol worship, and a great tragedy in many lives. Millions of people, called Christians, were worshippers of these relics, supposedly the perfectly preserved bodies of Saints of the Church. This was a great barrier to the acceptance of the Gospel. After the revolution something happened which almost entirely eliminated this hindrance.

## Elimination of the Church Relics

The Soviet Government did what no other Government had dared to do in ordering the opening of all the coffins containing the "holy relics." This opening took place officially, and in a lawful order, not as a sacrilege, but to confirm or forever refute the assertions of the priesthood.

In every city where the churches or monasteries had popular relics special committees were appointed, consisting of the bishop, priests, representatives of the workmen, peasants, law courts and police. The opening of each coffin was performed by the bishop, with the help of the priests. After the opening special minutes describing the contents of each casket were written and signed by all present, under orders from the Government.

What were the results? In all cases there was found something quite different from what the people had been told —not perfectly preserved bodies of saints, but only bones. Then the open coffins were put in the churches for the people to see. Naturally the worship of relics almost ceased from that time.

There may be different opinions regarding this action by the atheists, but nevertheless the results of opening those coffins, which became known throughout Russia, produced a very strong impression on the masses of the Russian people. They saw now that what had been called incorruptible was really corruptible.

## The Priests Attempt to Explain

In some places the priests told various stories in order to escape the odium of their deception, and one of them was that the saints, when they saw the atheists approaching to examine their relics, fled to heaven and left their bones behind. But the people would not believe such stories, and thus faith in the sacred treasures of the Greek Orthodox Church was lost, the worship of relics was considerably reduced and even stopped. One great obstacle to the evangelization of the Russian people was thus removed by the atheists.

 c. Some specific doctrines of the Greek Orthodox Church helped immensely.

In Russia the Greek Orthodox Church had taught for centuries that a man is justified by his "works", and also under the name of "works" understood the Church virtues: fasting, ascetic exercises and church contributions. Millions of souls sought their salvation in that direction, pouring into the coffers of the Church gold, silver and precious stones without stint.

I can testify from personal observation to their ascetic attempt to gain salvation, for I saw sights that I shall never forget. In the city of St. Petersburg I saw a man walking barefooted and with no cap on his head on a very cold winter day. In such cold any man would be expected to get sick and die, but he seemed not to suffer from it. If you asked him, why he was doing it, his reply would have been: "Of course, for my salvation."

In the Caucasus, my native country, not very far from the town of Vladikavkas, on the famous mountain Kazbek, there was an old Georgian Monastery. In the month of August every year hundreds of pilgrims came to that place to worship a famous ikon, a very old "holy image" of a saint. I myself saw how many of those pilgrims were creeping up the bare slopes of the mountain at the risk of falling into the abyss below.

Ask any of them why they came to the monastery, and why they climbed those slopes at such an awful risk, and they would have said to you the same thing: "For the salvation of our souls."

## Monks and Relics in the Old Monastery

On one occasion I made a visit to the very old Kievo-Pechersky Monastery of Kieff, in Ukraina, in which there were many relics of saints, lying in coffins in the long underground caves. A great many people used to come to that monastery to worship those relics.

Following our guide through those tunnels I saw many coffins with the holy relics, and also something still more remarkable. In the walls were small windows, through which were to be seen the pale faces of men. The monk explained that those were monks who decided to spend their whole life until death called them in cells in these stony caves. If you asked these monks what was their purpose in enduring such a hard existence in these horrible surroundings, you would have received the same reply: "For our salvation."

In the beginning of the World War with Germany I read in the newspapers that the German troops took possession of a Russian monastery in the Polish provinces. Among many other discoveries they found there three coffins with a live monk in each one. When asked why they were living in the coffins, they answered: "For the salvation of our souls." The three monks were ordered to leave their coffins, but they would not do so voluntarily.

Among the Greek Orthodox monks there were also some "pillar saints," who stood for a number of years and until nearly the time of their death, on a pedestal, "for the salvation of their souls."

### "Who Can Say That He Is Saved?"

All these men committed great feats of asceticism for one purpose: To work out their own salvation. But if you approached any one of them and said: "You believe that this is required for your salvation. *Are you saved?*" you would see a look of great surprise on their faces. They would surely have replied: "Who can say that he is saved? It would be a great arrogance, a presumption."

Is it not a tragedy! The greatest tragedy that has ever taken place in the world. Hundreds of millions of men and women deprived themselves of food, of comforts of life, and endured all kinds of hardships for the one single purpose of working out the salvation of their souls, and they died without any hope or assurance, with despair in their hearts, for they had no clear knowledge of their salvation.

Yes, it was a religion of pessimism, hopelessness and despair. But now the unlearned man, the workman and the peasant comes to these souls and reads to them: "Man is not justified by the works of the law, but by faith in Jesus Christ." — Gal. 2:16.

## A Religion of Everlasting Optimism

Like the rays of the sun, shining through the windows, this truth penetrates into the dark closets of the souls of these hopeless toilers, and they pass from a state of despair into the state of bright hope, from deadly pessimism into the light of optimism of the faith, for the real religion of Jesus Christ is the religion of everlasting optimism.

Here are two illustrations of how this great truth works miracles:

One of our missionaries informed me of an experience which he passed through in a certain village in the north of European Russia, where he was holding evangelistic meetings. After one meeting was over he was told that near this village, in an adjacent wood, there was a man who wanted to get salvation by his own method. This man had been a soldier in the war. There he had met another soldier who told him that if he wanted to have salvation he must return home, forsake his wife and his family, go to a wood or forest and live there. Together with other brethren, our missionary went to the wood, where he saw, in a kind of a cave or pit, a man in rags, pale and gaunt.

## Aescetic Abandons His Cave for Home

The missionary told the man that his salvation was not to be found in such a place as that, in a cave or pit, but on the hill of Calvary, where His Saviour was crucified. To this the man replied: "God sent you to me." He at once accepted the Gospel and left his cave and went back to his family.

Another missionary of our Union told me that a fellow messenger of the Gospel came to a village and held there evangelistic meetings. The people told the Evangelist of another man who was trying to save himself. When the

247

missionary came to the place he saw a man with an iron chain around his body which was bound so tightly that blood was flowing from the wounds made by it.

Our brother said to this man that there was no reason for him to wear this chain since his salvation was secured by the Saviour, who bought with His blood freedom for him. That man accepted the message of salvation in Christ, became saved and threw away his chain.

Many similar facts could be brought as evidence of the miraculous working of the truth of salvation upon the hearts of sinners by faith in Jesus Christ. The glorious contents of this truth and the power of it are the principle causes of the success of the Evangelical movement. The wrong doctrine of the established Church in this regard made of despairing hearts fertile ground for the Gospel, bringing hope in the place of despair.

## How Could Atheism Spread the Gospel!

4. Atheism helped the Evangelical Movement.

Atheism itself aided in the spreading of the Evangelical movement in Russia. This may seem to be a paradox, but it is absolutely true. As is known, atheism came to Russia together with communism and bolshevism. At first the Russian people thought that atheism was a kind of philosophy, but after observations and experiences, they concluded that atheism is a kind of emptiness, a vacuum, in which no real life is possible.

At first, under decrees issued by Lenin and the communistic party, atheism could be propagated in Russia only by peaceful means, i.e., by arranging meetings, lectures and debates; by spreading literature, tracts, books and periodicals. They printed their magazine, *The Atheist,* in great quantities, but soon were compelled to reduce it considerably for the people would not buy it. This periodical was bought, however, by the priests, pastors, preachers and missionaries, because it contained caricatures of these religious workers, which the men themselves enjoyed looking at. I also used to buy it, because frequently it contained my own caricature.

# CALAMITIES ADVANCE THE GOSPEL

I was pictured as a very stout man with a sack of dollars and with an inscription: "The representative of the bourgeoisie and capitalism."

## Free Advertising Brought Many Inquiries

After such caricatures appeared in *The Atheist* we usually received letters asking us to send our literature. It was in this way that atheism helped us in spreading the Gospel and enlarging our spiritual labors. It was really good advertising for our movement and undoubtedly was a source of new converts.

The atheists were very fond of arranging so-called anti-religious debates in the largest halls, filled with crowds of people. Usually the first speakers railed against God, religion and moral law. After them the defenders of religion were allowed to speak.

The audiences at these meetings usually interrupted the Evangelical speakers and other defenders of religion with applause and made for them great ovations at the end of the debates. Usually the people surrounded our Evangelical speakers and asked for the addresses of our churches. As a result, new hearers filled our meetings.

## The Atheists Confess Their Failure

Very soon the leaders of atheism began to realize that their propagation work brought results quite the opposite of what they aimed at, aiding our work instead of their own. In 1927 the atheists had their congress or conference at Moscow. One of their leaders made a report about their activities, in which he said that the results were most deplorable,—instead of the destruction of religion, assistance to it. As an illustration he mentioned an occurrence in Odessa.

He said that before the atheists came there with their propaganda the religious bodies lived in a condition of mutual strife, but when the atheists came all the religious bodies united and began to attack the atheists. In this way, he said, we do not destroy religion but strengthen it. Of course, from our standpoint it could not be otherwise. Atheism, consisting

249

of various denials of God, the immortal soul and conscience and moral law, cannot give to the people and their souls anything positive. The hearts of the Russian people, with their mysterious seeking after God, cannot accept the atheistic doctrine.

A new psychological condition was created in the minds of millions of the Russian people. On the one hand they were disappointed in the old system of the Greek Orthodox Church; on the other hand they had no desire to accept the new system of atheism.

## The Spiritual Hunger Was Unsatisfied

They desired to find the living religion of Christ, the religion of the Gospel and the New Testament, which was hitherto unknown to them. Probably no nation on the earth or in the history of the Christian Church, was so ready for the spiritual harvest as the Russian people, with their long centuries of seeking after God, unsatisfied by the deceptive methods I have described.

To no other nation can be applied with such fitness the the words of Jesus Christ: "Look on the fields, for they are white already to harvest."—John 4:35.

5. The laws of the new regime also helped the development of the Evangelical Movement.

During the period from 1917 to 1927, in spite of the fact that many religious leaders suffered (I myself being twice in prison), there was a large amount of religious liberty. Various laws were issued by the new Government favorable for religious activities, for arranging religious meetings and conferences; for sending out missionaries, for the publishing of religious literature and for the founding of Bible Schools. The most striking of these laws undoubtedly was the decree regarding liberation from military service on the basis of religious convictions. It was such a broad law that nothing like it has ever been carried out in any state on earth, and all the more wonderful because it was issued by an atheistic government.

## CALAMITIES ADVANCE THE GOSPEL

### Growth of Our Evangelical Movement

Under favorable laws it was possible for us to develop our missions, publishing and Bible educational work. We occupied the time to the utmost of our ability, and have every reason to thank God for the results attained, for souls won, for real knowledge of the Scripture, and also for the time to train those fine young preachers and missionaries who are now devoting their lives to His service. Though there is persecution and hindrance again, even as in the days of the old State Church, the Holy Spirit is working, and there is still the promise as of old:

"So shall my word be that goeth forth out of my mouth: it shall not return unto me void, but it shall accomplish that which I please, and it shall prosper in the thing whereunto I sent it."—Isaiah 55:11.

In Russia generally and at Leningrad in particular we often lived through very trying times. I frequently saw around me the gloomy faces of my fellow-workers. All were filled with trouble and apprehension. In these moments the optimism of faith helped me in a wonderful way. I usually stood up and said in a loud voice:

*"All things work together for good to those who love the Lord."*

Looking back over this period even as far as nineteen years, to the darkest days of persecution and exile for those who dissented from the old Greek Orthodox Church, and scanning all my own past, I can say with a deep sense of satisfaction and gratitude to the Lord:

"Yes, all things, including my arrests, worked for good in our labor of spreading the Gospel in Russia through the Evangelical movement. Greek Orthodoxy, Revolution, atheism and bolshevism alike plowed the soil of Russia, but they could not sow the seed which brought forth fruit unto righteousness. The messengers of the Gospel were the sowers, and the sowing is even now being followed by a glorious harvest. So I say: Glory be to Him who alone doeth wondrous things, for even the evil men would do was transformed into good.

# CHAPTER XXXI

## The Great Persecution
### (Beginning with 1929.)

*"In all these things we are more than conquerors
through Him that loved us."*    *Rom. 8 : 37.*

HAVING left Russia in May, 1928, I intended to return
within less than a year, but various lectures, meetings
and conferences delayed me too long.  On April 8, 1929,
while I was in Germany, a decree was issued in Russia which
considerably restricted the activities of religious societies, and
since that date a severe persecution of Christians was begun.

I soon received letters of appeal from suffering brethren,
asking for help.  These appeals were multiplied as the needs
over there grew, and I understood it to be the will of God
that I should remain abroad and try to organize continuous
help for the sufferers through their time of trouble.

What is happening now in the religious life of my country
since the alteration of the religious freedom decree?  An
actual persecution of all the religious denominations and
organizations.  Why did the Soviet Government change its
attitude with regard to the religious question, transforming
their comparative toleration into this severe persecution?

### Abolishing Religion from the Heart by Decree

As everybody in Russia knows, it was done under the
pressure of the Union of Militant Atheists.  The Atheists
have now declared a five-year program for the stamping out
of all religion in Russia (1932-37).  Before the above decree
was issued, the activities of the atheists were governed
definitely by the same laws under which all religious societies
labored.  According to resolutions of the Conferences of the
Communistic party, atheism could be propagated only by
peaceful methods, exactly the same as those which we were
permitted to make use of in spreading the Gospel,—by ar-

ranging lectures, meetings and debates and by publishing all kinds of literature.

The atheists were hopefully using their propaganda methods up to 1929, but, as I indicated previously, with negative results. Realizing their moral defeat, the atheists began to seek another method of struggling against religion. This they found in the old forms of oppression and persecution as practiced by the State Church before the days of separation. Becoming now a state-supported institution— *the State religion, in fact* — atheism is in a position to use the same tactics as the Greek Orthodox State Church formerly practiced to compel adherence to its tenets and at the same time to use pressure against all forms of true worship of the God they insist does not exist. Since they could not prosper and increase under the methods which they allowed to the Christians, they have reverted to means familiar to early martyrs in Rome, the days of the Reformation and known to the Evangelical Christians in Russia in the days of the Czar and the State Church.

### Three Methods of Atheistic Persecution

1. *Elimination of Places of Worship.*

The atheists began with closing the temples, monasteries, mosques, synagogues, prayer houses, meeting halls and places of worship. Many were converted into theatres, motion picture halls and business shops. We Evangelical Christians had in Leningrad seventeen places of worship, sixteen of which were closed. Only one hall was left open, a place holding up to 1000 people, but it is entirely too small for our people in that city.

The same thing has happened with our churches at Moscow and other cities. All the denominations have been subjected to the same restriction. Of course, atheism can have as many meeting places as it desires!

2. *Removal of Religious Leaders.*

A great many priests, pastors, ministers, preachers and active religious workers were arrested and exiled to the North of Russia or to Siberia. Many of them are in hard

253

labor camps under the most distressing conditions, suffering from the terrible cold in winter, starvation and the brutality of their guards. Sickness and death are the all too common result.

One can imagine something of what this means to their families! Wives and children are left without homes or means of subsistence. Hundreds of Evangelical preachers and missionaries are now going through this terrible experience in Russia.

3. *Deprivation of Food.*

The third method is perhaps the most terrible of all. All priests, pastors, preachers and missionaries, and even active members of the churches, are by a special decree deprived of their food cards and bread cards. Under the present condition it means actual starvation for all religious workers and their families, since there is no money for the purchase of food at the Government or private stores.

This makes of the present atheistic persecution in Russia a condition unparalleled in history of the Christian Church. Even the Roman Emperors did not deprive Christians, as a class of population, of means of existence.

### Great Mortality Among the Christians

All the above measures of persecution have resulted in a great mortality among the suffering Christians and their families. Their present lot is simply indescribable!

What is the relation of the Christian believers to this persecution? There are some Christian friends here in America, and in Europe also, who say that surely under this system of persecution religion has been strangled and wiped out in Russia, and no more religious activities are possible there. But this point of view is altogether incorrect.

When did persecution ever stop the spread of the Gospel? What was the condition in the first century of the Christian Church? If somebody acknowledged allegiance to Christ in those times he would be thrown to the lions and tigers in the arena of the amphitheatre or made into a torch to light the games at night. Nevertheless Christianity was never so widely spread or made comparatively so many converts as in the first century. The Christians, being unable to conduct open meetings, gathered secretly in the catacombs and continued the work of God.

The same thing is happening in Russia today. Although the persecution is extremely severe, the Gospel is being spread by secret means with great success. In the hearts of the Evangelical Christians in Russia now the same faith is to be found which was in the hearts of the Apostles and the early Christians, the faith which overcomes the world and gains victory through Jesus Christ.

This faith gives a perseverence in preaching the Gospel, at all times and everywhere. Their motto is: "Every Evangelical Christian a missionary!" They preach the Gospel in their homes, in their offices, in factories, in street cars and in the trains.

## Transferring Missionaries to New Fields

If the atheists discover that a certain man is too zealous in the preaching of the Gospel, they put him into prison or send him away in exile, and assure themselves that his preaching will be stopped, but of course they are mistaken. They have merely transferred him to a new field of action, given him a new group to whom he can witness as long as life remains.

All the Evangelical Christians have come to look upon the prison and exile camps as the best places for preaching the Gospel, because there are usually more sinners there. Many cases are being recorded where, through the testimony of our brethren, the criminals were converted and became good Christians. The Evangelical preachers cannot be silenced because of imprisonment nor is the testimony of any believer thus stopped.

In a provincial city one of our preachers was arrested for his zealous way of spreading the Gospel. He was put into a cell where there were twenty-six other prisoners. Of course, he did not cease his usual activity. Once the jail warden, passing through the corridor and hearing strange sounds, opened the door to that cell and looked in. What did he see!

The greater part of the prisoners were on their knees. It was a prayer meeting arranged among the prisoners by our brother, with many of them taking part. The warden was very excited. "How does this come about?" he exclaimed. "A prayer meeting in a Soviet prison!"

Our brother was immediately transferred by the warden to a cell of solitary confinement. Here he soon learned that there were prisoners in the adjacent cell, hearing their voices in conversation. Finding that the partition between the cells was of wood, he bored a hole in the wall and began to talk to the prisoners about Jesus Christ and His teaching. He also passed through the hole to them Bible texts written on scraps of paper. One day the same warden opened the cell for examination, and was astonished to see that hole in the wall through which our brother had been preaching the Gospel. He exclaimed:

"The Evangelist is a better propagator than we communists!" He did not know what to do with such a persistent prisoner. Nothing apparently can stop a Russian Evangelical preacher from bringing his testimony to Jesus Christ. If it becomes necessary, he is ready to bring a sacrifice for that privilege. The faith which was in the hearts of the Apostles still lives in the lives of those who have heard the call to "Go and tell" today, and the Holy Spirit gives the same power as He did in the days of Peter and Paul.

### Gives His Life for the Gospel's Sake

In my congregation at Leningrad there was a young brother by the name of Arseny, who came to see me one day and said:—

"Brother Ivan Stepanovich! I feel the Lord calls me to Siberia to preach the Gospel!"

"Very well," I said, "if it is the call of God you must go by all means. We will help you as we are able, with prayer and support."

Arseny went to one of the cities in the central part of

Evangelical Choirs of Sebastopol and Simferopol

**Brother Arseny's Funeral**  (See page 257)

Siberia. On his arrival he was told that the atheists were arranging there a series of anti-religious debates, and exclaimed:

"I will go there and defend the faith of the Gospel!"

For three nights Arseny spoke in those debates and produced such an impression that the audience frequently interrupted his speeches by applause. At the end of the debate he was usually the object of an ovation. On the fourth night an atheist came to his landlady and said:

"Tell Arseny that he should not come any more to our debates. Otherwise something will happen to him!"

On the next morning the landlady told these words to Arseny, but he said: "Whatever may happen, I will go to the debates and will fulfill there my duty!"

Eye-witnesses tell that on his last night Arseny spoke with special power and his face was shining like that of an angel. The audience was more than ever carried away by his testimony and made a great ovation as the meeting closed. But three young men came and took Arseny away.

## The Victory Which Overcometh the World

In the morning our brethren found him dead in the snow near the railroad station. He was in a half-kneeling position, with the New Testament in his hands. He was shot while praying. Is not this an illustration of the words of Jesus Christ:

"Be thou faithful unto death, and I will give thee a crown of life!" Surely it is the faith of such heroes which produces the power for spiritual victories. In the first centuries of the Christian Church there was a severe battle between heathenism and Christianity. Christianity was victorious. The same power produces the same result in our day. The victory which overcometh the world is still the faith of the Gospel.

From the standpoint of the teaching of Jesus Christ the persecution is not an evil. It is a means of spiritual purification of the Church, a power to increase the zeal of His witnesses, a trial of our faith, a school of patience in tribulation, and endurance even unto death.

"The blood of the martyrs has ever been the seed of the Church!"

The atheists think that by their persecution they will soon extinguish the Evangelical movement and bring it to a standstill, having even set a definite date for its end.

How surprising that these people, who pretend to be so conversant with all things material, are unacquainted with history! If they actually knew what the definite result of their persecution will be they would never have chosen such means in their effort to advance atheism and banish religion from Russia. Their persecution is like a wind which fans the flame. Instead of stamping religion out, they are aiding in its development. The believers in Russia who are suffering under the present persecution very well know that after atheism has done its utmost the Gospel movement will be found to have developed and grown while they suffered for Christ's sake. This optimism of faith has many times been justified in the history of the Christian Church and will be justified in Russia now.

*"This is the victory that overcometh the world, even our faith."*—1 John 5:4.

## The Spirit of Optimism Remains

While I am away from Russia and my beloved country is passing through the valley of great tribulation as I write the closing words of my autobiography, I am still possessed of a strong spirit of optimism regarding the future of the Gospel in Russia and for the final victory of the Evangelical movement. Should this book be received with favor sufficient to warrant a second edition, it may well be that in the reprinting I shall have additional events to record. History is not standing still and great changes may occur at any time in Russia, making possible my return to Leningrad, or Petrograd or to St. Petersburg.

———•———

# CHAPTER XXXII

## Russian Christian Message to All Christians

*"The watchman shall lift up the voice."*
*Isa. 52 : 8.*

AFTER I had written the previous chapter, I asked my-self: "How shall I finish this book of mine?" and answered at once: "I shall finish it as I began." On the first page I laid out my message, as the result of my life slogan, "The Optimism of Faith." But I desire to express the final message not in my own words, but with a message from my fellow-workers.

In the year 1928, when I was preparing to leave Russia for my journey to America and some of the European countries, I desired especially to take a message to Western Christians from the struggling Russian Evangelical Christians. Therefore we wrote a special letter of appeal to all the Christian denominations and churches in the whole world. It was entitled *"The Resurrection Call,"* and summons the Christians of the World to a more glorious life in Christ Jesus, even as I summoned the old Greek Orthodox Church in Russia to throw off her shackles of ritualism, tradition and fetishism.

The Russian Christians have had a unique experience under persecution at the hands of a ruling atheistic government. Nowhere else is the battle so hot between atheism and Christianity. As the early Christians during their persecution in Rome and elsewhere might have written, indeed, did write, messages of faith and hope and cheer to the whole world, even so the Russian Christians now call out to their fellow-believers throughout Christendom.

Many of our believers live in the remotest parts of that great land of Siberia. They are separated from the Western Christians, even those of Europe, by thousands of miles, and

259

nearly half way around the earth from the Christians of America. Nevertheless, amidst their trials and persecutions, they think of and pray for the Western Christians.

The chief appeal of their prayer is the great spiritual revival which they ask God to send to the people of Europe and America.

"The Resurrection Call" from which I have made excerpts below, is the expression of what my Russian Evangelical Christian brethren would say to every Christian brother throughout the world. The reader will find in this message not only outward characteristics of the Russian Christendom in all their persecution by the old State Church and now by atheism, but also its spiritual life, which has enabled it to go through the fires of tribulation steadfast and true to Him Who gave His life for us all.

———•••———

# All-Russian Union of Evangelical Christians

## Our Resurrection Call[1]

*Blow ye the trumpet in the land.*
*Jeremiah 4 : 5.*

*Awake thou that sleepest and arise from the dead, and Christ shall give thee light.* *Ephesians 5 : 14.*

*The work is great and large, and we are separated upon the wall, one far from another. In what place therefore ye hear the sound of the trumpet, resort ye thither unto us: our God shall fight for us.*
*Nehemiah 4 : 19-20.*

To all the Christian Churches and denominations in the world:

OUT of the depths of a land which, from the viewpoint of size, embraces a considerable part of Europe and Asia, and constitutes one-sixth of the entire surface of the earth, we desire to send the radiant Russian Easter greeting: "Christ is risen!" to all the churches and creeds throughout the whole world which find in Christ Jesus the foundation of their belief, the object and purpose of their life, their service and their hope. If we address you with this resurrection call, the reason therefor is not to be found in the external conditions under which we live; for these conditions are subject to constant change. It is only the problems of the inner spiritual life that have for us an unchangeable significance.

We in Russia have the deep conviction that, together with us, all the Christian churches and creeds in the world are passing through a terrible crisis. On the one side it is evident that the cause of this crisis is unbelief, which is con-

---

[1]Published by the Hars Graphic Art Association, Vernigerode am Harz, Germany, and translated into English by Miss Catherine Ruth Smith.

stantly increasing everywhere at an almost incredible rate. We must bow ourselves in humility before the realization that this unbelief itself is, in turn the fruit of a specific development which has reached its consummation in the life of the Christian churches and creeds. So it is natural for the question to arise: "What is the problem at issue in this crisis?" We will endeavor to answer this question from our own standpoint, as we believe we have come to see it in the light of our severest experiences and upheavals.

a. The Causes of the Spiritual Crisis — Biblical history shows that long ago the Old Testament Church passed through a similar crisis. No less a personage than the great prophet Isaiah referred to it, and pointed out its causes. Commissioned by God, he addressed his people in these moving words: "To what purpose is the multitude of your sacrifices unto me? saith the Lord: I am full of the burnt offerings of rams."[2] In another place he finds himself compelled to pass the judgment of God upon the religiosity prevailing among the people: "This people draw near me with their mouth, and with their lips do honor me, but have removed their heart far from me."[1] In the reference here to "lips" are included all empty prayers, and all forms of worship and religious observances which are lacking in spirituality. Closely to be linked with these words of the prophet is the severe reproach addressed by Christ to His pious contemporaries: "For laying aside the commandment of God, ye hold the tradition of men, . . . full well ye reject the commandment of God, that ye may keep your own traditions."[2]

The misfortune of the people of Israel consisted in the following circumstances:

1. For centuries people had been disregarding the one divine revelation in the canonical Scriptures, and had permitted themselves to be delivered over to the leadership of men. From this it followed that,

---

[1]Isaiah 29:18.
[2]Mark 7:6, 8, 13.

2. Their ceremonies, which had no basis in faith, and their religious activities, which did not touch the soul, were the death-blow to all healthy spiritual life.[3]

3. Formalism in religion acquired, for this reason, a power which it by no means deserved; and this power it used, not for the arousing and furthering of personal religious life among the people, but for the repression of such life, in the name of its own interests.[4]

4. The practical side of spiritual life, the "care of widows and orphans," and of those who had no possessions or rights of their own, the needy and oppressed, was entirely forgotten.

This was the situation of the people of Israel in the time of Jesus: their religion was characterized by impressive external forms, without any true divine content. The inevitable consequence was the constantly increasing growth of unbelief, as practised and manifested in the rationalism of the Sadducees.[5]

We meet with the same ideas in our own day. It is firmly held by all believers in Christ, apart from any distinction of name or creed, that the church of the first century, the church of Christ and the Apostles, as it is revealed to us in the Acts and in the letters of the Apostles, is in its ideal aspect the model for the Church through all the future centuries, and will ever remain so. But just as, from a mountain spring which is clear and transparent at its source, there may flow a dark and muddy stream, the churches have wandered from their old historical prototype, forsaken the sacred Scriptures, and have allowed themselves to be governed by traditions. They have developed cults and outward ceremonials in such a multitude that their inner spiritual life has been almost entirely extinguished. They have built up a complex hierarchy and assigned to it the power of direction in and over the church—a monopoly of the functions belonging in reality to the Holy Spirit. And, finally, they have

---

[3]Mark 7:1-8, 23, 25-27, etc.
[4]Matthew 23:1 f.
[5]Acts 23:8.

forgotten the "widows and orphans," that is to say, they have allowed the social side of religious life to pass out of their jurisdiction.

It is true that the great Reformers who arose at the end of the Middle Ages strove mightily to re-create among their people the original pattern of the Christian Church. A great deal was accomplished by them, but yet this was not sufficient to mend the harm which had been done. The power of tradition was still too strong. The successors of the Reformers should have made further progress along the paths which they had begun to follow, in the return to the spirit of ancient Christianity; but unfortunately the churches of the Reformation, in their historical development, came to a dead stop all too soon. As a result of this, in their case also, tradition, formalism, hierachy, and the abandonment of the social side of life among the people, became the most powerful influence at work.

Social injustices of all kinds have increased enormously. The majority of the people have lost their confidence in the Church. Closely associated with this is the rise of various kinds of sects which deny the fundamental truths of Christianity. Persons who reject Christ and His message attempt to carry out in social life the ideal of Christ, as that ideal is demonstrated in the New Testament and, in particular, in the history of the Apostolic Church.

The course of events will produce further upheavals in this direction, unless a healthy spiritual life once more makes its appearance among the Christian churches and denominations, and leads them to perceive what their duty is toward suffering humanity. Partial reforms are of no avail in the accomplishment of this end. Radical measures of a moral and religious nature must be employed. Above all else, the whole world must be brought to a realization of the fundamental fallacy of one belief, namely, the belief that the contradiction between the practice of the Christian churches hitherto and the message which they profess to believe is to be laid to inherent inadequacy of Christianity or to falling off in the power of the Gospel.

It must be proclaimed that the Gospel contains within itself the highest aims for the moral life of man, and that it supplies the power to accomplish them. The New Testament is the only book on earth which can lead sinners of all kinds into a new life. Today, as in the time of Christ, the same marvellous power is at work which could turn both the publican Zacchaeus and the murderer on the cross into new men. From this source still flows a stream of light, love and peace available for all the world. There sounds here now, as of old, the call to attain the true perfection of the divine stature. Men inspired by the Gospel are still receiving, even in our own days, the power to accomplish great deeds of self-forgetful love, for the healing of suffering mankind.

We know that all we have to do is to hold up a small sunshade, or to draw the curtains, and the light of the sun will cease to shine upon us. Similarly, all that men have to do is to make a few additions to Christian life and teaching, and the light of the Gospel will no longer be able to reach the mass of the people. It is not the sun of the New Testament which must bear the blame, but the churches and creeds which have hidden themselves behind the curtains of additions and new discoveries in the field of religion.

b. Our Attempt to Relieve the Crisis — In spite of the severe persecutions of the faithful in the latter half of the century, there arose in Russia a Free Evangelical Church for all the people, and as the direct result of the proclamation of the Gospel through service and sacrifice, there are now a large number of popular preachers, though many of them have had no preparatory training. Most of the Evangelical churches and parishes which have so arisen have affiliated themselves with an organization. The All-Russian Union of Evangelical Christians conceives its mission and task to be the re-creation of early Christianity upon earth in all its creative power, and, closely associated with this, the spiritual and moral rebirth of the individual, of the family, of society, of the people, and of all mankind. In the spirit of this task, as appointed for it in the Word of God, there burns within the heart of the Russian Evangelical Church the desire to have all the churches throughout the world share in the knowledge of the events which have transpired up to this time, and the experiences through which it has passed.

The Tenth General United Congress of Evangelical Christians at Leningrad, in November, 1926, following a detailed report made by I. S. Prokhanoff, resolved to dedicate itself with particular emphasis to the consummation, at the earliest possible date, of "living conditions in accordance with the Gospel," that is, of a new manner of living in the midst of the Russian people, upon the basis of the Gospel alone. The watchword for these conditions of living in accordance with the Gospel is to be found in the words of the Apostle Paul: "Be thou an example of the believers, in word, in conversation, in charity, in spirit, in faith, in purity."[1]

This ideal of life in accordance with the Gospel is already being realized, though in many of its phases only the first beginnings have as yet been made.

We hope to overthrow rationalism by virtue of the fact that we have taken our stand firmly, from the beginning, upon the principle that belief and knowledge must be coordinated, and that all civilization must be subjected to the penetrating influence of the Gospel. Quietism we shall avoid through strict adherence to the principle that all members of the Church, without exception, must take part in the life of the community, and must work together in unbroken unity.

No one, however, is to deduce that we, as Evangelical Christians, have an exaggerated idea of our own attainments, or that we would lay claim to special privileges of our own, in preference to the other Christian churches. We write this in the fear of God, as the brethren who are least among the saints, and as a true expression of our desires and hopes. We would, however, make you the partners of our experiences, and are desirous that all who read this call may test it by the Word of God, and, if they find it true, may be able to use it for the welfare of their own churches. For we

---

[1] I Timothy 4:12.

believe that only in this manner can a solution be found for the present religious crisis in the churches. Only the restoration of a Church which had its origin in the spirit of primitive Christianity, with its all-embracing and creative religious power, will be able to overcome the spirit of unbelief as manifested in atheism, materialism, and free-thinking, and to prevent its further growth among the people of the world.

The present religious combat with unbelief is the most burning question among all the Christian churches, and particularly among the heirs of the Reformation in the West. This burden, however, now lies most heavily of all upon the Evangelical Christians of Russia. Never yet in the history of the world has the line of battle between belief and unbelief been so clearly defined as it is today in the present Soviet Union. And furthermore, the spirit of unbelief which is now rampant in Russia in the form of atheism and materialism is the fruit and the creation of the pseudo-science of Western Europe, and, in particular, of the work of Feuerbach, Häckel, Büchner, Nietzsche and others, as well as of the faculties of Protestant theological schools, from that of Tübingen down to the present day.

### Only Spiritual Resurrection Can Conquer

We are therefore most deeply convinced that only a spiritual resurrection of the Churches of Western Europe can again conquer the thinking majority of mankind, and produce such a whirlwind of divine power that streams of new spiritual force will flow through the life of all people, with the result that then there will be no place left for unbelief among them. One of the first fruits of the spiritual awakening in Western Europe must be a science which will be the defender of the faith, since it will live by faith, and which will fully and irrevocably overcome all the atheistic, materialistic and other theories of unbelief, through the Spirit of Jesus Christ. The Reformation lands, which have produced this unbelief, are under obligation to uncover, by means of science, all the senselessness, the lack of a sure foundation, which characterize free-thinking, and, in the consciousness of their

267

own stupendous responsibility to the civilized world, to demonstrate the fact that Atheism or Free Thinking never has produced and never will be able to produce the power required for that new and exalted future which lies before us.

What a glorious and blessed task for the philosophy and science of Western Europe! The highest achievement to be desired along these lines is the creation of an Ecumenical Church in the spirit of primitive Christianity. This, however, can be brought about only in one way: "Not by might, nor by power, but by my Spirit, saith the Lord of Hosts."[1]

If anything is accomplished as a result of this proclamation, it can only be accomplished by the methods of peace and mutual understanding. An Evangelical Church can work only by means of following her convictions, by proclamations issued in the spirit of peace, and by voluntary cooperation. She cannot, she dare not have anything to do with violent upheavals, of whatever sort. God is not in the wind, not in the fire, not in the earthquake, but in the still small voice.[2]

This proclamation is written and issued in silent prayer and waiting upon God. May it be received in precisely the same spirit! He that hath ears to hear, let him hear what God saith to the Church: Christ is risen! Let us also rise and walk in His light!

*All-Russian Union of Evangelical Christians*

I. S. PROKHANOFF, *President*
I. I. JIDKOFF,
W. C. BYKOFF,
　*Vice-Presidents*
J. A. KARGEL,
A. W. KAREFF,
A. J. JIDKOFF,
　*Members*
P. S. KAPALYGIN, *Secretary*

[1]Zechariah 4:6.
[2]I Kings 19:11-13.

## MESSAGE TO WORLD CHRISTIANS

What is the significance of "The Resurrection Call?"

During the better part of the last fifteen years all religions and denominations in Russia have been under conditions of restriction and oppression by the so-called Russian militant atheism. There is now a "five-year plan" (1932-1937) during which the atheists hope to stamp out all religion and the very Name of God and His influence from the Russian life.

### Who Is Fighting This Battle?

Many religious leaders are suffering in prison, in exile, with nothing to look forward to apparently but continued persecution, starvation and death. Many have already died in loneliness away from all that they loved and cared for on this earth. A great battle is going on between Faith and Infidelity, actually between Christ and Anti-Christ.

But in other parts of the world things are not comfortable and joyous and easy for people. Awful economic difficulties arise, depressions, crises, unemployment, hunger. The atmosphere of life is very stifling. In the whole world there is hopelessness, despair, pessimism.

At this most gloomy moment a loud voice is heard from the depths of suffering Russia, the voice of the Young Suffering Gospel Church, crying out of a land officially announced to be atheistic.

This voice is similar to the words of the Apostle Paul, who wrote from prison a letter of cheer and hope to the Christians at liberty, admonishing them to *"Rejoice in the Lord alway."* (Phil. 4:4.) It is like a torch of flame raised in a world shrouded in darkness. The Russian Christians say:

### We Are Still Imbued With Optimism

"Having found ourselves in Russia under an unparalleled oppression under militant atheism, and though from the human standpoint we have reason to become pessimistic and filled with despair, we are in reality imbued with the crystal-like optimism of the Gospel Faith."

Christ was crucified and His little flock scattered, but He arose from the dead and gathered them again, sending them forth with the Gospel message. His victory over the powers of darkness and death was complete.

In the first centuries the condition of His followers was terrible. They were tortured, given to the beasts, burnt with fire. Nevertheless, the Christianity preached by unlettered men overthrew the Greek philosophy and the Roman military power, and on the ruins of that ancient civilization erected the Church, a wonderful building of Christian refinement, culture and religion.

Striving together now for the faith of the Gospel in the atheistic country, we believe that God will give us the spiritual victory over all doctrines of denial of the existence of God and will as an outcome create a new and happy life in our country.

With these beliefs strong in our hearts, we feel an inspiration to say to a world filled with pessimism a brotherly word of faith and optimism. Take the Old and yet Eternally New Gospel as the foundation of your life, to rebuild it in accord with the teaching of Jesus Christ, and then the earth and heaven will be new.

This is the sense of "The Resurrection Call."

"Christ is Risen!" All will rise!

I. S. PROKHANOFF.

March 17, 1933
New York

# One Body Ministries

One Body Ministries is dedicated to answering our Lord's prayer for unity, "that they all may be one . . . that the world may believe" (John 17:21).

In addition to this English version of *In the Cauldron of Russia,* One Body Ministries, in cooperation with Literature and Teaching Ministries, White Fields Overseas Evangelism and World Evangelism Global Outreach, has produced the book in the Russian language.

A Christian magazine, *Morning Star,* will also be produced in the Russian language.

One Body Ministries produces a quarterly magazine, *One Body* (founded by Don DeWelt), and a monthly newsletter, *The Knowlesletter.* The ministry also helps coordinate the annual unity meeting known as Restoration Forum.

If you are interested in learning more about One Body Ministries please contact the Executive Director, Victor Knowles, at P.O. Box 645, Joplin, MO 64802-0645. Tel. (417) 623-6280 or FAX (417) 623-8250.